JEWISH NOTABLES

IN AMERICA

1776–1865

Links of an Endless Chain

by HARRY SIMONHOFF
Author of *Under Strange Skies*

Foreword by Dr. David de Sola Pool

New York

GREENBERG : PUBLISHER

to Ilse
wife, friend, companion

INTRODUCTION

THREE centuries have elapsed since Jews settled in North America. Yet the conscious recording of their past started little more than half a century ago. It is true that in the year 1800 an inceptive attempt was made to summarize the 150 years of previous American Jewish history. This happened at the graduation exercises of Columbia College held in St. Paul's Chapel of New York. For his baccalaureate oration Sampson Simson, the subsequent founder of Mt. Sinai hospital, delivered a brief address in Hebrew. The original manuscript, now in the archives of the American Jewish Historical Society, has marginal corrections that reveal the guidance of Gershom Mendes Seixas, the patriotic minister of Shearith Israel, perhaps the most learned Jew in the young republic at that time.

Almost a century was to pass before that little bud would blossom and then flower forth. Recording the story of Jews in North America began in the last decade of the 19th century. Curiously enough, the most noteworthy of the pioneer Jewish historians was not a Jew. To Charles P. Daly, Judge of New York's Court of Common Pleas, we owe a volume which, after three score years, still has value among the historical writings that are beginning to catch up with the drama of American Jewry. The American Jewish tercentenary celebration in 1954-55 has served to stimulate public interest in the American Jewish past. Harry Simonhoff's collection of biographical sketches, presented here with imagination and vividness, is a welcome addition to that historiography.

iii

Jewish Notables in America brings to life some ninety American figures who made their mark in the forgotten past. They begin with the year when the Declaration of Independence was proclaimed and end when the curtain fell upon the War between the States to rise upon a unified and free nation. Of the ninety personalities whose stories are told, six were women—a pleasantly surprising proportion when one remembers how sheltered and in a sense how constricting a woman's life was two centuries and even one century ago.

We tend to think of the early Jewish settlers in North America as residents of the oldest established towns along the Atlantic Coast, such as New York, or Philadelphia, or Newport, or Charleston. The concise biographies in this book widen our horizon and take us afield to places such as Lancaster, St. Augustine, Aaronsburg, New Orleans, Richmond, and to states far beyond—to North Carolina, Georgia, Alabama, Texas, Kansas and California.

We also tend to place the early Americans in stereotyped pictures. Details of American history fade in our memory and leave a blurred image of refugees in search of freedom. Jews were indeed to be found playing their part as soldiers at Valley Forge and as pioneers in the back woods. But these succinct stories go far beyond such generalization. They fill out and clarify the picture. They bring before us Jews of early America who were also playwrights and artists, physicians and rabbis, philanthropists and organizers of communal bodies, merchants and bankers and stockbrokers. There are among them proselytes to Judaism, converts from Judaism, and those who battled against missionizing activities. They are soldiers, writers, sailors, poets, editors, poetesses, publishers, politicians, congressmen, senators.

These Americans out of the past come to us in this book not as bloodless silhouettes. Nor are they pen and ink pictures academically limned from dry historical research. They appear as men and women in their human embodiment, and as we read about them, we share in their interesting situations and are present at many a dramatic juncture. We become familiar with some

iv

striking personalities in well nigh a century of history in our land. At the very beginning, they mingled with and assisted the founders of the nation that became the United States of America.

By adding their distinctive Jewish character to the story, these men and women brought color to the bright and variegated hues of America with its stimulating philosophy of life in a pluralistic culture. They helped preserve the character of the land from merging into a neutral, colorless background. The very name United *States* negates the conception of a unilateral, monolithic empire. The Federal Union allows its forty-eight states, large and small, to retain much of their individual character. In consonance with this rugged individualism, the social, religious, and cultural philosophy of America has developed. It has given American Jewry a great opportunity and a great challenge.

One dare not generalize in one set phrase about the contribution of any one group to America as a whole. The Pilgrim Fathers brought far more than their puritanism. The Quakers have given us more than pacifism. The Jew brought more than the basic, everliving and overriding teachings of his faith, inherited from prophets, rabbis, and teachers of the past. This volume shows how individual Jews in their individual paths of life added their mite to the forging of a great democracy and to enriching life and freedom in America.

David de Sola Pool

Rabbi of the Spanish-Portuguese Synagogue of New York
President of the American Jewish Historical Society

COMMEMORATING
FRANCIS SALVADOR
1747 - 1776

FIRST JEW IN SOUTH CAROLINA TO HOLD PUBLIC OFFICE
AND
TO DIE FOR AMERICAN INDEPENDENCE

HE CAME TO CHARLES TOWN FROM HIS NATIVE
LONDON IN 1773 TO DEVELOP EXTENSIVE FAMILY
LANDHOLDINGS IN THE FRONTIER DISTRICT OF
NINETY SIX. AS A DEPUTY TO THE PROVINCIAL
CONGRESSES OF SOUTH CAROLINA, 1775 AND 1776,
HE SERVED WITH DISTINCTION IN THE CREATION
OF THIS STATE AND NATION. PARTICIPATING AS
A VOLUNTEER IN AN EXPEDITION AGAINST INDIANS
AND TORIES, HE WAS KILLED FROM AMBUSH NEAR
THE KEOWEE RIVER, AUGUST 1, 1776.

BORN AN ARISTOCRAT, HE BECAME A DEMOCRAT;
AN ENGLISHMAN, HE CAST HIS LOT WITH AMERICA;
TRUE TO HIS ANCIENT FAITH, HE GAVE HIS LIFE
FOR NEW HOPES OF HUMAN LIBERTY AND UNDERSTANDING.

ERECTED AT THE TIME OF THE BICENTENNIAL CELEBRATION
OF THE JEWISH COMMUNITY OF CHARLESTON, 1950.

APPROVED BY THE HISTORICAL COMMISSION OF CHARLESTON, S.C.

CONTENTS

viii

LIST OF ILLUSTRATIONS

1776

FRANCIS SALVADOR

Alien Patriot

THE SALVADOR COAT OF ARMS.

As the 18th century grew older, England forged ahead in political and economic power. Its London Jewish community began to
surpass the parent body of Amsterdam, descended of the famed
Sephardic Hidalgoes, who had fled the Spanish and Portuguese
Inquisition. A leader of the English Synagogue was the financier Joseph Salvador, who made loans to the government and
became the first Jewish director of the East India Company. At
the accession of George III, he was chairman of the committee to
present the respects of the Jewish community; it was an expression of loyalty which pleased the King, judging by the gracious
reply of the Lord Chamberlain.

His nephew Francis Salvador was born virtually grasping the
legendary silver spoon. Given a good education, he traveled on
the continent after the manner of the English gentry. On attaining his majority, he received an inheritance of £60,000, to which
Uncle Joseph added £13,000, the dowry that went with his daughter. Like other gentlemen of quality and fortune, Francis at-

tended the stock exchange and frequented the theatres and coffee houses, wearing his powdered wig, velvet clothes, embroidered linen shirts, silk stockings and silver buckles on low cut shoes.

Life with a loving wife and four children was just too pleasant to last. Suddenly reverses hit Joseph Salvador. The catastrophic earthquake at Lisbon and failure of the Dutch East India Company swept away his fortune. All he had left was 100,000 acres somewhere in the wilds of South Carolina. Francis had to come to the aid of his proud and sensitive uncle, who just could not bear the thought of losing prestige and leadership. He "bought" of his father-in-law 6000 acres for £8000, probably more than triple its selling value. But Uncle Joseph was not satisfied. He had to stage a comeback. Too old to cross the ocean himself, he insisted on his nephew investigating in person the possibilities of his vast land holdings.

In 1773, Francis Salvador landed at Charleston and proceeded to Ninety-Six District, now called Greenwood. He was warmly entertained by the sun-bronzed planters, who had transformed a wilderness into an agricultural colony. He listened to their calm recital of the many irritations they were experiencing from the English Tory Government and sensed the approaching crisis. Something within him responded to these determined, wholesome farmers ready to defend their convictions with their lives.

Salvador grew ashamed of the idle life as a London dandy and soon discarded his velvets, his brocades, his silver chains. He donned the homespun shirt and the leather jerkin of the frontiersman and settled down with the help of 30 slaves to cultivate the soil purchased from his father-in-law. The backwoodsmen quickly recognized the sincerity and mettle of the Jewish newcomer. A year after his arrival, they elected or selected him a delegate to the first South Carolina Provincial Congress.

In Charleston, the aristocratic slave owners were attracted by the polished manners of the London man about town. But as Salvador entered heart and soul into the struggle for colonial freedom, they also sensed his capacities. They were qualified to judge, for never again did South Carolina produce simultaneously such a galaxy of ability, character, intellect, and patriotic fervor. Among them were the signers of the Declaration of Independence and the drafters of the Federal Constitution. John Rutledge, the first President of South Carolina, was subsequently appointed the first Chief Justice of the U. S. Supreme Court. It was Edward Pinkney who declared: "Millions for defense but not one cent for tribute." Salvador earned the friendship and esteem of such eminent Carolinians as William Drayton, Charles Cotesworth Pinkney, Edward Rutledge, Patrick Calhoun and John Gervais.

The Congress set up the Republic of South Carolina, and Salvador was appointed a commissioner to sign and stamp the new currency. His knowledge of finance came in handy, for the new state was in dire need of funds. He kept down salaries and even prevented the Assembly from voting £10,000 a year for the President. He helped to reorganize the courts and participated in the selection of the magistrates. He advised the Assembly as to proper election districts and managers to receive the votes of the electorate. Though not a lawyer, he took part in drafting the State Constitution.

As the Congress adjourned, Salvador returned to his plantation at Coronaca Creek. His new task was to keep a close watch on the Indians stirred up by British agents. The numerous Tories loyal to England presented a difficult problem. He caused the arrest of their leader, the notorious Patrick Cunningham, and became involved in that Tory *cause celebre,* which aroused the whole state. The new Chief Justice, William Drayton, lived at Salvador's home and directed the defense against the perilous combination of Indians and Tories poised for attack upon the patriotic settlements.

The Cherokees finally struck, and Major Andrew Williamson took command with Salvador as his chief adviser. The frontier was now on fire. Salvador urged President John Rutledge to send reinforcements of men and arms. His advice even as to military matters was respected by the High Command. But fighting the

Indians was not nearly as difficult as holding in check the undisciplined militiamen bursting at the seams with rugged individualism.

With a force of 1200 men, Salvador urged an all-out attack against Indians and Tories. On the night of July 31, 1776, the little army of 330 picked men proceeded in the silence of the moonless night. Suddenly a fusillade of shots poured from behind bushes, trees, and fences. The Americans were ambushed. Major Williamson had sent a detachment to ford the Keowee River and remained with Salvador at the head of the company. With the first volley, Salvador swayed heavily in his saddle. The Indians closed in on all sides, but the militia soon repulsed them. Williamson found Salvador lying in a bush, scalped but still alive. He asked whether the enemy was beaten. "Yes," was the answer. He shook Williamson's hand, said farewell, and died in his 30th year.

The short career of Francis Salvador in South Carolina registers the approaching change in status of the Jew in Christendom. Heretofore a pariah at worst, or a tolerated enemy alien at best, the Jew henceforth emerges in the Western world a citizen and patriot ready to give up life for his Christian fatherland. Neither the alien Salvador nor his South Carolina hosts were aware of this momentous step. Actually the Constitution that Salvador helped to draft recognized only Protestants as citizens with full political rights. The first Jew in the modern world to hold an elective office and die on the battlefield a willing martyr for freedom, Francis Salvador opens the chapter of Jewish participation and integration in Western society.

1777

AARON LOPEZ

Merchant Prince

İɴ Lɪꜱʙᴏɴ, Aaron Lopez was born of a family, which for centuries knelt at mass, said *gloria patria* fervently at the conclusion of prayers, went regularly to confession, and celebrated every holy day on the Catholic calendar. But secretly they prayed in Hebrew, fasted on Yom Kippur, and ate matzos on Passover. Aaron's half brother was scented by the hounds of the Inquisition; his father's gold saved him from torture and burning. He managed to get away on an English boat. Aaron finally induced his aged father to permit him to follow his brother to the new world. It was well the brothers got away, for three years later they would have perished during the great Lisbon earthquake. In 1752 Aaron landed in Newport, Rhode Island, and immediately entered the covenant of Judaism.

Newport was booming. In 1750 a business man declared resignedly: "New York can never hope to rival Newport as a shipping center." The cause of its prominence in the commerce of Colonial America is sometimes overlooked. It is also often forgotten that

5

religious freedom was not a vested right in the colonies of the Atlantic seaboard.

The Pilgrims, who had tasted persecution in old England, established their own brand of intolerant theocracy in New England. To escape the fanaticism of Puritan rule, Roger Williams founded the first colony to welcome people of all religions. As soon as the news got around, Jews found their way to the new Utopia in Rhode Island. A Masonic source reports that the fifteen Jewish families, who settled Newport in 1658, were the first to bring Masonry to America. It did not take too long for this town to become the leading Jewish settlement in Colonial America. Before the American Revolution, Newport reached its pinnacle of prosperity, and the Jewish community its peak of affluence. Evidently there was a connection between the two.

The Jewish community of 1100 souls contributed not only to Newport's trade but to its manufacturing. James Lucena introduced the making of soap, a skill he had acquired in the King of Portugal's workshops. Abraham Riviera, uncle of Aaron, produced candles made out of sperm oil. Aaron's half brother Moses Lopez obtained a license from the General Assembly for the manufacture of potash, a rare commodity even in 18th century England. In this busy port all kinds of merchandise, from candles to carriages were bought and sold. The repute of Newport Jewry can be judged by the famous "no sanction to bigotry" letter written to the congregation by George Washington when he became President.

In this beehive, Aaron Lopez proved himself a business genius. In a short time he became one of the leading, if not the leading merchant and shipper in all the English colonies. The entire city felt the impact of his phenomenal rise. He is said to have owned, in whole or in part, 30 transatlantic ships and over 100 coastwise vessels. They carried lumber, fish, horses, whale oil, manufactured articles, molasses and rum to and from Newfoundland, Surinam, Madeira, West Indies, Lisbon, Gibraltar, Cape Nicholas, Cape Francois, Amsterdam, Bristol, Curaçao, besides the ports of the

American colonies. He had agents in the ports of call and traded in tobacco, flour, meats, tar, pitch, and turpentine. Following the custom of the times, his ships brought slaves from Africa and carried ivory, gold dust, palm oil, and camwood to European ports. Newport became the American export-import clearing house, with Aaron Lopez as director.

Lopez followed rigidly the tenets of Orthodox Judaism. Lay leader of the community, he contributed liberally to the Synagogue and personally laid the corner-stone of that famous building, which stands today as a Federal shrine. No ship ever left his dock (still called Lopez wharf) on Saturday, and out of deference to Christian sentiment, his large business was also closed on Sunday. Prominent in establishing friendly relations between Christians and Jews, he was able to settle 40 Jewish families in Newport. He had a strong sense of public relations and conducted himself with a dignified modesty that evoked respect and admiration from Christian and Jew, competitor and associate. Ezra Styles, Christian Pastor and President of Yale, wrote in his eulogy: "He was a merchant of the first eminence; for honor and extent of commerce probably surpassed by no merchant in America."

Yet this merchant prince, who raised Newport to the top in Colonial commerce, could not altogether escape racial or religious prejudice that evidently existed even in the haven of tolerance founded by Roger Williams. Under the Colonial Naturalization Acts, he applied for citizenship. The court and assembly turned down his petition on trifling grounds. He applied to the neighboring colony and became the first naturalized Jew in Massachusetts.

As a public spirited citizen, he helped generously in the founding of the Newport Public Library, perhaps the finest in all the colonies. His portrait was painted by Gilbert Stuart, of whom he was an early patron. His entertainment of high public officials brought to his home the best society of the city. In strong sympathy with the patriots of the Revolution, he fled Newport and relinquished his extensive holdings to the British, who woul' gladly have come to terms with a leading merchant of the 13 colonies.

The war brought ruin to the opulence of Newport. Lopez was able to rescue a pittance out of the wreckage of his vast holdings. After Washington's victory at Yorktown secured peace, Lopez set out in 1782 with his numerous family to rebuild his commercial empire and restore the prestige of Newport. On the road his horse suddenly bolted and threw him into treacherous quicksand. He struggled helplessly until submerged. With his death, Newport lost the opportunity to regain its commercial prestige. Today it ranks among the foremost summer resorts for fashionable society.

THE NEWPORT SYNAGOGUE
DEDICATED BY AARON LOPEZ.

HOLY ARK OF SYNAGOGUE
IN JOSEPH SIMON'S HOME.

JOSEPH SIMON

Of Lancaster

By the middle of the 18th century, Jews were better established in Pennsylvania than in most colonies. That they stood quite well in the esteem of their neighbors was partly due to the liberal charter of William Penn. But not altogether. The constitution of Roger Williams was as tolerant. Yet the legislature of Rhode Island refused to grant citizenship to Aaron Lopez, and the Supreme Court upheld the assembly. Other influences operated in Penn's colony.

Jews encountered a certain sympathy from Quakers, still aware of the persecutions directed against their own immediate forebears. But Germans had immigrated in large numbers and became ancestors to the group later known as "Pennsylvania Dutch". Divided into a score of sects, they gravitated in small settlements, separated from each other, and far removed from the birthplace of their respective credos. The age was pietistic, and religious enthusiasms became infectious. Hostile to each other, these sectarians were open to the influence and example of Jews who came to trade with them and the Indians.

9

Many took over Jewish practices. They circumcised the children and observed the dietary laws. In Lancaster County they built a log house and called it the "Shul". They employed a Hazan, who chanted the prayers and blew the Shofar. They greeted the new moon with prayer and buried their dead near the Synagogue. Many of these Judaized Germans actually turned to the old dispensation and followed the Old Testament. Nothing like it had happened since the old Romans were turning to Judaism, prior to the advent of Christianity.

So when the 22 year old Joseph Simon came to Lancaster in 1735 he opened shop in a milieu of friendly feeling. Soon he ran the biggest business in the county; but storekeeping was but an open sesame for the ambitious entrepreneur. He sensed the enormous possibilities in the vast hinterland that was just opening up. Indians had become attracted to blankets, red cloth, paint, beads, hatchets, trinkets, guns, armbands, cheap laces, earrings, and tobacco. Here was a good consumer's market, but the red men had no money, nor raw material, nor commodities in exchange, except furs and skins in varying quantities.

Of course, Indians had land, plenty of land, which they were willing to trade for required articles. But with such abundance of earth about them, what chance could a merchant have to turn land into cash? William Penn had sold 100 acre tracts for $10 on easy terms to his settlers. It took a bold, constructive imagination to foresee that land had real potential value. The age of invention had scarcely begun. Transportation had not changed since the days of the Phoenician sea traders. It seemed impossible to forecast the vast population that would migrate to the American shores. Thomas Jefferson declared later that it would take 1000 years to fill up the territory east of the Mississippi.

Joseph Simon followed his hunch and acquired land, little tracts and huge tracts. He was fond of partnerships, and among his Christian associates were some of the notable landholders of the day: Captain William Trent, after whose father Trenton is named; Ephraim Blaine, great grandfather of James G. Blaine, presidential candidate who lost to Grover Cleveland; George Croghan, a wily Irish frontiersman, who negotiated an important treaty between the British and the Indians. His Jewish partners, besides the noted David Franks of Philadelphia, were the capable young men he chose as his sons-in-law: Michael Gratz, later a famous merchant prince; Solomon Etting who never ceased his labors until Maryland permitted Jews to hold public office, and Levy A. Levy, a promising business man, who survived most of his contemporaries in the fur trade.

The mere owning of unproductive land was not profitable. Something had to be done to make barren country valuable. Here Joseph Simon did his bit in the upbuilding of Colonial America. Settlers were encouraged and directed to make their homes in the beckoning hinterland. And when farms were cleared and villages started, the pioneers could not be left to their own devices. The merchant stepped into the hiatus. Joseph Simon's pack horses traveled the Indian trails that wended over mountains through forests, gorges, and valleys, ever in danger of the aborigines smoldering with resentment at the white intruders. His bateaux floated down the precarious waterways. Both carriers brought to the sparse settlements essential foodstuffs, coarse clothing, ammunition, blankets, soap, shoes, and such heavenly luxuries as sugar, coffee, spices, rum, and tea. Without the pack trains, the rigorous pioneer life would have atrophied and settlement delayed.

Simon became one of the important colonial landowners, and in conjunction with Gratz, Croghan, and others, he secured vast tracts in Virginia which later became the state of Kentucky. With his old time partner John Campbell, Joseph Simon was the original founder of Louisville. Their agent George Croghan advertised property in Louisville as the new city at the Falls of the Ohio. At first Virginia disputed this grant but ultimately the rights of Campbell and Simon were upheld by the legislature. Another syndicate, in which Simon participated, organized the Indiana Company. It received a grant of 2,500,000 acres from the Six Iroquois Nations, but royal confirmation was withheld. In the

Wabash Grant and the Grand Ohio Company, Simon was associated with the most distinguished men in the colonies, among them Benjamin Franklin.

Supplying armies in wartime was big business that required capital, influence, and European connections. So during the French and Indian War the pack trains of Joseph Simon met the army of General Braddock on schedule at Big Crossing. The Reverend William Barton who knew Joseph Simon well spoke highly of him in a letter to Sir William Johnson in the summer of 1767.

Naturalized in 1749, Joseph Simon was later a loyal patriot to the Revolutionary cause. He furnished supplies to the troops and waited patiently for the impoverished government to order payment. He seemed to thrive on arduous labor, many partnerships, and continuous excitement. Among his many enterprises, he set up a gunsmith shop to manufacture flintlocks for Washington's army. A supporter of Mikveh Israel Congregation at Philadelphia, his home was the synagogue for the Jews of Lancaster. Bold entrepreneur, intrepid Indian trader, merchant and landowner, he died in his 93rd year, respected and honored, surrounded by the large family of his numerous descendants.

MORDECAI SHEFTALL

Commissary General

Iɴ 1770, the Georgia Legislature refused to confirm the title to a cemetery on the Savannah Commons owned by Jews who ostensibly had "imbibed principles entirely repugnant to those of our own (Christian) religion." This act of bigotry might be interpreted as anti-Semitic had not the self same assembly rejected a similar petition for a Presbyterian cemetery on the same Commons. The Anglicans simply would not recognize the legal right of any other denomination to exist in Georgia.

Yet sectarian narrowness was absent when Mordecai Sheftall was made chairman of the Parochial Committee of Christ Church Parish, the most important county in the colony. The War for Independence was on and Sheftall threw himself heart and soul into the struggle. Georgia like other colonies was divided into Whig and Tory camps, and the Parochial Committee soon became the *de facto* government. The leader's importance became apparent when the Royal Governor James Wright in a letter to a high British official complained that "one Sheftall, a Jew, is chairman

13

of the Parochial Committee, as they call themselves, and this fellow issues orders to captains of vessels to depart the King's port without landing any of their cargoes legally imported."

In 1777, Sheftall was given the state rank of Colonel and became Commissary General of Purchases and Issues to the militia of Georgia. He must have given satisfaction, for the following year the American General Robert Howe extended his command to the Continental troops of South Carolina and Georgia. Before confirmation by the Congress in Philadelphia, Sheftall was taken prisoner.

The British controlled Florida and sent out fighting contingents from St. Augustine. They effected a junction with the Northern expedition that sailed from New York. Georgia was caught in the pincers and Savannah fell. Mordecai might have escaped but his son could not swim. Captured with 185 officers and men, he had the satisfaction of hearing the British commander refer to him as a "very great rebel". Refusing to talk, he was thrown into the guardhouse for Negroes. Ill treated by drunken soldiers and denied food for two days, his end seemed near. But German-Yiddish saved him. A Hessian officer, delighted to hear some one speak his native tongue in a wild foreign country, took good care of the Jewish prisoner.

Mordecai spent several months on a prison ship. His jailers thought it good fun to feed him pork. Paroled with others, he was confined to Sunbury, a town in Georgia. Ultimately the British garrison withdrew and left the prisoners in charge of Tories. Now trouble really began. The Colonials loyal to England were far more vindictive towards their rebel fellow countrymen than the professional soldiers of Britain. Some patriots were killed. It was high time to flee. Mordecai Sheftall and several others managed to escape in a brig. On their way to Charleston, they were recaptured by a British frigate and kept on the hot West Indian island of Antigua. Mordecai and his son were released on their word of honor not to fight England for the duration. They reached Philadelphia, and six months later the parole was cancelled when they were exchanged for other prisoners.

Mordecai Sheftall was born in Savannah two years after the founding of Georgia. At the outbreak of the war, he had a farm and cattle ranch; he operated a sawmill and tannery; he kept store and shipped out produce. In keeping with his environment he owned slaves. But in Philadelphia, he was in dire need. His property, business and slaves were held by the enemy. His wife and four children had taken refuge in Charleston and were in distress. He had no alternative but to petition the government for repayment of the money and provisions he had advanced. Actually he had sacrificed everything for his country. The bill for back pay and provisions ran up to $139,800 in paper money. An additional claim for financing an expedition against the Indians, for supplies to the troops, and for his share in a brigantine captured and burned by the enemy amounted to £1900 sterling. He succeeded in getting back $7,682 in paper money, which had negligible buying power.

In recognition of Mordecai's services, probably, the Board of War did accord a high honor to his 18 year old son. Sheftall Sheftall was commissioned to take a boat through the British blockade under a flag of truce to Charleston and deliver money and food to the starving American prisoners. Mordecai managed to extract another $20,000 in paper money from the U. S. Treasurer. Of this sum, he spent $12,800 to clothe his son. Inflation of paper money did not originate with the 20th century.

In Philadelphia, Mordecai promoted a deal that promised the ready money he needed so badly. He fitted out a schooner for privateering and obtained the cash by selling shares in the venture. Legalized piracy was patriotic. Encouraged by the government, the privateers played havoc with British commerce, a pursuit that influenced English business men to favor the cessation of hostilities. It also brought in scarce supplies and hard money that was still scarcer. Mordecai's venture did not justify his high hopes.

After bringing in one prize, the "Hetty" was captured by the British and scuttled.

While in Philadelphia, Mordecai actively participated in the reorganization of Mikveh Israel and, though financially disabled, donated £3 for building their first synagogue. He made a tiresome journey to Charleston in order to be present at the dedication of Beth Elohim. In his own community he took a leading part. Besides donating ground for a cemetery, he furnished a room in his home for group prayer and assisted in the reestablishment of the Mikveh Israel Congregation of Savannah.

The Sheftall family had a literary bent. Benjamin Sheftall, who came over in 1733 on the second boatload to Georgia, left a Hebrew diary of his pioneering days. His son narrated his adventures in a journal, "Capture of Mordecai Sheftall, Deputy Commissioner General of Issues". Mordecai's brother, Levi Sheftall, as president of Mikveh Israel, wrote the letter of congratulation to the first president of the U. S. in the name of the Savannah community. His son Sheftall Sheftall also left a record of his adventures.

CEMETERY PRESENTED BY MORDECAI SHEFTALL
TO SAVANNAH'S JEWISH COMMUNITY.

1780

ABIGAIL MINIS

Matriarch

THE AMERICAN HIGH COMMAND in 1779 decided it was time to re-take Savannah from the British. General Lincoln and Count d'Es-taing selected Levi Sheftall and Philip Minis, both born in Geor-gia, to help guide the expedition. After the patriots launched their attack they were sorely in need of supplies. The commanders ap-plied to Abigail Minis, a matron past 80, for the necessary pro-visions. The keen old business woman knew the Continental Army to be a poor credit risk. But how could she fail her own beloved state in the cause of independence? She had lived 56 years in Georgia, in fact since the colony was founded.

The retaking of Savannah turned out a failure; the American forces suffered a disastrous defeat. Repayment by the defeated Americans was the least problem. Far worse was the resentment of the English, who had mistaken the old dame for a Tory. The British decided to prefer charges that she was a Whig, the open-ing measure for confiscation of property. Her son Philip, already branded a vile rebel and on the blacklist, could never hold office under any Royal Governor.

The old lady acted with ready decision. She and her five daughters petitioned Governor Wright and the Royal Council to permit them, including their Negroes, to leave for Charleston. She also prayed for a trustee to oversee her property, and even had the temerity to request a boat to transport them with their personal property under a flag of true. Surprisingly the petition was granted. Was it an act of gracious clemency? Or were the British swayed by political considérations? Georgia was equally divided between Tories and Whigs, as the patriots called themselves. Courtesy might be a better gesture for retaining the Loyalists and possibly winning over the patriots than harsh treatment to a group of helpless women. Apparently it did not hurt the Minis cause to have some friends in the enemy camp.

The female octogenarian struggled hard to support her household; but she seemed equal to the task. She requested compensation of the military leaders for supplies advanced to the American forces. They could not or would not help her. Believing Mordecai Sheftall might possibly be in Philadelphia, she wrote her old friend to dig up documents and file her claim with the National government. In the same letter, she suggests that he use the money—should he secure any—for goods that might bring a good return. Her alert mind never missed an opportunity to do business.

Abigail Minis represents a type by no means rare in Diaspora Jewry. She belongs to the class of matriarchs evolved in the checkered history of a minority hovering on the periphery of danger and exile. After the destruction of the state, the anomalous Jewish position was summed up in the annual Seder of the Passover feast: "In every generation adversaries rise up to annihilate us; but the Blessed Holy One saves us from their hands."

Physical survival and preservation of Judaism were the objectives to which everything else was subordinate. The men repudiated all Gentile values of glory in physical prowess for unarmed pacifism. Newly married women sacrificed romance and beauty by shearing their locks of hair. The ancient spiritual tradition would die out unless the sensitive could dedicate their lives to its preservation. The scholarly spent night and day in the study chapels. The women became the breadwinners.

Glueckel of Hameln left a fascinating biography of the Jewish wife, mother and business woman of the 17th century. Conditions might have favored her development. Yet the ideal for the Jewish matriarch is poetically delineated in the closing chapter of Proverbs. Central and Eastern Europe saw many "women of valor" earning the family livelihood while husbands devoted their lives to the Torah.

In her 22nd year, Abigail demonstrated sturdy character when she accompanied her husband to pioneer in a new colony. In January 1733, Gen. Oglethorpe had transported a cargo of impoverished Protestants to make a fresh start in Georgia. Three months later, a boatload of Jewish settlers followed in defiance of the trustees in London. Abraham Minis was not compelled to take any desperate chances. He was one of the few well-to-do on board. After some hesitation, Gov. Oglethorpe permitted the Jewish pioneers to land. The first deed to real estate in Georgia is recorded in Abraham Minis' name. He had the cash. Later the Governor distributed free plots among the colonists. It would seem that life in London would be more comfortable for a young couple with two little girls. The following year, Philip Minis was the first European child born in Georgia.

In 1740 a number of Christians and Jews left Savannah. The restriction against slavery made it very difficult to survive in an agrarian economy without hired workers. But the Minis family stuck it out. In 1757, Abraham Minis died leaving his horses to three sons, his cattle to five daughters. The estate and business went to his capable widow, who increased the farm by 1000 acres and owned 17 slaves, now permitted.

In Savannah, Abigail occupied a house of 4 bed chambers, a sitting room, a large kitchen, a business office. The hall had 10 mahogany chairs resting on a carpet and rug. Looking glasses, abundant silverware and cutlery aborned the walls. The parlor contained 12 mahogany chairs, candlesticks, a sofa, card tables.

Tall 4-post bedsteads of mahogany with a profusion of linen stood in each bedroom. The kitchen was stocked with pots, kettles, and pans of brass, copper, iron and pewter. Gridirons, spits, tongues, flat irons, hooks served the fireplace. An assortment of dishes, bottles, measuring cups and cooking utensils were used by the slaves in preparing meals for the large family and visiting guests.

Her son Philip helped in the business, which took him to Cuba and Jamaica. He found a wife in Newport, Rhode Island, in his 41st year, an advanced age for marriage in Jewish circles of the 18th century. Significantly, none of his sisters were married until after their mother's death. Matriarchal authority was evidently dominant. In 1776, Philip Minis acted as Pay Master and Commissary General of the Continental troops. He advanced $11,000 to the Virginia and North Carolina troops and was lucky enough to get some of it back. He served as President of Mikveh Israel and City Warden of Savannah. Abigail Minis survived her three sons. A matriarch of classic proportions, she conducted business, ruled the household, and died in her 96th year.

ONUMENT TO HAYM SALOMON.

1781

HAYM SALOMON

Patriot Financier

THE STORY of Haym Salomon poses the most intriguing picture of any Jew in the American Revolution. Born in 1740 in Lissa, Prussian Poland, he remains a figure not easy to comprehend. For example, how he managed to acquire a knowledge of French, German, Italian, Dutch, Russian, or even the native Polish, remains a mystery.

In the closed Ghetto world of the 18th century, Central and East European Jews spoke Yiddish exclusively; some knew a smattering of Hebrew from the prayer book or study chapel. There was little enough contact with Christians when Chassidism sprang up as if by magic and closed Jewish life in Poland, not only to the Gentile environment, but even to Jews outside the charmed circle of Israel Baal Shem Tov. Haym Salomon left Poland in 1772 for America. What could a Polish Jew, sunk in the stupor of Chassidic obscurantism, know of New York, or how to get there?

More surprising was his western *weltanshauung,* his patriotic fervor for freedom. He sensed the importance of the coming struggle and, it is believed, threw in his lot with the Sons of Liberty, the underground of colonial patriots—quite in contrast with the merchant class, largely loyal to wealthy England just rising to commercial-industrial preeminence. Salomon was arrested and later released when found useful as interpreter for British officers with the Hessian mercenaries. Evidently doing a job for the underground, especially among the Hessians, who began to desert the English, he was apparently rearrested, charged with treason, and court-martialed to be hanged. It is supposed that he escaped with the help of Minutemen and fled to Philadelphia. Strange doings for a husband and father, for a merchant worth $30,000, equivalent to a quarter million in our day.

His marriage would indicate an unusual, if not a superior, person. At 37 the recent immigrant married 15 year old Rachel Franks of the most influential Jewish family in all the Colonies. Col. Isaac Franks, supposedly on the staff of General Washington, is said to have been her brother. Her beautiful and witty 2nd or 3rd cousin, the Tory belle Rebecca Franks, charmed the British in her Philadelphia home, married an officer, and subsequently became Lady Rebecca Johnson. Considering the gap between German and Polish Jews that continued almost to our own day, it is surprising that a born American would marry a "greenhorn" with a thick accent.

Haym Salomon came to Philadelphia penniless, the British having confiscated his property in New York. But in the capital city of the new nation there were business and speculative opportunities for a hustling trader with imagination. Prices fluctuated hourly on rumors of a boat getting through the British blockade. Merchants gambled on the prospects of privateers hauling in captured cargoes. Salomon soon got on his feet. He gave generous handouts to wounded or distressed soldiers, and donated a fourth of the cost for building the Mikveh Israel Synagogue.

We have no evidence that would establish Haym Salomon as the Financier of the Revolution. There is, however, positive proof that he was "Broker to the Office of Finance" of the Continental

Congress. He also advertised as "Broker to the French Consul General and the Treasurer of the French Army". The difficulties of such a position should be noted here. Colonial America was agricultural, and hard money is always scarce in a farming economy. The merchants and bankers, if not outright Tories, were friendly to England. A broker for the Treasury Department had the thankless job of selling the certificates of a government which had little if any power to tax the several states or their people. The outcome of the war was doubtful, and the U.S.A. under the Articles of Confederation was weak, unstable, and chaotic.

The miracles performed by George Washington were not on the battlefield exclusively. His force of character held together the hungry, freezing, ragged soldiers in those terrible winters at Valley Forge, at Morristown. The Commander-in-Chief could get nowhere with the Continental Congress. He wrote to Robert Morris direct for clothing, food, and supplies. The Finance Minister would send for Haym Salomon imploring him to find money. The latter charged a brokerage fee of one-half per cent for every bond he sold. So the sale of $200,000 securities would net him the munificent sum of $500. The importance of the Jewish broker can be judged from the diary of Robert Morris in which the name Haym Salomon appears 75 times.

Many stray facts, upon which history is built, come down in letters intended only for the eyes of intimates. Thus a number of references attest to the benefactions of Haym Salomon to the Founding Fathers. One of them, a young chap from Virginia, never dreamed of becoming President of the new Republic. In the direst need of expense money, James Madison attended his Congressional duties at Philadelphia. He was told of a certain Haym Salomon on Front Street who often helped out a fellow in distress. Madison wrote home complaining, "I have been for some time a pensioner on the favor of Haym Salomon, a Jew broker." In his next letter to John Randolph he could not conceal his annoyance at the Jew moneylender who refused to take interest.

Haym Salomon died at 45 and left his wife and children penniless. His bank account showed cancelled checks in excess of half a million dollars paid to the government treasury. For over a century his descendants petitioned Congress for a return of the money which, they alleged, helped to achieve independence. But nothing was ever done.

A legend sprang up that Haym Salomon advanced the Continental Congress over half a million dollars which was never repaid. In the 1920's the Federation of Polish Jews projected a monument to Haym Salomon to stand in New York as a tribute to the memory of one who gave his entire fortune so that freedom would prevail.

The monument project came to the attention of Max J. Kohler, Vice President of the American Jewish Historical Society. It seemed odd to a cautious lawyer that generous Uncle Sam would refuse to honor a just obligation. The detached historian directed a research job into the Revolutionary era. Examination of source material convinced Mr. Kohler that the large sums in the bank account represented sales of securities for the government by Salomon the broker, and not personal loans to the U.S.A. This candid opinion discouraged the plan for a monument, at least in New York.

Perhaps evidence does not support the claim that Haym Salomon was the financier of the Revolution. Probably he did not lend the large sums credited by legend. But he did assist Robert Morris during very trying periods to obtain money that was sorely needed. He may or may not deserve a monument, but there is little doubt that Haym Salomon was a patriot who during crucial times labored and sacrificed for American Independence.

1782

REBECCA FRANKS

The Tory Belle

Eᴠᴇʀʏ Jᴇᴡᴇss is not a heroine, nor were all Jews devoted to the American cause during the Revolution. A handful were Tories; which merely shows that Jews reflect the society in which they live. The conventional attitude has changed towards those Colonials who were loyal to England. Modern historians have concluded that some of the "best people" did not think it necessary to separate from the Mother Country. Tories were convinced that the general public were better off in the 13 Colonies than elsewhere in the world.

Among these Anglophiles was David Franks, a merchant and landowner of large dimensions. His father had come over from Hanover to London in the entourage of George I. He did well, and his son David settled in Philadelphia. David had a grateful respect for the King. Probably his commercial interests were tied too closely to British business; perhaps he contrasted the barbarities of the walled German ghetto with the more humane treatment in England. When hostilities erupted in 1775, David

Franks was numbered among the wealthy and educated, with unexpressed leanings toward the Crown.

His immediate family shared his Tory sentiments. His daughter Rebecca was one of those fortunate girls who had everything. Beauty and brains were her birthright. Reared in wealth, educated remarkably for that century in a provincial world, and trained socially in all the graces and niceties of the *ancien regime,* she made her home the most sophisticated in Philadelphia, then the intellectual center of English America. Its atmosphere was cosmopolitan and assimilationist, its tone set by the Episcopalian gentry. Her mother was Christian, and her sister Abigail married Andrew Hamilton, nephew of the governor of Pennsylvania. Unlike her older brother and sister, Rebecca was not baptized; but raised as a Christian, her Judaism was far more lukewarm than her father's.

Rebecca Franks was sparkling, witty, and clever—perhaps too clever. Folks more naive and less educated intuitively grasped the significance of a bell ringing out the news that a certain Declaration had just been signed. That evening the well-born Tories snickered at the naivete of the yokel statesman, one Tom Jefferson, who could write that all men are created equal. Rebecca probably amused the gay house party by rolling off extempore some of the doggerel for which she had a talent.

> *"From garrets, cellars, rushing through the street*
> *The new-born statesmen in committees meet*
> *Legions of Senators infest the land*
> *And mushroom generals thick as mushrooms stand."*

While popular with the patriots, 20 year old Rebecca came into her own when the British took over. The Franks' home became the center of fashion, wit, and gayety. Philadelphia belles flirted with the officers in red coats, white powdered wigs and pigtails, and swords dangling. Sir William Howe, the British Commander, dropped in occasionally for a drink and a chat. Tories and English gloated over a booklet of rhymes entitled "The Times—a Poem by Camilo Querio—Poet Laureate of the Congress." Every one suspected Rebecca Franks as the author, who took some vicious stabs at George Washington:

> *"Was it ambition, vanity, or spite*
> *That prompted thee with Congress to unite?*
> *Or did all three within thy bosom roll?*
> *Thou heart of a hero, with a traitor's soul."*

Had General Howe bestirred himself, he could have destroyed the ill equipped forces of Washington. He preferred to idle away in hilarious revelry. In 1778 a gorgeous fete was given the British General, under the direction of Major Andre, the unfortunate officer soon to be hanged by the Americans in anger over Benedict Arnold's treachery. The Meschianza, a revel Renaissance in scope, began in the morning at the water side. An English Lord flanked by six *Knights of the Blended Rose* appeared in honor of a Philadelphia belle. Captain Watson with a similar retinue of *Knights of the Burning Mountain* appeared for Rebecca Franks. In the most exquisite apparel, she together with the other lady was crowned Queen of Beauty. In the evening fireworks were followed by a sumptuous supper, while not many miles away the American troops suffered cold and hunger.

After the British evacuated Philadelphia, Rebecca continued a favorite of the incoming patriots. They even put up with her sharp tongue and biting wit. Col. Jack Steuart of Maryland was glad to exchange his ragged Valley Forge regimentals for a scarlet coat. He addressed Rebecca as Princess, and expected to find favor wearing "her colors". She turned to her companions and declared "How an ass glories in the lion's skin." But the Continentals jailed David Franks; probably through the influence of his relatives on the American side, he obtained permission to leave with his daughter for New York.

In the last Tory stronghold, Rebecca took up where she left off. Again the round of parties and frolics. At a ball of the British officers, Sir Henry Clinton requested the band to play *Britain, Strike*

Home. "The Commander-in-Chief meant to say Britain, Go Home," quipped Rebecca and got away with it. Col. Henry Johnson had been in love with her since Philadelphia. In 1782 they married. He was made a general and subsequently a baronet. The daughter of David Franks became Lady Rebecca Johnson, the ancestress of many British nobles.

In his Memoirs, General Winfield Scott tells of meeting Lady Johnson. The former beauty was old, tired, and sick. Only her eyes retained their brilliant lustre.

"Is this the young rebel?"

"My dear, it is your countryman," interposed her tactful husband.

"Yes, it is," she continued, "the young rebel, and you have taken the liberty to beat His Majesty's troops." After a slight pause, she added:

"I have gloried in my rebel countrymen." Another pause, "Would to God I too had been a patriot." Sir Henry remonstrated gently, and she added: "I do not, nor never have regretted my marriage. No woman ever was blessed with a kinder, a better husband, but I ought to have been a patriot before my marriage."

General Scott comments sentimentally that of all the party, only her eyes were dry. In the stuffy atmosphere of British aristocracy she evidently felt a nostalgia for her native land, even if she had no longing for her Jewish family.

HOME OF REBECCA FRANKS.

1783

JACOB PHILADELPHIA

Mystic and Scientist

Mystery attaches to the first Jew born in Pennsylvania. We know neither his birth year nor the name of his parents. Under the assumed name of Jacob Philadelphia, he attained fame in Europe as lecturer, scientist, mystic, astrologer and magician.

In 1750 Jacob sailed for England, armed with a recommendation that got him an appointment in the experimental laboratories belonging to the Duke of Cumberland. How he got training for scientific experimentation in a sparsely settled land without the facilities for elementary learning remained an open question until answered by Julius F. Sachse. This investigator unearthed a community of mystics who lived near Philadelphia at the close of the 17th century. In this communistic group known as "Woman of the Wilderness" were Rosicrucian pietists who lived in seclusion as hermits and cultivated the Jewish Cabala with other occult speculations. One of them, Dr. Christopher Witt, practiced medicine and lived in semi-retirement at Germantown.

This Dr. Witt was reputed to be a botanist and astronomer. He had knowledge of Cabalistic and esoteric lore; he seemed well versed in physics, chemistry, horology and the mechanical arts. Astrology fitted in with his astronomy, as the occult with the scientific. All this amazing learning would perish in the wilderness of a new world unless passed on to disciples. It appears that the German doctor imparted his science and learning, the mystical and the occult, to the Jewish lad thirsting for knowledge in the woodlands of Pennsylvania surrounded by red savages.

The letter from Dr. Witt had great weight with Lord Henry Frederick, Duke of Cumberland, who became patron to the American student. Jacob spent several years on the Duke's estate. He studied mathematics and perfected himself in the mechanical sciences. When the Duke died in 1758, Jacob was proficient enough to lecture before learned societies in England and universities on the continent.

The 18th century was a curious blend of contrasts. Against the Divine Right of Kings revolutions were brewing. In the face of despotic churches, a widespread deism and agnosticism prevailed. In this era of *Aufklaerung* (Enlightenment) the Inquisition was still roasting heretics in Spain and Portugal. Learning and philosophy attained high respect, yet ignorance was rampant. Mechanical and physical sciences began to astonish with their marvels, while the popular mind quaked under superstitious terrors.

In this combination of reason and obscurantism Giuseppe Balsamo, an Italian physican calling himself Count Cagliostro, could befuddle even the intelligent with his charlatanry. Casanova, a talented rascal, passed for a wandering philosopher. The Austrian Dr. Franz Anton Mesmer, who gave his name to the new phenomenon of hypnotism, had to indulge in mummery and quackery at his seances.

Jacob Philadelphia was qualified by nature and training for this European ambivalence of erudition and necromancy, of reason and mysticism, of physics and astrology, of science and crystal gazing. For good fees he delivered lectures before learned bodies and groups not so learned. While demonstrating scientific experiments, he evidently was not above resorting to hocus-pocus. Consequently, he impressed his contemporaries as part scientist and part magician, as a combination of physicist and sorcerer, of pioneer in the mechanics of submarines and astrologist. He traveled extensively, probably to Egypt, India, and even to Portugal, the latter country just beginning to shake off the incubus of the Inquisition.

Success and fame usually provoke envy. Jacob Philadelphia became the butt of some racy, if not malicious, satire on the occasion of his scheduled lectures before the University of Gottingen. A wag printed a number of derisive pasquinades and posted them all over the place. They announced the coming by post-chaise, "although it would have been an easy matter for him to have come through the air," of the renowned magician, who two centuries earlier in Venice had thrown a ball of twine into the clouds and climbed the rope until out of sight. Ironically, the wit lists seven superhuman tricks for each performance at one thaler admission. Perhaps the joker meant nothing more harmful than rollicking fun, but the travesty seemed too vicious for the scientific lecturer who couldn't see the humor. Immediately on seeing the posters he left Gottingen with his retinue. Nothing could induce him to return or ever to address the university.

By 1783, Jacob surmised the American Revolution to be over. Probably tired of travel, he prepared to become a man of affairs by utilizing his knowledge of American and Prussian business. He drafted a letter to the Royal Director of Maritime Affairs for Prussia, hoping it would reach Frederick the Great. It contains sound observations on the benefits that would accrue to Prussia by establishing commercial relations with the new American Republic. He enumerates the commodities and manufactured products that could be exchanged and suggests a trading company to handle the business at great profit to the shareholders. Of course, Jacob offers his services as the best expert on American matters in Europe. The letter was ignored; yet the following year King Frederick signed with the U.S.A. a commercial treaty, which substantially embodied the ideas set out by the "magician-scientist".

The career of Jacob Philadelphia is shrouded in obscurity. In fact, he was completely forgotten but for a small engraved portrait hanging on the walls of the Pennsylvania Historical Society. Starting with this photo, Dr. Sachse has traced his story in the files of German universities. No evidence has been discovered of any Jewish associations. His picture reveals strong Dutch features. It would have been as easy to suppress his Jewish origin as the family name. Perhaps he did. It was no religious sacrifice, for like most eminent men of his time he was, no doubt, a deist or agnostic.

As a professing Jew, he could hardly have received invitations to lecture before learned societies at a time of religious intolerance, when Jews were shut up in ghettoes of Germany and Italy. Yet the German sources do state he was Jewish. After returning to his birthplace he seems to have had no affiliations with his brethren in Philadelphia. Evidently he could not find his place in the new world and returned to Europe. The time or place of his death is unknown.

1784

HAYMAN LEVY

Indian Trader

Recent arrivals in colonial New York might have watched the Indians with fear and wonder as they crowded Beaver Street in front of Hayman Levy's warehouse. Were they seeking trouble? Why was the store locked and barred in broad daylight? A Jewish holiday might be the answer. Then they came to scalp the Jew trader for some advantage taken, the newcomers were sure to surmise. Yet the Indians were peaceful enough. Brave and squaw sat on the ground, their backs leaning against the wall ready for the night's sleep.

The following daybreak the clerks arrived, perhaps accompanied by a Negro slave or two, and ready to unlock and unbolt. Among the workers was a German immigrant, possibly John Jacob Astor, glad to earn a dollar per day beating out furs and peltries. Unnoticed he kept eyes and ears open, learning all he could about furs from one of the largest fur traders in the Colonies. The European onlookers then saw Hayman Levy coming. Yet the Indians stood or sat in stolid silence while the sachem or

33

chief gravely handed his smoking pipe to the paleface merchant for several puffs. The red men brought skins, wampum belts, maize, antler horns, medicinal bark to trade for calico, hatchets, blankets, beads, or rings. The primitive folk appeared satisfied that the white trader gave them the best deal obtainable in the big city of wood and stone wigwams. He might even explain in their own tongue why he would not give them firewater or fire-arms.

Born 1721 in Hanover, young Hayman followed his Hano-verian King George to England, then found his way to the Colo-nies. Trading in the northern wilds of the New York province, he formed early friendships with Indians. That he also knew the cruel streaks of Indian nature can be judged from a letter sent by his agent in 1757 after the fall of Fort William Henry. Manuel Josephson described graphically the ferocity of the red savages scalping the white officers, as well as the women and children, whom the French General Montcalm either could not or would not protect.

In the midst of the French and Indian War, Hayman Levy fitted out ships to prey on the enemy's commerce. Privateering was a hazardous business, approved and encouraged by govern-ments before submarines sank belligerent shipping on the high seas. Instead of enriching himself, he was bankrupt. The new restrictions which the British imposed upon colonial business added to his troubles. Perhaps resentment against measures de-signed to ruin American merchants induced Levy to sign the historic boycott not to import or use English merchandise.

Business troubles brought Levy into court as a plaintiff. A char-acter assassin went about making slanderous statements about Hayman's integrity. This libel was altogether without foundation and Levy, quick tempered and sharp tongued himself, filed suit for defamation of character. The entire community stood ready to testify as to his sterling honesty. The defendant felt happy to get off with payment of court costs and publish a most abject apology in the newspapers. The trouble maker probably learned that Levy's creditors had received full payment of principal and interest, after helping him make a fresh start.

Energetic, capable, vigorous, and worshiped by Indians who continued to bring their furs, Hayman Levy succeeded again. Soon he owned a string of buildings on Beaver (formerly Duke) Street. But misfortune came back. A fire reduced his houses to ashes. By now the Revolution was on in full blast. A patriotic reputation enabled him at once to do business with the armed forces. Two resolutions adopted by the Continental Congress of 1776 authorize payments to Hayman Levy for supplies. But the fortunes of war turned against him. George Washington retreated from Long Island and the Americans prepared to abandon the heights on Manhattan overlooking the Hudson, later named after their general. Together with other patriots, Levy fled New York and took refuge in Philadelphia, the capital of the young nation, and the only Jewish community left functioning in the new free republic. He took the oath of allegience to Pennsylvania and, although in his late fifties, joined the state militia as a private.

Patriot, merchant of capacity, Indian trader, and perhaps for a time the most extensive colonial fur dealer, Hayman Levy's true significance lay nevertheless in leadership. His talent in the direction of communal affairs was early recognized. Talking freely in the synagogue yard, he was fined 20 shillings for using "indecent and abusive language" to the Parnass. Yet his guilt could not have been too black, for at the same meeting he in turn was elected Parnass, or president. The 35 year old trader, up to his neck in furnishing army supplies and commissioning ships for privateering, paid a second fine that day for declining the honor!

His prestige may have been increased on marrying the sister of Myer Myers, the noted artist-silversmith, native born and rooted in the community. His influence rose still higher when the up and coming merchants Isaac Moses and Benjamin Mendes Seixas became his sons-in-law. His authority was felt in closing Shearith Israel and removing the Torahs and ritual silverware to Stratford, Connecticut, as the British advanced towards New York. At the order of Hayman Levy, supported by Isaac Moses, the minister Gershom Mendes Seixas left Stratford and brought along the ritual objects to Philadelphia. Hayman Levy became an active reorganizer of Mikveh Israel and contributed to building the Philadelphia Synagogue the then considerable sum of £73—the third largest donation. At the dedication he was accorded the honor of opening the Holy Ark.

After the war Hayman Levy, his family and in-laws returned to New York. They found Shearith Israel standing and somehow in operation. Even a hazzan was officiating. But to the patriot exiles the synagogue without their favorite minister Gershom Seixas was simply unthinkable. The reorganized congregation quickly reelected their spiritual leader at the salary of £200 a year, 6 cords of hickory wood, matzos, the usual perquisites, £6 and 8 shillings for the expenses of coming home. Hayman Levy wrote demanding the return of Seixas in time to officiate for Passover. Two weeks seemed little time for preparations and traveling. Mikveh Israel begged a respite of several months longer, and Seixas pleaded sickness and bad weather. But the parnass was adamant that the Minister return for Passover. He did.

Hayman Levy, his son-in-law Isaac Moses and brother-in-law Myer Myers addressed a letter of welcome to DeWitt Clinton upon his return. They reminded their governor that though "the antient congregation of Israelites lately returned from exile . . . . is but small when compared with other religious societies . . . . yet none has manifested a more zealous attachment to the sacred cause of America in the late war with Great Britain."

1785

DAVID FRANKS

The Tory Man of Business

THE ASSIMILATIONIST is essentially a climber. He desires to improve his status by changing religion or by marrying into a higher caste. David Franks had reason to be grateful to a kind fate. His father, though born in Germany, prospered in New York and became the King's agent for the northern colonies. How else could he have married Bilhah Abigail, daughter of Spanish born Moses Levy?

David's parents were devoted to Judaism. A special prayer was recited every Yom Kippur in memory of his mother for helping to build the Shearith Israel Synagogue out of stone to replace the small frame building on Mill Street, worshipped in by the Spanish-Portuguese Jews in early 18th century. Yet the Franks' standard of living embraced the patronage of art. Colonial paintings of Moses and Abigail Franks have come down to us. Another picture shows their son David, a tall well-formed lad of 16, holding a bird on his forefinger, together with his sister Phila, of dark eyes and black hair, about two years his junior. Later Phila mar-

ried Oliver De Lancey of Van Cortland stock, and her surname
is preserved on New York's Lower East Side highway of Delancey Street.

New York for some reason cramped David's style. The Dutch
city probably seemed dull and provincial alongside Philadelphia,
the social and cultural hub of Colonial America. There he would
mingle with the English elite of the Governor's party, and ignore
the democratic Quaker group with their drab clothes, their boor-
ish manners, their quaint speech. In Penn's capital he married the
High Episcopalian Margaret Evans and attained his social ambitions when invited in 1748 to become a member of the City Dancing Assembly, restricted to the "best citizens". All his children
were lost to Judaism.

David Franks at no time left the fold; but he was never affili-
ated with the only synagogue in Philadelphia, where he spent
most of his life. Nor did his assimilation notions prevent friendships and close associations with his coreligionists. His first partner and guide was Nathan Levy, the father of Philadelphia's Jewish community. The Gratz brothers were introduced to American
business in his counting-house, the 18th century term for a business office. He joined in many ventures with Joseph Simon of
Lancaster, his son-in-law Levy A. Levy, and the Gratzes.

As a business man, David Franks rose to great importance. He
ranks with Joseph Simon and the Gratz brothers as an Indian
trader. He also acquired vast tracts of land and contributed his
share in their colonization. But in furnishing provisions to the
British forces in the French and Indian War, he outstripped any
victualler in the colonies. Such contracts were eagerly sought after
by the biggest merchants. It was no doubt due to his brother
Moses in London, a member of the firm of Colebrooks and Nes-
bitt and influential with the government, that David Franks became the chief provider to the English and Continental troops.
The London firm shared in the profits by exporting the necessary
provisions. The fact remains that David Franks is mentioned in
the Amherst Papers far more than any other purveyor.

With the war over, the colonists anticipated a peace that would promote industry and commerce. Instead Parliament passed the Stamp Act, which aroused bitterness and hostility. David Franks sided with the patriots and signed the Non-Importation Resolution. It was to his advantage as a large purveyor to be free of the burdensome new taxes. But as the situation deteriorated, circumstances forced him to veer to the side of England.

His Tory partisanship could not have been very pronounced. At the war's beginning, the Continental Congress voted him the contract to feed and house prisoners in the Philadelphia area. The entry of the British brought him together with other merchants in closer contact with the military authorities. The Franks' home became the center of entertainment and gaiety. His daughter, the beautiful and brilliant Rebecca, held sway over the English officers and amused Tory circles with her doggerel, lampooning Washington and his ragged Continentals. Yet when the patriots returned, David Franks was not molested. Rebecca was even sought after by the American officers. Only with the treachery of Benedict Arnold did resentment turn against all suspects. That Rebecca Franks was friendly with Margaret Shippen, the beautiful young wife of General Arnold, did not help matters. David Franks was arrested and tried. A jury found him not guilty. In London Moses Franks implored Lord North to exchange his brother for some American prisoners. When the offer reached the American lines, David Franks and his daughter Rebecca were already free. This mild treatment contrasted sharply with the tragic fate dealt out to another Jewish Loyalist. About the same time Isaac Hart of Newport was virtually torn to pieces by some patriots on Long Island.

After much difficulty, David Franks and daughter reached New York. She remained the favorite of the English and married Col. Henry Johnson. When peace was signed, Franks accompanied the married couple to England. Here, with all his sacrifices for the British cause, he found himself but a Tory refugee waiting for governmental aid. Evidently his brother Moses could not or would not help him. David wrote a letter in 1783 to Joseph Simon in Lancaster, complaining of loneliness, of coolness the English show to the impoverished, of the impossibility to borrow money in London. Yet he still had considerable land in America. He could hardly suppress bitterness in contrasting his own miserable plight with the esteem enjoyed by his former associates who remained loyal patriots.

It did not take too long to find out the ingratitude of governments. He petitioned Parliament for a grant of £1125 sterling, a small return for his losses. His application was strongly supported by Sir William Howe, the commander in the American war, and Peter DeLancey, another Tory residing in London. Both were in a position to know the price he paid for his loyalty to Britain. Franks was allowed £125 for his claim, and the commission recommended £100 a year as a pension. There was nothing else to do but return home and face the sneers and insults of his former associates.

The former tycoon found his way back to Philadelphia. In the changed world, his previous contacts turned a deaf ear to pleas for assistance. He could only turn to his Jewish associates for help in his time of need. His lands were a drug on the market, with Congress giving away 400 acre parcels to almost anyone who shouldered a musket in the War for Independence. Joseph Simon and Michael Gratz advanced him small sums. His misery was finally ended when the yellow fever swept the city in 1793. Instead of an honored grave in the Mikveh Israel cemetery among the first Jewish families of Colonial America, David Franks, the assimilator whose daughter married a nephew of Pennsylvania's Governor, found his final resting place in Potter's Field.

1786

AARON LEVY

Of Aaronsburg

THE LITTLE TOWN of Aaronsburg tucked away in the forests of eastern Pennsylvania witnessed a unique celebration on October 23, 1949. About 30,000 visitors from far and near came to this town of about 400 residents. The Governor of Pennsylvania spoke. Dr. Ralph Bunche, fresh from mediating an armistice between Israel and the Arab States, delivered an address and Justice Felix Frankfurter of the U. S. Supreme Court read a paper. The day was taken up with pageants, symposiums, and panel discussions, participated in by eminent figures in religion, education, journalism, and government.

Ostensibly it was all in commemoration of the 150th anniversary of Salem Lutheran Church. Actually, the assemblage turned into an inter-faith demonstration, dedicated to religious, racial, and social toleration, with Aaron Levy as a symbolic figure dominating the celebration. Honor was paid to the memory of the Jewish founder of Aaronsburg, who in 1786 donated the ground upon which the church was built.

In 1760, Yiddish speaking Aaron Levy then in his late teens arrived in Philadelphia. An emigrant from Holland, his origins seem German or Polish and, judging from the books brought over by his nephew, the family background was religious and Talmudic. For about a decade, Aaron trafficked about between Philadelphia, Northumberland and Lancaster, where the example or advice of Joseph Simon induced him to trade with the Indians.

But merchandising and Indian trading were incidental. Aaron Levy's fame rests on real estate. As a real estate operator, he ranks with the foremost among the numerous land speculators in all the colonies. The number and extent of his transactions are astonishing. He appears to have owned land in every county of Pennsylvania. In his study on Aaron Levy, Dr. Sidney S. Fish tabulates 74 transactions in Northumberland and 88 in Centre County. The deals range from single lots to 26,000 acre tracts, as revealed in recorded documents. One must bear in mind that the population in all the 13 colonies scarcely reached 3,000,000 souls.

One of these tracts lying in Penns Valley and situated in Centre County was particularly beautiful. Thirty miles from Northumberland, surrounded by fertile soil, the spot promised to be ideal for farmers to sell their produce. Located in the very center of the new county about to be incorporated, this tract, it was presumed, would become the seat of county government. It was on the road leading to Philadelphia. A newly projected highway to Ft. Pitt (Pittsburgh) would surely cross at this strategic point. The nearby navigable water could link the town with the large cities on the coast. Good timber and stone quarries in the neighborhood provided building material for homes, churches, stores, schools, and public buildings. The imagination of Aaron Levy envisioned a thriving community that would become a prosperous city of commerce and civilized living.

The projected town he named Aaronsburg. The planning, the prospectus, even the advertising show that the modern realtor has nothing to teach the land prospector of the 18th century. The ordinary 50 foot streets intersected each other at right angles. The main avenue 160 feet wide, called Aaron's Square, was prepared for public buildings. He named the intersecting 100 foot boulevard Rachel's Way, in honor of his wife. The lots averaging 60x220 ft. were auctioned off at $6 each, with a dollar annual ground rent, the purchaser to receive full title on paying 20 "Spanish silver milled dollars". Plots reserved for churches were presented as gift parcels to several Christian denominations.

The great expectations for Aaronsburg did not materialize. Aaron Levy anticipated a large immigration to the free Republic of the West following the Peace Treaty. But the new government, without stability and deeply in debt, had to sustain a severe economic depression that settled on the new country. Revolutions and Napoleonic Wars prevented a sizable immigration. Levy suffered keen disappointment when Centre County selected Bellfonte as its seat of government instead of the better located Aaronsburg. At the turn of the century only 32 families inhabited the town. Aaron Levy left nothing undone to attract settlers. He authorized a relative in London to sell land to prospective immigrants. Perhaps the economic crisis reduced Levy's commercial resources. Possibly Christian prejudice militated against settling in "Jewstown," as Aaronsburg was often referred to. Today, in spite of American prosperity and with all the industrial development of Pennsylvania, the town has not more than 400 inhabitants.

Aaron Levy experienced the ups and downs of real estate speculation. The buying splurge following the French and Indian War was halted with the Revolution. Hard money, not too abundant in the pre-Constitution days under the Articles of Confederation, made selling real estate difficult, especially since Congress gave away public lands to war veterans. Overloaded with properties, Levy found himself land poor. Aaronsburg strained his resources and caused him to mortgage such holdings as would attract a lender. Instead of a tycoon, he turned agent and placed his abilities at the disposal of powerful land interests.

Robert Morris, War Director of Finance for the Continental

Congress, headed a real estate syndicate and used Levy to discover large tracts of at least 40,000 acres. Morris agreed to pay for warrants, surveys, patenting, the cost of chaincarriers, pack horses, and provisions. Levy's compensation was £15 for each 1000 acres. This connection was profitable for a time. The Morris interests swung large deals and collapsed. Aaron Levy was among the heavy losers, yet his confidence in Robert Morris remained unimpaired.

Association with James Wilson was more satisfactory. This distinguished jurist, statesman, signer of the Declaration of Independence, drafter of the Federal Constitution, and Washington's appointee on the Supreme Court was interested in acquiring large acreage, but for colonizing rather than speculation. Levy contracted to furnish James Wilson with 500,000 acres.

Aaron Levy and wife spent their last days in Philadelphia. Childless, they adopted as their son and heir Simon Gratz, brother of the famous Rebecca. It is rather surprising that Aaron's will makes no bequests for charities, not even a plot of ground for Mikveh Israel of which he was a member. He did, however, during the darkest hour of the war make a loan to the U.S.A.; and in spite of all the influence of Robert Morris, he was not repaid—at least not in full.

1787

COLONEL
DAVID S. FRANKS

Treaty Bearer

IN QUEBEC some one smeared on the monument of George III "This is the Pope of Canada and the Fool of England." An excited Frenchman fumed that the culprit should be hanged. The youthful merchant David Salisbury Franks remarked, "In England men are not hanged for such a small offense." A fracas ensued, and David knocked the Frenchman down. A warrant was sworn out, but not for assault and battery. In the high tensions of 1775, Franks was held on £10,000 bail, exorbitant even in our day of inflation. After a week he was released without trial.

Shortly thereafter he had occasion to show more concretely his sympathy for the Revolutionary Colonials. When General Montgomery occupied Quebec, Franks helped with money that was badly needed. Having stuck out his neck, he had to follow through and join the American forces on their withdrawal from Canada. After leaving Montreal, he served until Burgoyne surrendered at Saratoga, then reenlisted in the forces of the French Count D'Estaing.

45

By 1780, the humble private had become Major David S. Franks on the staff of Gen. Benedict Arnold. Normally he would have served to the war's end and gone back into business, possibly with his chief, who liked money and talked of a partnership with his Jewish aid-de-camp. Franks' memory would have been preserved on the army roll, a name among many others. But he got into history through the treason of his commander. With Benedict Arnold's defection, Major Franks and Col. Varick were arrested and court-martialed. This was routine procedure, and the trial cleared both staff officers of any possible guilt in connection with Arnold's treason.

But Franks felt uneasy. There were too many whisperings and insinuations. People knew of his friendship with the traitor general, who entrusted his beautiful wife and children to the Major's care. Besides, David Franks and his daughter, the fascinating Rebecca, suspected as Tories and possibly enemies of the republic, were evidently in some way related; unwittingly they cast aspersions on their namesake. He therefore sent a well written letter to Gen. Washington urging a new trial that would investigate fully his conduct prior to Arnold's flight. This was unnecessary, since Benedict Arnold had the decency to inform the Commander-in-Chief by letter that neither his wife, nor Col. Varick, nor Major Franks had any part or knowledge of the affair. A new trial was ordered. Franks requested the State Council of Pennsylvania to send all pertinent records and papers to be read in evidence. The minutes of this trial make exciting reading. Major Franks and Col. Varick cross-examined each other minutely as to all their actions. A complete vindication was handed down. But Franks was still not satisfied. He requested of Gen. Washington that all proceedings of the trial be made public.

After Yorktown, the army having little to do though technically the war was still on, Franks obtained a mission of honor and trust. He carried dispatches to Benjamin Franklin in Paris and John Jay in Madrid. Detained by them in Europe, he got back somewhat late in June 1782 and delivered their answers safely.

Now he was amazed to find out that his name had been struck off the army roll. This was especially mortifying since his salary was cut off and the mission specifically stipulated no other emoluments than his army pay. How did it happen? Possibly he did not apply for army leave, thinking that Robert Morris, the Director of Finance who sent him, would attend to that minor detail. One could venture a guess that such bungling could not happen to an Adams, a Laurens, or a Pinckney. He had to go through the red tape of a memorial to Congress for reinstatement and back pay. Robert Morris joined his petition, and the Secretary of State ultimately reissued his commission, pursuant to a resolution of Congress.

While Franks was, what we would call today, a go-getter, a business career, after his army experience, appeared no longer attractive. He longed for one of those consulships the young republic needed in many foreign countries. His application, studded with prominent Gentile recommendations, was filed and pigeonholed. Instead he received an assignment which many ex-officers would have accepted gladly. In Jan. 1784 Congress resolved to send Lt. Col. David S. Franks to deliver the signed Treaty of Peace to the American Ministers in France. Time seemed of the essense and the date for sailing was fixed not later than Feb. 3rd. But New York harbor was frozen and no boat could break through the ice. On Feb. 8th he wrote Congress of the necessity of his transgressing the law and embarking when the weather permitted. After a disagreeable voyage of six weeks and four days he landed at Dover only to learn that Messrs. Franklin and Jay were in London. Proceeding to London, he found they had returned to Paris. After more shuttling and the ratification of the treaty, he delivered additional dispatches to Amsterdam.

Remaining in Europe, he accepted the vice-consulship of Marseilles from a reluctant Mr. Barclay, who probably did not have the authority for such an appointment. But with the approval of Thomas Jefferson and John Adams, Franks felt secure. Later he accompanied Mr. Barclay as secretary to negotiate a treaty with the Emperor of Morocco, as he called himself. Franks carried the original document to Jefferson in Paris and to Adams in London for their signatures. When he returned home, the new Constitution of the United States was awaiting the ratification of the thirteen states.

Franks persisted in his appeals to Pres. Washington and Sec. Jefferson for a consular appointment to France. Jefferson found him honest, active, affectionate, of more than common understanding, yet a bit indiscreet in conversation, especially among the ladies, with whom the Colonel was a favorite. The real reason that no consulate was forthcoming remains hidden. His qualifications seem adequate. Meanwhile he helped found the Society of the Cincinnati, a secret organization for officers of the late war, subsequently to become a citadel of reaction and snobbery for their descendants.

Congress also voted 400 acres for his war services as additional compensation under the Land Grant Law. He became involved with a real estate company in a French settlement in the Ohio Valley, the location of his land. The tactics of his associates caused extreme dissatisfaction. Before long the Indians were on the trail and massacred all the French settlers. Meanwhile Franks had accepted the important post as assistant cashier of the Bank of the United States. His career was brought to a sudden close in 1793 either by the yellow fever, or perhaps he was among the French colonists in Ohio massacred by the Indians.

Who was this David Salisbury Franks? Probably a member of the numerous Franks family, which participated on both sides of the Revolutionary struggle. Born apparently in Philadelphia, he moved to Montreal, and when quite young served as president of its Shearith Israel Synagogue. After leaving Canada, he seems to have had no further Jewish associations, not even with the elite Franks menage in Philadelphia.

1788

JONAS PHILLIPS

Staunch Libertarian

Jᴏɴᴀʜ Fᴇɪʙᴜsʜ, born about 1736 in Rhenish Prussia, managed somehow to reach London. Unaware that his paternal surname was the ghetto version of Phoebus Apollo, the Greek sun god of music and poetry, he cast off all Judeo-German handicaps by Anglicizing into Jonas Phillips.

Jonas no doubt worked hard to make a living in the English capital until meeting the ebullient Moses Lindo. This loquacious, self-advertising promoter, expert of indigo and cochineal, painted a glowing picture of the unlimited opportunities in the lands beyond the western sea. In fact Lindo himself was contemplating a change from misty, fog-laden London to the cheerful, sunny atmosphere in South Carolina. But how could an impoverished alien obtain passage across 3000 miles of ocean? Quite simple. Just sign a paper to serve Moses Lindo several years for the passage, for food and clothes.

Thus like a gentleman of quality, Moses Lindo traveled with a footman on board the *Charming Nancy*. Master and servant

49

settled in Charleston, and Jonas worked faithfully, judging from a letter written years later by Lindo "that he believes the said Jonas trustworthy even of Gold untold." He even saved a neat sum. For at the termination of the indenture, he was able to travel a long stretch and start business on his own. One might question the necessity of going to far away Albany, an outpost of New York's white civilization, when Charleston with its balmy climate and substantial Jewish community offered as good if not better prospects.

In Albany, Jonas opened a store, became a Master Mason and felt lonely. After two years, he advertises his intention to leave and offers his "best Hyson green tea in pound canisters, wines, brandies, tea, raisins by the cask, Florence Oyl by the box, milk and butter, biscuits in the cask" in exchange for "Beavers and deer skins, small furs, etc." The following year he married Rebecca, daughter of the Hazan David Mendes Machado and Zipporah Nunes Ribiero; a rise in the social ladder for Jonah, son of Feibush, now three years a freeman of Albany.

The marriage might offer a clue for his leaving Charleston. The liberated servant of Moses Lindo could never hope to be received by the snobbish Sephardim. But 1500 miles removed in the wilds of New York made all the difference for the ambitious Ashkenazi whose handsome face, according to the old painting, is more typically Anglo-Saxon than the features of Thomas Jefferson or John Hancock. This union was happy, if 21 children in 23 years is any indication of domestic felicity. It certainly assured his place as an outstanding ancestor in Jewish annals of early America. His grandsons, the quixotic editor and politician Mordecai M. Noah and the naval officer "Commodore" Uriah P. Levy, are among his numerous descendants, Jewish and Christian.

As the family grew, business declined. It became harder each day to do business against the British restrictions that were driving the colonies to war. Jonas Phillips assigned his assets for the benefit of creditors and obtained a court release as an insolvent debtor. Now his knowledge and orthodoxy came in handy. The New York community appointed him *shohet* and *bodek* (slaughterer and overseer of ritual meat) at a salary of £35 a year. He held on four years, then tried business again. Following the Hebrew maxim that a change of place is a change of luck, he moved to Philadelphia.

This time he was successful. The coming war created boom conditions, and scarce merchandise brought high prices in the soaring market of the national capital. In contrast to other merchants with strong Tory leanings, Jonas Phillips was an ardent patriot. He signed the Non-Importation agreement. Father to a brood of children, merchant on the main street and 43 years old, he joined the Philadelphia militia.

In Jewish affairs he took a leading part. His donation of £145 for the construction of a new synagogue was second only to Haym Salomon's and larger than the contribution of the far wealthier Gratz Brothers. Elected president of Mikveh Israel Congregation, Phillips is said to have written a letter inviting Gen. Washington to the dedication ceremony. The General did not attend, but the same source alleges that he sent a gracious reply. The legend, however, persists that George Washington was present at the wedding of Phillips' daughter Zipporah to Manuel Noah, the future parents of the famous Mordecai M. Noah.

Jonas Phillips has the distinction in American history of being the only outside person to address the convention assembled in Philadelphia to formulate the Constitution of the United States. He pointed out the defective provision embedded in the Pennsylvania Constitution which required of any one holding public office to swear to the belief that the Old and New Testament were both given by divine inspiration. In the letter to the delegates, he wrote:

"It is well known among all the Citizens of the 13 United States that the Jews have been true and faithful whigs, & during the late Contest with England they have been foremost in aiding and assisting the states with their lifes and fortunes, they have supported the cause, have bravely fought and bled for liberty which they cannot Enjoy.—

"Therefore if the honourable Convention shall in their Wisdom think fit and alter the said oath & leave out the words to viz— and I do acknowledge the scripture of the new testament to be given by divine inspiration—then the Israelites will think themselves happy to live under a government where all Religious societys are on an Equal footing."

Jonas Phillips did not know that two weeks earlier the Convention had already inserted into the new Constitution a provision that no religious test shall ever be imposed as a qualification to any office or public trust under the United States. Another incident reveals his vigorous and staunch Judaism. He was cited to appear in court on Sabbath and testify as a witness. Jonas Phillips ignored the summons and proudly paid the fine of £10.

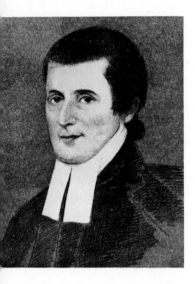

1789

GERSHOM MENDES
SEIXAS

Patriot Rabbi

In 1766, the vestry of Shearith Israel received an application for the position of Hazan from 23 year old Gershom Mendes Seixas. American born, he was related to the elite Sephardim of the congregation. His father, a New Christian in Portugal, had entered the covenant of Judaism and married the daughter of Moses Levy, Parnass and leader in the New York community of early 18th century. There were no other applicants, and the trustees elected the youthful "rabbi" with enthusiasm.

Gershom Seixas was hardly an ordained rabbi in the technical sense. He had neither the required learning nor the traditional *semicha*. Yet with him emerges a new kind of religious leadership that answered the needs of sparse settlements in a new world. The ancient concept of rabbi was neither priest, levite, pastor, monk, nor preacher. No intercessor or intermediary with the Almighty, and without function in the synagogue, he was simply one of a *minyan*, the minimum unit of ten males devised by Orthodox Judaism for public prayer, which required no altar or ceremonial, no vestments or effigies, no rabbi or priest.

53

All through the Middle Ages and almost to our own century, the rabbi was the repository of learning, adviser and leader, the judge whose decisions rested on a religious code. No spell-binding maggid (preacher), he delivered a learned discourse once or twice a year. Obviously the small communities in a new world could hardly afford the learned *Haham,* without a place in the Ritual. Religious direction fell perforce upon the Reader, who assumed the additional duties of Shohet, Mohel and became the true shepherd of the flock.

Gershom Seixas did not originate a new officiant for the Synagogue; but in him the Hazan-Preacher found complete expression as minister and religious director. Not until 1845 did a rabbi ordained in Europe officiate on any pulpit in the U.S.A. Yet the Hazan-Shohet-Mohel continued to function as religious head of many a community, until displaced in our own day by the seminary trained rabbi, who resembles the Protestant Pastor far more than the *Rav* of bygone days.

The youthful Hazan soon had occasion to show his leadership. As the struggle with England loomed, it was no simple matter to discern the underlying issue. Patrick Henry might declaim with passionate eloquence, "Give me liberty or give me death." Yet there were no actual persecutions. The "best people" of wealth and talents stood by the Crown. Most Christian preachers in New York were Tories. It took courage and insight for Gershom Seixas to throw in his lot with the "rebels", looked down upon by his more wealthy parishioners as mere rabble.

The revolutionary spirit swept Seixas along in its current. Possibly identified with the Minute Men, he had reason for apprehension after Washington's retreat from Long Island. Seixas refused to remain in New York. The English did not interfere with religious freedom, yet the *Hazan* took no chances; he preached a patriotic sermon and closed the Synagogue. He took along the Torahs, the silverware, the candlesticks, and found refuge in Stratford, Connecticut.

Most members of Shearith Israel, being patriots, fled. In

Philadelphia they, together with other refugees, swelled the existing congregation into the largest Jewish community in America. A spiritual leader was necessary, and the New Yorkers sent to Stratford for their Hazan. He assisted in organizing Mikveh Israel, the congregation that ranked second in the early republic. Two distinguished New Yorkers rallied to his side. Haym Salomon and Jonas Phillips, former constituents, made liberal contributions to the building fund of a new Synagogue. With the end of the war in sight, the dedication took place and included a special prayer in English for the President, the Congressmen and "His Excellency George Washington, Captain General and Commander in Chief."

After the Treaty of Peace, many war refugees returned to their homes. Seixas might have remained with Mikveh Israel but for the insistent demand that he return to New York. Before leaving he, as Rabbi of Philadelphia's Synagogue, with Barnard Gratz and Haym Salomon and others petitioned the Pennsylvania authorities to amend the State Constitution by removing the requirement of any one taking public office to declare upon oath that the New Testament was of divine inspiration. This was but a variant of the British oath "on the true faith of a Christian," devised against would-be Jewish members of Parliament. No action was taken. But the petition was not wasted. Four years later, the framers of the Federal Constitution assembled in Philadelphia adopted a provision that no religious test shall ever be required to hold office under these United States.

The swing towards liberalism ushered in by the long war for independence affected the first native born rabbi. He was obviously influenced by the new currents sweeping through the America of Thomas Jefferson. Orthodox and pious, he nevertheless foreshadowed the coming reforms in America Judaism. In sermon and service, he discarded Portuguese for English. The first to attempt inter-faith good will, he lectured on Jewish history in St. Paul's Church of New York, something hitherto unheard of in America or Europe. When President Washington called upon the nation to set aside the last Thursday in November for prayer and gratitude, Seixas set an example to Christians and Jews by opening the Synagogue for the first Thanksgiving Day.

The capable, patriotic Hazan was recognized as religious leader by Jews and Christians. Christian scholars consulted him on questions of interpretation in the Hebrew Bible. A trustee of the Humane Society, he was elected by the state legislature on the first Board of Regents for the University of the State of New York. At the inauguration of George Washington, he was present among the Christian clergymen, though not on the platform which was too small for the large concourse. One of the incorporators of Columbia College, he served as trustee for 30 years and rendered services on committees of this institution, which in its early days was Protestant and denominational. Columbia University struck a medal in honor of Gershom Mendes Seixas and on its 175th anniversary unveiled his portrait, which hangs among the institution's celebrities.

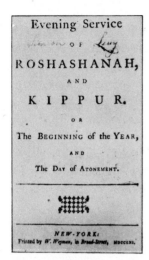

1790

ISAAC PINTO

Of New York

Lᴎᴛᴛʟᴇ ɪs ᴋɴᴏᴡɴ of the Pintos in Colonial New York or Connecticut. Research has not yet disclosed whether they were all related or even members of the same clan. Names do not reveal much, since Pinto on the Spanish Peninsula is as common as Jones in England.

Most of the Pintos lived in New Haven. Abraham, Solomon, and William, sons of Jacob and Thankful Pinto, had graduated from Yale. They are mentioned in the diary of Ezra Stiles, the liberal Congregational minister and learned President of Yale College. Their mother's name, *Thankful,* shows Puritan influence of early America upon the tiny Jewish group. The family appears to have become well integrated into its environment. Some of its members, perhaps, had become Christians. Two of the brothers were wounded in the battles of the Revolution. Solomon Pinto rose to be an officer of the Connecticut Seventh Regiment, and after the war he was a founder of the Society of the Cincinnati.

The same Ezra Stiles also mentions another Pinto as "a learned Jew of New York." The President of Yale evidently meant the Isaac Pinto who, born in 1720, was never married and died in his 72nd year. Buried in the Chatham Square Cemetery of the Congregation Shearith Israel, he has the distinction of being "Etched in Stone" 161 years later by the scholarly Dr. David deSola Pool, Rabbi of the famous Spanish-Portuguese Synagogue.

For a scholar, Isaac Pinto seems to have done well in business; or he would hardly in 1747 have been assessed almost £5 for communal dues. Three years later he paid £1 and 6 shillings for his synagogue seat, substantial assessments for the economy of two centuries ago.

His part in practical affairs is recorded in a protest. The New York Legislature of 1761 devised a measure for protection against the spread of fire, an ever present hazard to life and property almost to our own era. The law required all new buildings south of a certain *Fresh Water Pond* to be of stone or brick, with the roofs of tin or slate; the enactment to take effect 15 years later.

Such legislation would seem a reasonable protective measure. We might understand Pinto's protest if he were an active builder of new structures. Wood in the colonies was cheap and plentiful. But a hardship to the public becomes apparent when we read further that the same roofing material had to be used in the repair of old houses. This law hit tenant as well as landlord. All such materials had to be imported. Each purchase thus brought profit to British manufacturers, while the reactionary policies of George III prohibited manufacturing in the colonies.

But when we see Isaac Pinto signing the resolution to continue the Non-Importation Agreement, which the merchants adopted in 1765 to boycott British made articles, we then understand the patriotic reasons behind all these petitions. They were economic sanctions imposed by the American Colonials, the prelude to the Revolution, the opening phase of the conflict that was settled on the battlefields.

Wars are waged on many fronts, and each combatant can best

do his bit in his special field. A scholar and writer, Pinto appears to have contributed to the literature that promoted and justified the Revolution. It seems quite probable that he wrote articles and tracts under the typical 18th century pseudonym of Philalethea. It is even more probable that Isaac Pinto was author of a pamphlet with the heavily scented Hebrew title, *The Chapters of Isaac the Scribe,* which describes in Biblical language the voyage of the vessel, the *Duchess of Gordon,* from New York to London.

Pinto evidently suffered financial reverses during the war. In 1784 when the scattered membership of Shearith Israel returned to reorganize communal life in New York, he was offered in his 64th year the secretaryship of the Congregation. Up to and including his last day, an advertisement appeared in the *Journal and Patriotic Register* that Spanish was taught by Isaac Pinto at 14 Duke Street.

The deeper interests of Pinto were scholarly rather than political or financial. On learning that Rabbi Isaac Karigal was in Newport, he corresponded with that colorful *meshulach* who traveled far and wide gathering funds for the poor or the learned in Palestine. The New Yorker was anxious to ascertain the meaning of certain Arabic words used by Abraham Ibn Ezra in his commentary on the Torah.

The chief reason for remembering Isaac Pinto stems from his two books, which any collector would prize as rare finds. If we except Judah Monis, the Harvard apostate and compiler of a Hebrew grammar, then Pinto ranks as the earliest Jewish author to appear in English America. In 1761 an English translation of the New Year and Yom Kippur evening service appeared. Its anonymous author expressed in the preface the pious wish: "not without Hope that it will tend to the improvement of many of my brethren in their Devotion." Five years later Isaac Pinto translated and had printed a more complete rendition of the Sabbath and High Holiday prayer book, "according to the order of the Spanish and Portuguese Jews." Both volumes contained no Hebrew text.

Those are the first English translations of the Hebrew Prayer Book in America. They antedate the German rendition of the Scriptures by Moses Mendelssohn, but were preceded by translations into Spanish, Portuguese, or Dutch. The need or motive for this self-appointed task is not too clear. In the 18th century Jews were anchored in orthodoxy. No one thought in terms of reform. To substitute any modern vernacular for Hebrew, the sacred language of the Torah, was unthinkable. Consequently, the value of his efforts are doubtful. For 20 years Pinto's rendition of the ancient service into English remained unsold. The Hebrew prayer book retained its primacy in the synagogue and at home.

Perhaps Isaac Pinto desired to enlighten Christians of the free new world as to the "mysterious" content in Jewish prayer. But if he saw the coming necessity for rendering the Hebrew service in English, then he anticipated Isaac Harby and Isaac M. Wise and becomes the earliest pioneer in the new world to blaze a trail for the reforms that took root in the synagogue a century later.

PRAYERS

FOR

SHABBATH, ROSH-HASHANAH, AND KIPPUR;

OR

The SABBATH, the BEGINING of the YEAR,

AND

The DAY of ATONEMENTS;

WITH

The AMIDAH and MUSAPH of the MOADIM,

OR

SOLEMN SEASONS.

According to the Order of the Spanish and Portuguese Jews,

Translated by ISAAC PINTO.

And for him printed by JOHN HOLT, in New-York.
A. M. 5526.

No. 45.

ISAAC PINTO'S TRANSLATION
OF HIGH HOLY DAY SERVICE.

1791

MICHAEL GRATZ

Colonizer and Trader

In his essay on character, Emerson devotes an illuminating paragraph on the merchant. "There are geniuses in trade, as well as in war, or the state, or letters; and the reason why this or that man is fortunate is not to be told. It lies in the man; that is all anybody can tell you about it." Emerson's observation might well apply to Michael Gratz, the capable business man of the 18th century, before big business had become departmentalized and bureaucratized in the modern corporation.

Michael Gratz was born in Silesia, not too far from the Polish border. Besides "learning" in the Yiddish speaking *cheder,* he somehow got some modern education, at least enough to long for a broader life removed from the medieval restrictions of Germany. Following his brother Barnard, he tarried in Amsterdam, then arrived in London to work for his relative Solomon Henry, a merchant of considerable importance. Together with good English manners he acquired a business background in a land which at that time excelled all others in commerce and shipping.

Longing for travel he sailed for India, to which the fabulous legends of Marco Polo still clung. In Madras, he found the chance of becoming a nabob shut off by the monopolistic East India Company, which had its own Clive or Hastings eagerly awaiting the opportunity to start fortune hunting. Returning to London, he found a letter awaiting him from his older brother, now in Philadelphia, offering to turn over his job in the flourishing counting-house of David Franks, one of the most successful traders in Pennsylvania.

Before long, Barnard and Michael, now in America, formed a partnership which lasted all their days. Following the example of their kinsman in London, they aimed at importing and exporting. In a short time, brigantines were taking their cotton and grain to France to be exchanged for wine and fruit. From Amsterdam cargoes of spices, silks, and tea sailed back to Philadelphia. With Solomon Henry in London to make connections in Europe and other associations in the West Indies, the partnership was on the way to gigantic international trade. Their wares were sold in all the colonies and new agents were solicited in New Orleans and Guadaloupe, in Quebec and Halifax. In touch with coreligionists in affluent Newport, Michael sought to emulate Aaron Lopez and own a fleet of ships. Acquiring *The Rising Sun* in 1770 further improved his growing status.

With Barnard taking care of the counting-house, Michael traveled incessantly on land and sea, on pack horse and flat boat. Voyaging to Curaçao he survived a ship wreck in the Caribbean. A ship captain was preparing to hoist sail and carry dispatches to Philadelphia. Sunset was about to usher in Friday eve and no time remained for a lengthy letter without violating the Sabbath. "Being just Shabat" in a short dispatch was enough notice to Barnard of his safe landing.

On his return, Michael found the province surging with the excitement brought about by the Stamp Act. A reactionary English cabinet had pushed the law through Parliament, blissfully unaware of the impact it would have on the colonials.

Instead of producing revenue, the hated Act generated a patriotic spirit which pledged the Americans to boycott stamped products. Mass meetings were pledging patriots not to wear imported clothes. A petition to cease all importation was circulated among the merchants; a policy which, if carried out, would put exporters-importers out of business. But B. and M. Gratz threw in their lot with their adopted country and in 1765 signed the Non-Importation Resolution.

While journeying about to establish a network of trading posts, Michael had visited Joseph Simon of Lancaster, then the outpost town of Pennsylvania's white settlements. The nabob of Lancaster recognized a kindred spirit in the young go-getter. Fond of partnerships, he offered the Gratz brothers a share in one of his many enterprises. The association became invaluable to the young business men as yet strange to the ways of a new world. It provided additional outlets for imported merchandise; it opened new vistas to their energies and capacities; it enabled them to grasp the possibilities of acquiring and colonizing land. But most important, it enabled Michael to marry Simon's daughter and raise that large famous family of capable sons and beautiful daughters, one of them Rebecca Gratz, the original of Scott's Rebecca in *Ivanhoe*.

Parliament ultimately repealed the Stamp Act, but Lord North's Cabinet continued its restrictive policies aimed at confining American business to rum, tobacco, and slavery. It was, therefore, opportune for the Gratz brothers to turn their attention towards the hinterland. They happened to strike the right time. Activities on the seaboard were shifting to the interior and the ablest minds foresaw that continued immigration would create a demand for the plentiful soil that was less valuable than money. Large land companies were forming with the participation of such prominent men as Franklin, Washington, Patrick Henry, Jefferson, Robert Morris, James Wilson, and many others. Some Jewish merchants joined these syndicates, others organized their own companies. B. and M. Gratz became deeply involved in land deals and finally surpassed Joseph Simon as Indian traders and landowners.

The Gratzes had to turn their backs to the sea and send to their trading posts such articles as were crudely manufactured in the colonies. They entered the fur trade, by far the most profitable in colonial America. But as a result of Indian depredations they lost heavily in goods and pack trains. As compensation, the Gratzes and other merchants received large tracts of earth from the Indians. Other lands they bought outright. But their vast tracts without settlements were useless; they were forced to become colonizers. With such associates as Joseph Simon, the keen-witted Scotsman William Murray, the shrewd negotiator George Croghan, who left the Benjamin Franklin group to join them, Barnard and Michael Gratz operated on the grand style and played an important part in linking the Ohio and Mississippi valleys to the Atlantic seaboard.

The Revolution curtailed business and colonization, and Michael Gratz transferred his energies to the war effort. The government could not muster a single ship to oppose the mighty sea power of Britain. The Continental Congress urged all patriots to fit out "private-men-of-war to seize and destroy the enemy." Gratz moved to Virginia and became active in fitting out boats on the Potomac. His privateers preyed on English commerce and helped to break the blockade.

Another important service was helping George Rogers Clark in his dash through the wilds of Illinois as far as Detroit. This expedition secured the great Northwest Territory to the U.S.A. Michael furnished the supplies for which he was paid back only a small part of the $7000 he advanced.

The contributions of Michael Gratz to early American colonization have not been adequately studied. References to his enterprises lie buried in the archives of many states. There is, however, sufficient data to indicate his part in founding many "governments", as the early settlements were called, in the Mississippi and Ohio valleys. After the Revolution he became involved in the project of draining the Dismal Swamp and planning a new colony in what is now West Virginia and northeastern Kentucky. He had a goodly share in opening the West as far as the Mississippi. From his own correspondence, we can see his activities in the wild regions of Pennsylvania and Virginia, and in that vast territory that subsequently became Ohio, Indiana, Illinois, and Kentucky. If history has been remiss, then geography has preserved his memory in "Gratz" on the Kentucky River and "Gratztown" in the Pittsburgh area.

SILVERWARE FASHIONED BY MYER MYERS
(SEE FOLLOWING CHAPTER).

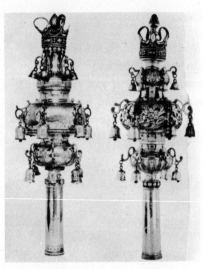

REMONIM BY MYER MYERS
IN NEWPORT SYNAGOGUE.

1792

MYER MYERS

Artist and Craftsman

On DISPLAY in museums of New York, Boston, Brooklyn, Philadelphia, Dearborn, and St. Louis can be seen old American silver objects, embossed MM in rectangle, or *Myers* engraved in script. This plate reflects the taste and style that obtained in the 18th century era of refinement, which received its tone from royalty and aristocracy, particularly of the *ancien regime* in France. Their line and proportion reveal artistry in craftsmanship.

Their artificer, Myer Myers, ranks high among the silversmiths of Colonial America, an honorable calling that claimed such prominent names as Brevoot, Van Dyke, and Roosevelt. Myer Myers is probably the first native born artist of English America—certainly the first Jew who made a contribution to American art. Yet both Jewish Encyclopedias fail to mention his name. To enjoy the grace and beauty of the gifted silversmith's work, one must consult the recent book on *Myer Myers* by Jeanette W. Rosenbaum.

The parents of Myer Myers sailed from Holland long after the

English changed New Amsterdam to New York. In 1723 Solomon Myers had a banner year. The Colonial Legislature passed a special act which naturalized him and other Jews, a privilege not granted for the mere asking, and unthinkable in Europe even amid the tolerance of Holland. At the same time his wife gave birth to the future artist. The legal phrase "freedom of the city" carried the right to exercise any handicraft. Young Myer could therefore be apprenticed to a master artisan who worked in gold and silver. After completing the legally required seven years training, the master craftsman Myer Myers opened his workshop.

Nothing is heard of him for seven years. The presumption points to his shop being kept busy. In 1753 he advertises in the New York *Gazette* offering a reward of £3 to the finder of his indentured servant, a jeweler and engraver. The following year the same paper carried a news item about the home of Isaac Seixas being robbed of two large silver tablespoons, stamped MM. Evidently the quality of his work was soon recognized, for we find among his customers the most distinguished names in the colony: the prominent Livingstons; the Murrays who survive in the Murray Hill of New York's telephone exchange; the historic Schuylers of Revolutionary fame; Samuel Johnson, the first President of Kings College, subsequently Columbia University.

Before the rise of large scale manufacture, when artistic plate indicated taste in every home, the English aristocracy were reputed good judges of workmanship in silver. We find Myer Myers estimating costs of a five-quart silver tureen, plain or chased, for Sir William Johnson, the Major-General of the French and Indian War who broke French power in America. The Jewish silversmith made sauce boats for the Commander in Chief of His Majesty's forces in North America, the Earl of Loudoun, who presented them to Colonel Meserve of New Hampshire for distinguished service in 1756 at Fort Edward. These powerful noblemen could easily import silverware from London by boats constantly crossing the ocean.

The fifty years activity of Myer Myers mark three changes of style in the 18th century. Rococo is imitated in his early coffee pots, salvers, sauce boats, candlesticks, snuffers with tray. Then follow the chaste and more restrained lines of the classical period in his covered and open *canns,* his saltcellars, teapots, table or tea spoons. The post-Revolutionary epoch is revealed in the solid practical tankards of the young nation on its own, no longer in need of currying favor. But the Federal era with a growing sense of dignified elegance is suggested in the sugar bowl containing the Goelet crest, reflecting an inner self-assurance of rising to noble heights.

Contrary to the rule, the art labors of Myer Myers paid off— at least enough to follow the general trend of speculating in land. After the French and Indian War, the Province of New Hampshire, no longer in dread of Indian attacks, is opened to settlers. Among the 100 grants of land in what later became Vermont, a deed is recorded in the name of Myer Myers. In 1765 he and two partners purchased a tract in Connecticut. In fact, he seems to have been prosperous all through life. Even as a patriotic exile after the British capture of New York, he was affluent enough to make a liberal donation towards building Mikveh Israel Synagogue in Philadelphia.

A devoted follower of Judaism, the artist-silversmith seems to have been free of the fanaticism which shrinks from making ritual objects for another creed. The Museum of the City of New York displays a baptismal bowl he cast for the Brick Presbyterian Church, and the Metropolitan Art Museum cherishes the broken alms basin he did for the First Presbyterian Church at the request of Peter H. Livingston.

But for the Synagogues of Newport, Philadelphia, and New York he reserves the emotion felt towards his ancestral faith. Unlike the Roman Church, the Synagogue offers few opportunities for expression in the plastic arts. But the *Rimonim* (pomegranates) with crown and silver tinkling bells that decorate the handwritten Torah scrolls have their origin in the high priestly garments described in Exodus. Like all religious art, these

Rimonim have long been stylized in conventional moulds. Yet Myer Myers lavished on them a wealth of design and detailed ornamentation, despite the limitations imposed by time and custom.

Besides artist, Myer Myers was father of a large family, patriot, community leader, and businessman. It was during his presidency of Shearith Israel that £149 were contributed for constructing the famous Newport Synagogue. In fact, congregational records are the chief source for the biographic details of his communal activities. Myers' standing in his profession was recognized when he was elected in 1786 chairman of the *Gold and Silver Society*. Like his fellow silversmith, the patriotic rider Paul Revere, Myers was attracted to Masonry and became Senior Warden of King David's Lodge in New York.

In the Revolutionary crisis he threw in his lot with the patriots and quit New York in 1776 before the British took over. Together with other refugees, he lived for a time in Norwalk, Conn., where his child Rebecca was born, then joined the ingathered colony of Jewish exiles in Philadelphia. His loyalty was such that he signed an affidavit reporting the New Haven merchant Ralph Isaacs for pro-British talk; he testified in court against the Jewish Tory Barrak Hays. The sash leads of his home were melted into bullets. After the war, Myers and two other prominent members of the congregation signed a letter conveying the loyal sentiments of New York's returned Israelites to Gov. DeWitt Clinton.

Myer Myers married twice and died in his 73rd year. Many of his descendants had distinguished careers in law and politics, in letters, in business and banking, and especially in the army, fighting on both sides in the great Civil War.

1793

MOSES MENDES SEIXAS

Sephardi Parnass

INTERIOR OF NEWPORT SYNAGOGUE
OF WHICH MOSES M. SEIXAS WAS WARDEN.

THE SEPHARDIM have been oversentimentalized. The tragic fate
that engulfed Spanish Jewry has left a deep scarred tissue in
Jewish consciousness together with illusions as to Marrano
heroism. The sufferings of the *Anusim* and their underground
adherence to Judaism have served to cast over them an aura of
martyrdom.

Stagnation had already set in when the inexcusable, though
understandable, ban was imposed on Baruch Spinoza. The last
Sephardi event, the final concerted public effort, ended with the
multitude milling around fraudulent Sabbatai Zevi. After that
humiliating display of decadence, there were no more movements
among Sephardim, nothing equivalent to Hasidism, *Aufklaerung,*
Emancipation, Haskalah, Reform, Nationalism, or Neo-ortho-
doxy. As individuals only did they participate in Zionism. Not a
single Sephardi of stature has emerged in Medinat Israel.

Nor were Sephardim a cohesive element that fused easily into
community life. A static arrogance inhibited their amalgamation

with the *Kahal*. Ever ready to take over on their own terms, they either dominated or remained aloof in sullen isolation. The Portuguese *Minhag* had to prevail in the synagogue ritual even if the majority might be Ashkenazim. They prided themselves on being a select group, direct descendants from the aristocratic society which in the 10th century created the Golden Age in Spanish Judaism. Yet these Sephardim were as far removed in spirit, learning, or creative energy from the contemporaries of Ibn Gabirol, Maimonides, Halevy, and Ibn Ezra as the modern Greeks are from the Athenians of Plato, Aristotle, Sophocles, or Aeschylus. They possessed the faults of an aristocracy with a minimum of its virtues. Like true Bourbons, they simply could not perceive that rising forces were surpassing and transcending their own ossified caste.

In early American settlements the Sephardim exercised an influence altogether unwarranted by merit or number. A minority in the six congregations at the close of the Colonial period, they nevertheless dictated the ritual. When impoverished they might marry Ashkenazim. But their offspring preserved and often exaggerated the inherited vices of exclusion and separatism. The Seixas clan, a mixture of both stocks, might be deemed exceptional. Yet even this eminent family, which furnished shining examples of Sephardic virtues, also helped perpetuate the narrowing spirit of unchanging status quo.

The Marrano, Isaac Mendes Seixas, came from Portugal in 1738 and settled in New York. Manfully fighting the *Tedesco* prejudices of his uncle, Roderigo Pacheco, he married Rachel Levy of the Franks family. Their son Gershom, the learned patriotic Hazan of Shearith Israel, seems as free of Hidalgo condescension as his father. Gershom's daughter, Sarah Abigail, married the German scholar Israel Baer Kursheedt, who eventually broke away from the Spanish-Portuguese Congregation to become a founder of B'nai Jeshurun in New York. Another son, Benjamin N. Seixas, also appears liberated of class prejudice, at least enough to marry Zipporah, daughter of rich Hayman Levy, originally from Hanover. With success, Benjamin became a distinguished citizen and a founder of the New York Stock Exchange. But when Parnass of Shearith Israel, he was meticulous about the niceties of Sephardic formality. Because a letter was addressed to him individually and not as President of Shearith Israel, he refused to answer. Even the intercession of his brother Gershom, Minister of the Synagogue, was of no avail.

Proud punctilio stemmed from Spain, where simple orders to home servants called for ceremony and propriety. Even the children in Velásquez' paintings carry themselves with stiff formality. Such conventions modelled after the Spanish diplomacy of the Baroque age were also insisted on by a brother of Benjamin and Gershom Seixas. Moses Mendes Seixas served as Warden of Newport's 18th century Synagogue after the election of George Washington. The opportunity to exercise formality together with authority soon presented itself.

The inauguration of the First President evoked strong interest, especially in minority sects with political rights not yet secured in the several states. It is sometimes overlooked that at the outbreak of the Revolution, each colony had its established church, which looked awry at Catholics, Jews and dissenting Protestants. The upsurge of the war established religious freedom. Yet in spite of the Declaration of Independence, Catholics, Dissenters, infidels or atheists did not attain equal rights in New York until the Constitution adopted in 1777 granted to Jews—but not to Catholics—full citizenship. Some states followed suit. Yet even after the Federal Union began to function, eight states, including Rhode Island, retained discriminations that affected Jews.

Congratulating the First President was not the simple proceeding it is today. In 1789 Jews evidently did not feel over secure. Should they act jointly? Should each congregation send its own felicitations? Hesitation and slow communication consumed a whole year. The six synagogues could not get together. Moses Seixas stood on his dignity and voiced displeasure over the lack of formalities in the letter from New York's Shearith Israel. The

Newport Synagogue had ceased functioning during the war, and the congregation shrank almost to nil. A year later the famous house of prayer closed its doors for a century. Yet Moses Seixas insisted on the Newport community acting on its own.

His course set, Moses Seixas acquitted himself creditably enough. The family gift for expression served him well. He wrote to the President and his letter has stood the test of history and criticism. Beginning his respectful tribute from "the Children of the Stock of Abraham" he goes on to state:

"Deprived as we hitherto have been of the invaluable rights of free citizens, we now—with a deep sense of gratitude to the Almighty Disposer of all events—behold a government erected by the majesty of the people—a government which to bigotry gives no sanction, to persecution no assistance, but generously affording to all liberty of conscience and immunities of citizenship, deeming every one of whatever nation, tongue or language, equal parts of the great governmental machine."

The Seixas letter evidently impressed George Washington, who repeats its punch line, which has became a classic phrase of American humanism. In a letter that ranks with the best documents of Hamilton or Jefferson, the Father of his Country answered the Newport Congregation:

"It is now no more that toleration is spoken of as if it were by the indulgence of one class of people that another enjoyed the exercise of their inherent natural rights, for, happily, the Government of the United States, *which gives to bigotry no sanction, to persecution no assistance,* requires only that they who live under its protection should demean themselves as good citizens in giving it on all occasions their effectual support."

1794

COLONEL
ISAAC FRANKS

Alleged Aid to Washington

Yellow fever struck Philadelphia. The national government was disrupted and President Washington looked about for a suitable dwelling in Germantown. The best house available stood on Main Street. Built in 1774, it had been occupied by Sir William Howe after the battle of Germantown. Here the British commander entertained the future King William IV, then a midshipman in the Royal Navy. In 1782 the building was purchased by Col. Isaac Franks, said to have served on the staff of General Washington.

For two months the Presidential family lived in the two-story house at the rental of $66.66—not high by our standards. But the total cost ran up to $131.56. The submitted bill lists such expenditures as: traveling costs of Franks and wife to put the house and furniture in order; cleaning the premises before and after the President's occupation; rent and expenses of Franks during the occupancy. The Colonel expends $10 in traveling merely to ascertain when he could get back his home. Probably ice and snow on the bad roads rendered the post unreliable.

The statement goes on to charge for 2 ducks, 4 fowls, 1 bushel potatoes, a missing flat iron. It was a frugal age and no one even intimated that the charges were somewhat picayune. Besides times were hard, and the President was reputed the richest man in the infant republic. But what impression did the thrifty Jewish landlord make upon the hero President?

This suggests a more intriguing speculation. What was the general attitude of Washington towards his Jewish fellow citizens? There is no private letter, no reported conversation, not even heresay on the subject. And yet he came in contact with Jews during the Revolution and the French and Indian Wars. Surely he was approached often enough by Major David Salisbury Franks for a special court-martial following the treachery of Benedict Arnold. Another Franks brought from John Hancock of Philadelphia $250,000 in cash for supplies and pay to his soldiers at Boston. He undoubtedly heard from Finance Director Robert Morris how Haym Salomon, Isaac Moses, and Simon Nathan helped the cause of independence. At the dinner table, some visiting patriot of South Carolina might have related the story of Francis Salvador and his death at the very beginning of hostilities.

But Washington had occasion to state his attitude in explicit language. On his election, all six synagogues sent letters overflowing with reverence for the winner of American liberties. At the same time the writers expressed gratitude on finally attaining the equal privileges of free citizens. The first President acknowledged these tributes with the quiet courtesy of a great gentleman. In the formal and stately prose of the era, he assures them of the right inherent in all men to practice their own religion and enjoy the immunities of free citizenship. In one letter he expresses hope that "the inhabitants of every denomination participate in the temporal and spiritual blessings of that people whose God is Jehovah."

There are critics who regard these letters as distant, official, and without concern for Jewish welfare. Evidently they misread the character of America's No. 1 hero, or they mistake aristocratic reserve for frigidity. Perhaps they cannot understand the detachment of a public man risking clerical displeasure, as Washington did, by inserting in the treaty with Tripoli: "the government of the United States of America is in no sense founded on the Christian religion. The United States is not a Christian nation any more than it is a Jewish or Mohammedan nation."

The value of the letters to the Hebrew congregation lies, perhaps, in their objectivity. Neither philo-semitic nor anti-semitic, the "Father of his Country" seeks impartially to secure for Jews the rights of human beings. Yet he goes a step further. The probable recollection of Jewish contributions to the war effort causes him to show annoyance at the word tolerance when applied to freedom of worship. One cannot but detect compassion, or even anxiety, in his letter to the Newport Congregation: "May the children of the stock of Abraham who dwell in this land continue to merit and enjoy the good will of the other inhabitants —while every one shall sit in safety under his own vine and fig tree and there shall be none to make him afraid."

There is no record of any contact between George Washington and Isaac Franks, who was born in New York City. On Franks' reaching his 17th year great tension prevailed. General Washington had succeeded in driving the British out of Boston. He was coming to New York for a similar encounter with Lord Howe, now occupying Long Island. Isaac Franks rushed to enlist in Col. Lesher's New York regiment and furnished his own uniform with equipment. These volunteers were immediately annexed to the regular army under the direct command of General Washington. One morning in July 1776, the regiment stood in formation and listened to a newly written document. General Washington thought it good for army morale that the soldiers hear the Declaration of Independence set forth the reasons why they were fighting. With one voice, Franks records, the soldiers shouted they would support and defend the newly declared freedom with their lives and fortunes.

On Long Island, Isaac Franks took part in the "heat of the battle" and retreated with Washington's army to New York City. Here he stood on detached guard at the Fly Market on the East River. The enemy took the city and took him prisoner. Confined for three months in Cunningham's notorious Provost, he escaped at night and embarked on a leaky skiff at Division Street on the North River. He paddled with a single oar and reached the Jersey shore. He then joined the Quartermasters near Peekskill as assistant to the Forage Master. In 1778 he was appointed Forage Master of the Garrison at West Point and served until commissioned Ensign of the Massachusetts Regiment. Stationed at West Point, he was later transferred to Stony Point on another command. For the first time in six years of constant service he applied for and received a furlough. While visiting friends in Philadelphia the news of peace arrived.

Franks seems to have inherited money. In 1782 he married (out of his faith) and purchased the house in Germantown. For the next 25 years he prospered. Associated with the celebrated Dr. Benjamin Rush, he acquired 19 tracts of land in what became Indiana. In 1789 he became "a Notary and Tabellion Public" which helped him support his growing family. In 1794 Governor Mifflin honored him with the title Lieut. Colonel in the Pennsylvania militia as a result of the Whiskey Rebellion. The following year he becomes a Justice of the Peace. He attained sufficient prominence for the artist Gilbert Stuart to paint him in oil and present him with the portrait.

But luck gave way to distress. Hard pressed, he applied for a pension as a war veteran in need. From his applications we glean the sketchy outline of his life. The Federal government rewarded his loyal service with $20 per month; the pension terminated with his death four years later. His descendants, long Christianized, preserve the tradition of their ancestor serving on Washington's staff.

Franks had little Jewish contact, even with his sister, the wife of Haym Salomon, who rendered far greater, if less spectacular, services to the Revolutionary cause than his soldier brother-in-law. After Salomon's death in 1785, the impoverished widow had difficulty in raising her children. Yet Isaac Franks showed the same indifference to his bereaved sister as to his ancestral religion. He never left Judaism, but in his will urged his children to be good Christians.

COL. FRANKS' HOME, IN WHICH
PRES. WASHINGTON RESIDED.

1795

COLONEL SOLOMON BUSH

Office Seeker

U NDER THE Naturalization Act of 1740 Matthias Bush was able
to become a citizen of Pennsylvania. In 1777 his son Solomon was
appointed Deputy Adjutant General of the State Militia. Fighting
several months later in the skirmishes near the Brandywine, he
received an ugly wound in the thigh, but was lucky enough to be
taken to his father's house. The doctor pronounced the wound
fatal, yet the patient managed to live on. Philadelphia was then
taken by the British. On being discovered and made prisoner,
Solomon Bush retained his freedom of movement by pledging not
to escape or fight the English.

A British army doctor helped the paroled prisoner but could
not cure him. The thigh wound never healed completely. One day
he went to British headquarters, either for medical treatment or
to report periodically on his parole. He happened to see a civilian
bringing a letter to General Howe. His curiosity was aroused.
Perhaps he knew the messenger and suspected treachery. Adroit
enough to learn that the civilian, a Colonial no doubt, brought the

message from a British spy behind the American lines, he forwarded the bit of information to Gen. John Armstrong, who reported it to Gen. Washington.

In Solomon Bush, the Jew emerges from the apologetic alien uncertain of his rights into the citizen proudly conscious of his worth and his services. Philadelphia was reoccupied by the Americans, yet Bush remained a prisoner on parole until exchanged. He applied for rations and pay. The Supreme Executive Council studied his case and reported that the distinguished military career of Major Bush had been brilliant, especially during the winter of 1776 "when the service was critical and hazardous." The Council recommended pay and rations equal to his rank. The Board of War went even further. He was promoted from Major to Lieutenant Colonel. Bush appears to have been the Jewish officer who held the highest rank in any combat unit of the Continental Army.

After the war, Col. Bush was unable to find himself. Like many others whose careers were interrupted by the struggle for independence, he desired some governmental post in preference to prosaic business, which after the dash and excitement of battle seemed dull and routine. Besides, his wounded condition disabled him for heavy work. In 1780 he petitioned Congress for a secretaryship of the Treasury. Four years later, he solicited the job of health officer for Pennsylvania's port. In 1793 he applied to President Washington for the naval office post of Philadelphia. His contribution to the war effort must have been important, for in 1785 tight-fisted Benjamin Franklin, while President of the Pennsylvania Council, granted him a pension.

Unrest drove Col. Bush to England. He went there on a Masonic mission and in all probability in search of medical aid not procurable at home. In London he was able to serve his fellow countrymen. The British still smarting from the loss of the American Colonies made their power felt on the sea. Capt. Watson and part of his crew were seized and charged with being English born seamen serving on a New York ship. This was an early case of the new British policy, which insisted on searching and seizing American boats and impressing their sailors into the British navy. Britain refused to recognize any new allegiance or changed citizenship for seamen born in England. Her own sea dogs often decided the birth place of the unfortunate sailor. This shortsighted policy ultimately led to the War of 1812. Abuses soon became so irritating that President Washington sent Gouverneur Morris from France to warn the British of the serious consequences that would follow such high handed action.

At the time no ambassador or consul was present to intervene, so Col. Bush took it upon himself to act in behalf of fellow Americans. Surprisingly, he succeeded in getting the captain and crew released. Reporting the achievement to the President, he demonstrated his fitness to serve his country. The letter hinted quite broadly that Bush would be happy to represent his government in London. He also sent through the painter John Trumbull a book compiled by an English admirer of Washington. This volume included petitions, statements, and appeals of Englishmen in sympathy with the Colonists at the time of the break with the Mother Country. Washington's answer contained warm commendations for the Colonel's energetic and successful intervention. The first President also thanked him for the book but maintained a discreet silence about any diplomatic or consular appointment.

Yet the Colonel was not easily discouraged. A vacancy in the President's Cabinet was caused by the promotion of Timothy Pickering from Postmaster General to Secretary of War. Solomon Bush felt equal to the post and applied for it. He might have attained a satisfactory position if his unhealed wound had not hastened premature death.

But if the Colonel failed to reach Cabinet rank, at least his ego found its compensation in Freemasonry. This secret society had a powerful lure for a people whose religion set them apart from general intercourse with the majority. In the lodge room a fraternal spirit obliterated the walls which millennia of persecutions had raised and maintained. Masonic ritual, pass words and symbolism had their traditional origin with the builders of King Solomon's Temple in Jerusalem. Jews rose to the highest degrees within the Order and helped to spread its power and influence.

All sense of deficiency must have vanished when the son of a German-Jewish emigrant during the era of the Divine Right of Kings could indite a letter to puissant Frederick the Great, King of Prussia and head of the Masonic Grand Council at Berlin and Paris: "I, Solomon Bush, Grand Elect, Perfect and Sublime Knight of the East and Prince of Jerusalem, Sovereign Knight of the Sun and of the Black and White Eagle, Prince of the Royal Secret, and Deputy Inspector General, and Grand Master over all Lodges, Chapters, and Grand Councils of the Superior Degrees of Masonry in North America within the State of Pennsylvania, etc." Signed—"Your very humble and most affectionate brother."

The intellectual monarch probably exploded a polite French oath, since he regarded German fit only for swineherds. On the other hand, the royal cynic might have laughed sardonically and remarked to his minister, "Mirabeau should see this. The French radical may then understand my refusal to admit that little Jew hunchback Mendelssohn into the Berlin Academy."

JOSEPH SIMSON.

1796

SOLOMON SIMSON

Merchant and Correspondent

Nathan Sampson left Frankfort for London and thought it good business to Anglicize his name to Simson. In 1718 he brought his nephew Joseph to New York, then a one street town laid out largely in orchards. A successful business man himself, Nathan had little patience with a kinsman who preferred Hebrew studies to storekeeping. How could his own nephew value a handwritten Hebrew Bible, even with annotations and vocalizations, above a title-deed to real estate? In disgust Uncle Nathan returned to England and left Joseph to his own devices.

Joseph Simson married, and to support his growing family took the job of beadle at Shearith Israel. When made a freeman of the city in 1747, he opened a store and began to prosper. Success came, however, because of his son Sampson, who showed all of Uncle Nathan's business acumen. Joseph resigned his post of *shamas,* and the same year was elected Parnass or president. He now had the leisure and standing to correspond in Hebrew with Dr. Benjamin Kennicott of Oxford and Dr. Miles Cooper of Kings (later Columbia) College of New York.

83

Evidently Joseph Simson never forgot the restrictions in the Frankfort ghetto of his youth. Throughout his long life he cherished deep love for the New World. A member of the Orange County Volunteers in his fifties, the old patriot when 90 left New York in 1776 refusing to live under British occupation. In 1786 the French miniature painter, Joseph Ramage, happened to pass the Simson home and saw through a window the sturdy 100 year old patriarch. He went in and begged permission to paint the remarkable Old Testament figure. The stubborn oldster finally consented. His orthodoxy was evidently tinged with modernism. The miniature shows us the determined face and full silvery beard of a priest in the old Temple. Yet the massive head is uncovered. He died the following year.

His two sons Sampson and Solomon operated the business. Sampson had the makings of a tycoon. Beginning with his father's small shop, he gradually acquired vessels that carried on extensive commerce with foreign lands. He became a founder and leading spirit in New York's Chamber of Commerce. On the way towards becoming one of Colonial America's top merchants, he died of tuberculosis in his 48th year. Rivington's *New York Gazette* carried a eulogy that expressed the public estimate of the man.

The younger brother Solomon continued Sampson's business ideas, his father's respect for learning, and the patriotic liberalism of both. Partner in a spermaceti oil factory and a proprietor of the United Whaling Company, he also carried on importing and exporting, before and after the Revolution. One of his ships touched Cochin, a port near the southern tip of India. The captain went ashore and visited a section named *Jew Town* by the English. He brought back a letter in Hebrew.

An epistle coming from the far end of the earth would naturally create a sensation in the small New York community, which considered itself pretty remote from the centers of Judaism. But in Cochin were Jews completely isolated from all Jewish life. Yet on the Malabar coast this group had maintained Judaism since its ancestors had emigrated from Palestine after the destruction of the Second Temple. The letter went on to relate that in the 4th century C. E. the king of the land granted to Joseph Rabban certain feudatory rights over Cranganore, where Jews lived for centuries under limited self government until the Portuguese came and began their usual persecutions. In the 16th century, they left Cranganore and were kindly received by the Rajah of Cochin. Yet they continued to suffer from Portuguese discrimination until Holland took over in the 17th century.

With the Dutch came Jewish merchants who brought back to Holland the story of their coreligionists in India. The Sephardim of New York were no doubt proud to learn that their fellow Sephardim of Amsterdam had sent to Cochin prayer books, Torahs, ritual objects and religious tracts that effected a revival of religion. They were doubtless relieved to hear that the "white" Jews looked down upon the "black" Jews as descendants of converts and not of pure Abrahamic stock.

Replying to this letter, Solomon Simson expressed interest in establishing trade relations. The answer came back that business was bad and that the goods which Simson wanted were not obtainable. Evidently the English overlords discouraged trade with the recent American rebels.

The Cochin incident stimulated curiosity in Solomon Simson about other Jews of the Far East. So when he read in a travel book that a missionary, with the suspicious name of Alexander Christian, had met Chinese Jews in the province of Honan, he felt excitement over the belief that the Lost Ten Tribes had at last been found. In a Hebrew letter, he informs the Jewish mandarins that 72 Jewish families in New York live peacefully and worship in a synagogue; that Jews together with Christians sit on juries giving judgment in civil and criminal cases. He instructed Capt. Howell to deliver the letter to the Jews of Kai-Feng-Fu, called by the natives Tiaokiu Kiao. The letter was returned with the notation: "Capt. Howell could not discover them."

During the war, Solomon Simson furnished cannon to the Colonial troops and supplied lead for making bullets. He had also served in the militia. While the British occupied New York, he lived in various Connecticut towns together with other patriotic exiles.

The most interesting phase of his political activity came after the war. Economic interests would point to his identification with the monied Federalists of Alexander Hamilton. Instead he became an active leader among the radical followers of Thomas Jefferson. A founder of the Democratic Society of New York, he served in 1796 as Vice-President, and a year later became President.

The last five years of the century were marked by political bitterness. Active participation by a respected businessman in the ranks of the hated Jeffersonians exasperated the Federalists. This party of "wealth and talents" loved to label Democrats as scum. Solomon Simson came in for a snide anti-Semitic attack from the same Rivington's *Gazette* that had extolled his brother Sampson a decade earlier. The Rivingtons had been violent Tories during the Revolution. Yet the Federalists did not balk at using the vituperative talents of former traitors. James Rivington attacked the Democratic Society by heaping scurrility upon its Jewish members. He wrote: "Its itinerant gang will easily be known by the physiognomy; they all seem to be, like their Vice-President, of the tribe of Shylock; they have that leering underlook, the malicious grin, that seem to say to honest men—approach me not."

But there are two sides in a political fracas. With equal punch Thomas Greenleaf, publisher and editor of the *New York Journal and Patriotic Register,* replied: "If, by the word Shylock, you mean a Jew, from my knowledge of the Vice-President, I dare say he would think himself honored by the appellation. Judaism being his religious profession as Democracy is his political creed."

Shortly after President Jefferson's election, 63 year old Solomon Simson died. He lived long enough to hear the Hebrew commencement address delivered at Columbia College by his son, the Sampson Simson who later founded Mt. Sinai Hospital.

1797

BARNARD GRATZ

Colonial Enterpriser

THE ANCESTRY of most American Jews is forgotten. Little would be known about the roots of the famous Gratz family but for the researches of Dr. Sidney M. Fish of Philadelphia. He brought to light the prominent roles played by the forebears of Rebecca, Michael, and Barnard Gratz in Polish and Silesian Jewries.

In the 16th century, Poland was the bright spot for Jews in Europe. Learned in Talmudic wisdom, they enjoyed prosperity and had a degree of self rule under that system known as the Council of the Four Provinces. The Gratz ancestors held top positions in that limited Sanhedrion. One of them became Chief Rabbi of the City and Province of Cracow and head of its Rabbinical Academy. Another was a senior member in the Court of Rabbis. Married into the best families, they enjoyed the social prestige that Jews derive from the combination of intellectual distinction with economic welfare.

The peaceful life of relative safety came to a sudden stop. The savage Cossacks of Chmielnicki broke into Poland and committed the most gruesome barbarities. Jews suffered even more than the Christian population. Hundreds of thousands were murdered. The roads of Europe were cluttered with refugees. Rabbi Jonathan Bloch ultimately found a precarious refuge in the Silesian village of Langendorf and there became the grandfather of Barnard and Michael Gratz.

Life was intolerable enough for Jews under Austrian rule when Charles VI ordered their expulsion. He died several days later and before his widow, the bigot Maria Theresa, could get around to execute the decree, Frederick the Great invaded Silesia. The jubilant welcome to the enlightened young conqueror turned out premature. The yoke of Prussian junkerdom soon weighed even more heavily than the archaic feudalism of Austria.

The crushing restrictions of Prussian laws together with travelers' tales of a better life beyond the continent stirred enterprising youth to seek far away lands. One boy had found his way to England, and the fabulous tale of the merchant prince, Solomon Henry, furnished a continuous topic of conversation in and out of Langendorf's little synagogue. The orphan Isaacher Ber decided to follow his kinsman's footsteps, and after lengthy stops in Berlin and Amsterdam, reached London still in his teens. Solomon Henry welcomed Berel, changed the name to Barnard Gratz, and put him to work in his own thriving business. For several years he learned the language, the ways and business methods of England.

Solomon Henry had a brother Jacob who ventured to the New World. Returning to London, he described Philadelphia, its promising opportunities, the tolerance of its Quaker inhabitants. Barnard crossed the ocean and set foot upon the soil of Pennsylvania.

In Philadelphia, Barnard made a fortunate connection when entering the employ of David Franks. Born in New York, Franks had moved to Philadelphia and rose to the top in colonial business as a merchant, Indian trader, fur dealer, land baron, and sutler to the British army in the French and Indian Wars. Obviously he could not all alone furnish army supplies to the tune of

£764,672, equivalent in our day to $100,000,000 in purchasing power. His brother Moses was a member of Colebrook, Nesbitt, and Franks, the English concern with a pipeline to the government in London. For such vast undertakings in a primitive country, unequipped for large scale operations, he needed agents, partners, and associates. In the 1760 decade, his combine with Joseph Simon and Levy Andrew Levy of Lancaster, and other commercial houses made David Franks for a while the dominant tycoon of Pennsylvania, if not of all the 13 Colonies.

Barnard received a small salary and lived in the home of David Franks. Occupying a position of trust, he was also permitted to go into private deals on his own. With such contacts, it is not surprising that Barnard could make his way. But his most fortunate stroke came when his brother Michael returned to London from India, disillusioned with the East and ready to try his luck in the Far West. Barnard wrote a cautious letter, offering Michael his job with the Franks firm. After a while the brothers went into partnership and remained interested in various ventures for the rest of their lives. The operations of B. and M. Gratz were large, varied, and extensive. They succeeded and supplanted David Franks and Co., just as the latter virtually displaced the influential Quaker firm of Boynton, Wharton, and Morgan.

It is doubtful whether Barnard could have achieved success without his brother. Michael excelled in daring, energy, drive, vision and enterprise. Yet they made a good team, each correcting the extremist tendencies in the other. The conservative Barnard possessed more prudence and ballast, better social gifts, and capacity for inspiring lasting friendships, especially among Gentile associates. With a stronger feeling of public obligation, he played a more active part in communal affairs, assisted in building the synagogue and served as parnass of the Mikveh Israel Congregation. Michael was the audacious speculator; Barnard the solid, methodic, cautious man of business.

The range and extent of the Gratz enterprises are surprising even in our day of specialization. During half a century of operations they built up, and were later compelled to sacrifice, an import-export business with European, Canadian, West Indian and Caribbean ports. They tried coastwise and trans-ocean shipping, only to be stopped by the British restrictions that brought on the Non-Importation boycott and the Revolutionary War. They turned their attention to inland commerce and traded in native products, including grain, lumber, cattle and tobacco. The profitable fur trade claimed their attention, nor did they overlook barter and exchange with the Indians. Individually or as partners, the brothers acquired and disposed of parcels of land. During the war, they purchased and built schooners or brigs, which ran the tight British blockade to transport commodities in demand at high prices in foreign markets, and brought back goods sorely needed at home. At the urging of the government, they fitted out privateers to capture or destroy the enemy's commerce. Between the Ohio and the Mississippi, they owned jointly or with syndicates huge tracts of land on which pioneers were attracted to form new settlements. With signers of the Declaration of Independence and drafters of the Federal Constitution, the Gratzes shared considerably in the settling, civilizing, and opening of the "West" as far as the Mississippi.

As the 18th century was closing, Michael began to fail in drive and in health. Barnard, also weary, turned to his only daughter for affection. But her husband Solomon Etting had decided to make a new start in Baltimore. Barnard joined them and found a situation that demanded action. In Maryland, Jews had since 1776 all civil rights; but if elected to any public office they were required to take the oath of a Christian. In 1797 Barnard, his son-in-law and others petitioned the General Assembly to grant Jews equal political rights with Christians. The memorial was pigeonholed. A quarter of a century later, after the intensive labors of Christians and Jews, the initial efforts of Barnard Gratz were realized.

1798

MOSES MICHAEL HAYS

Grand Master

A week after the Declaration of Independence had been signed, several members of the Rhode Island General Assembly met at Newport. They were there to receive sworn signatures to the Test of Loyalty demanded of 77 Americans suspected of pro-British sympathies. Moses Michael Hays refused to sign his name to the declaration. Ironically, with him patriotism was so fervent that he resented any one questioning his loyalty to America.

Before a large gathering, Hays demanded the right to confront his accusers and hear their charges. Avowing deep attachment for his native land and approving the war, he pledged allegiance to the government, obedience of its laws and willingness to pay his share of its demands. Then boldly he threw down his own challenge: Why a Test of Loyalty without a corresponding right to vote? Neither the Continental Congress nor the Legislatures of the various colonies had taken any notice of existing religious restrictions against the "Society of Israelites".

Today such outspoken demands appear quite normal. But in

1776 the rights of man were yet to be recognized. A German king was selling his able-bodied Hessians to George III at $50 a head for cannon fodder in the American war. In France crops could be destroyed by aristocratic huntsmen, without compensation to the starving farmers; yet if a peasant poached on the game preserve of his betters, he was shot without the semblance of a trial for the murderer. Poland, partitioned in 1772 among three royal banditti, saw its Christians and Jews pillaged and oppressed. Enlightened Frederick the Great issued edicts restricting the rights of Jews in Prussia to trade and labor, transit and marriage. Squalid ghettos, locked each night and holiday, lingered on century after century in the cities of Germany and Italy. Against that world of absolute monarchy, of feudal prerogative and clerical tyranny, the words of Moses Michael Hays resound in dignified protest and reflect the growing self-respect of Jews awakening from the nightmare of millennial persecutions.

One of six brothers, Judah Hays came to America from Holland; in 1739 his son Moses was born, it is believed, in New York. Moses Michael first mastered watch-making and then entered business. The amazing success of Aaron Lopez drew ambitious young men like Hays to Newport. Emulating Lopez as the ideal merchant, Moses aspired to importing and exporting. With Meyer Polock as a partner, he succeeded in building and outfitting a ship.

The "Mary" started for Amsterdam, sprung a leak, and returned for repairs. Five days later, the boat ran into a tropical hurricane, labored through 27 hours of terrific wind, lost two topmasts, sprung a leak for the second time, yet somehow managed to hobble back to Newport, with the pump never stopping a moment. It took nine days to restore the brigantine. The captain would take no further chances. He anchored the boat off an island and secured its mooring with cables. While waiting for good weather and proper winds, a twister blew up a storm such as no one ever remembered. The "Mary" was cast ashore, its cargo ruined, and the crew thankful that their lives were saved. The disaster bankrupted both partners and threw them into the debtors' prison.

After his courageous patriotic stand, no one dared ever again to question the loyalty of Hays. During the British occupation of Newport, he sought refuge in Philadelphia. Later he settled in Boston and prospered in the insurance business. He was equally active in large scale merchandising, exporting and money lending. Instrumental with others in establishing an iron foundry, he was also a co-organizer of the Massachusetts Bank, today the First National Bank of Boston. As a man of business acumen, he corresponded with Robert Morris, the famous financier of the Revolution, about taxation, finances, and the creation of a sound monetary system. In 1798 his name appears on the petition for a charter of the Massachusetts Mutual Fire Insurance Company, a pioneer venture in Boston.

Hays moved in the best society. He enjoyed the esteem of U. S. Senator Harrison G. Otis, son of James Otis, patriot of the Revolution. He was visited by Thomas H. Perkins, pioneer of American railroads. Robert Treat Paine, son of a signer of the Declaration of Independence, wrote his epitaph in sonnet form, which appeared in the Boston *Sentinel*. Ezra Styles, President of Yale, speaks of Hays in his diary. Rev. Samuel J. May, a prominent Unitarian, left a friendly account of the close intimacy between their respective families.

The political aspirations of Moses Hays were never satisfied. His inability to win an election may partly be attributed to affiliation with the conservative Federalists, rapidly in decline before the triumphant advance of the Jeffersonian Republicans. Hays was ready to turn over all business to his son for the Federal post of Collector of the Port of Newport. He applied to his friend, Secretary of War Henry Knox, and wrote to President Washington, but there were numerous office seekers more deserving or in far greater need. Nothing came of his political or office holding ambitions.

Political disappointments were, however, amply repaid with

high honors in Freemasonry. The portrait of Moses Michael Hays hangs today in the Masonic Temple of Boston. During the Colonial period he held important positions in the Order. As Grand Master of the Masonic Grand Lodge of Massachusetts, he was largely instrumental in bringing the "Ancient Accepted Scottish Rite" into the U. S. The eleven deputies he appointed exercised high powers in the lodges of different states.

No criticism can be leveled at the ethical purity of Masonry. But fraternal orders have succeeded no better than religion in transforming human nature. Like other humans, Masons have also been known to harbor anti-Jewish bias. Not without surprise therefore do we see Hays mount to the top leadership in the 18th century when Masonry attracted the elite. Many Gentiles were envious of his extraordinary powers. After his death, considerable criticism was voiced by the discontented opposition. His direction, however, stood and all powers and titles traced through his appointees in the Scottish Rite remain approved in Masonic history.

Like most of his contemporaries, Hays exhibited strong attachment to his own religion. With patriarchal authority, he instilled in his family circle devotion to Judaism and respect for the faiths of others. Philanthropy and patriotism were taught by precept and example. There is, however, a flaw that mars the record of an otherwise upright and humane character. A foolish prejudice made him act with the cruelty of a despot. An absurd notion that marriage between cousins is harmful caused him to ruin the lives of his daughter Catherine and his nephew Judah Touro.

1799

SIMON NATHAN

Ancestor

The Nathan family has made a deep impression on American Society. Poetess Emma Lazarus and her lesser known sister, the essayist Josephine Lazarus, novelist Robert Nathan, and writer Gershom Nathan have all contributed to American letters. Annie Nathan Meyer, author, playwright and lecturer, founded Barnard College, while Maud Nathan, President of the Consumers League, was a writer, social worker and a leading figure in the suffrage movement. Edgar J. Nathan, Jr., active in communal, legal, religious and political matters, now on the New York Supreme Court, is far eclipsed by his kinsman, the distinguished jurist Benjamin Nathan Cardozo, one of the most sapient in the long line of Justices of the United States Supreme Court.

The ancestor of this capable family was born in England. We first see Simon Nathan as a business man operating in British Jamaica yet in sympathy with the patriots of the Revolution. He jeopardized his freedom and business by shipping powder, canvas, and rope to a free port for transportation to the newly proclaimed Thirteen States. Discovery led to flight for the French colony of New Orleans. Abandoning a goodly part of his property in Jamaica, he still retained possession of considerable cash, which he invested in a new untried enterprise: a free government of, by, and for men created equal.

Simon Nathan acquired £35,000 in bills of exchange issued by the State of Virginia. In Havana he rendered real service to the American cause by purchasing $52,000 of the drafts earmarked for George Rogers Clark's expedition to capture the Northwest. The Spaniards were impressed with the confidence of a Jewish man of business in the new republic. His purchase in Cuba helped to stabilize the credit of a weak government engaged in warfare with the most powerful of empires commanding the strongest navy. Jewish finance, long held in great esteem by the Spanish for unerring acumen, would never be risked on a doubtful venture.

In Williamsburg, Simon Nathan received thanks from Governor Thomas Jefferson and from the Council of Virginia. Instead, he would probably have preferred the cash advanced. Yet in 1780 when the Governor announced in council that 500 men stationed at Fort Pitt (later Pittsburgh) were in the direst need of clothing, Nathan came again to the rescue. He raised for Virginia 300,000 continental dollars. Currency had depreciated 60 to 1. When the dollar declined 500 to 1, the State had an easy time paying back the loan. The last installment was made with paper that declined 1000 to 1. Nathan had opened business in Richmond on the strength of bills of exchange which the State of Virginia had assured him would be honored. His store was seized and sold by the sheriff when the Virginia debentures he had used in covering debts were protested for non-payment.

After the Richmond debacle, Nathan turned to Philadelphia. He enlisted in the militia and sent out ships to break through the British blockade. Several vessels were captured together with their cargoes. We do not know whether these boats were his. Either he used hidden resources or could mobilize capital. Perhaps the want of caution served him well in a highly speculative market. He never seemed to lack funds for new and often hazardous ventures. He carried himself like a man of substance and attained a respected place in the Philadelphia community, which included everybody who was anybody in American Jewry of the Revolutionary era.

In his late thirties, Simon Nathan married the brilliant Grace Mendes Seixas and thus became a member of the influential family that embraced Hayman Levy and Isaac Moses. He held an important office in Masonry, which then indicated high standing. One of the trustees who reorganized Mikveh Israel, he contributed over £37 towards building the synagogue and became President in 1782.

As head of Mikveh Israel, the only synagogue functioning during the war, Simon Nathan co-signed a letter in December 1783 to Pennsylvania's Council of Censors. The memorial states that in the Constitution of 1776, Section 10 prescribes an oath for each state legislator taking his seat that he acknowledge the Old and New Testament to be of divine inspiration. The signers felt this restriction of civil rights to be a stigma upon their "nation and religion". Respectfully and firmly the censors were reminded of the part Jews played in the war. The letter prays that their request be presented to a future convention called for revising the Constitution. The memorial was tabled, yet not forgotten. Seven years later, the Jewish disability was removed by the 1790 Constitution of Pennsylvania.

Another letter, co-signed by Simon Nathan, reveals a dog in the manger attitude of certain Philadelphia Germans. The trustees of Mikveh Israel purchased a lot and prepared to build a synagogue. Strenuous objections came from the Reformed German Congregation occupying the adjacent ground. Who ever heard of a synagogue built next to a church? Living in a Quaker city through a war for freedom had evidently made little impression upon the stolid Teutonic soul, accustomed to swinish behavior in the Old Country. The "Pennsylvania Dutch" must have been objectionable, or else the liberal and tolerant Benjamin Franklin, who incidentally contributed £5 to Mikveh Israel, would never have suggested that the voting rights of Germans be restricted. The trustees could have ignored the objections and gone ahead with the building. But was it dignified or practicable to be at constant loggerheads with churlish neighbors? At least the Germans could take the lot at cost. This the church vestry refused. Mikveh Israel built its synagogue elsewhere; a more suitable piece of ground became available.

As time marched on, the lucky streak in Simon Nathan waned. He really went overboard in his patriotic impulses. Besides the money already invested, he paid out additional £53,406 for supplies and guns to the Indians of Virginia. All told he advanced £323,000 in Continental money. Reduced to poverty and distress, he had no means of supporting his family. He drew drafts on the State, and they went protest. In desperation, he attached Virginia property in Pennsylvania. A *cause celebre* followed. Were the assets of a sovereign state subject to attachment and execution under the Articles of Confederation? To the relief of jurists, the courts decided that the property of Virginia was exempt from any judicial process of attachment in a sister state.

Yet he staged a comeback. Going to New York with his in-laws after the war, he became active in community affairs and served four terms as Parnass of Shearith Israel. In 1797 he became prosperous enough to advance £100 for buying a plot behind the Synagogue. Simon Nathan completed a satisfactory life, all in all, of 76 years, replete with good works. In 1932 the Manhattan Chapter of the Daughters of the American Revolution placed at the foot of his grave in the Chatham Square Cemetery a plaque that certifies to his patriotism.

1800

MAJOR
BENJAMIN NONES

Jeffersonian

THE AMERICAN WAR OF INDEPENDENCE had its repercussions in
France. The intelligentsia was elated. The middle class felt intuitively that the struggle was theirs too. Strangely enough, the feudal nobility, born to privilege and caste-ridden, enthused over such
catchwords as liberty, independence, the rights of man. Public
opinion favored aid for the struggling colonists and influenced the
King to act against his better judgment. When Louis XVI signed
the American Treaty he sealed his own death warrant.

Young Marquis de Lafayette, intent upon helping the Americans, fitted out his own ship at Bordeaux. Britain's strong protest
forced the King to forbid the nobleman's departure. Before the
lettre de cachet could arrive, Lafayette skipped over to Spain,
while his ship slipped out of the harbor. Such Utopian adventures
of a 20 year old aristocrat could not but affect the future of a
Jewish idealist of the same age living in Bordeaux.

In Bordeaux, a peculiar community evolved out of the exiles
from Spain and the *conversos* of Portugal. For two centuries they

99

had been following punctiliously all Catholic rites. When complete Church integration seemed finally achieved, they reverted to Judaism. Only in the growing tolerance of 18th century enlightenment could such heretical goings-on flout canon law and get by. And yet the community had slowly atrophied. These Sephardim actually petitioned the King to deny civil rights to fellow Jews out of Alsace or Germany.

These proud Hidalgoes naturally chafed at their alien status. After several centuries of French residence, they bristled up at hearing *they were not citizens.* Such resentments might have incited Benjamin Nones to forsake Bordeaux for a new world where "all men are created equal." Then too Sephardic hauteur and stratified conservatism perhaps repelled the budding democrat, stirred by the refreshing breezes that were ushering in a new era of rights for all people.

Nones seems to have arrived in America in 1777, although there is evidence that he might have come earlier. Soon in uniform, he fought in nearly all the battles of the Carolina campaign. Gallant conduct gave him distinction and subsequently the rank of Major. An apocryphal source maintains that he commanded a battalion of 400 men, fancifully called the "Hebrew Legion" either because of its commander, or on account of the large number of Jewish enlistments. A legend also persists that at the Battle of Camden Gen. DeKalb, mortally wounded, was carried off the field by Maj. Nones and two other Jewish officers. Additional myths cling to the Major as having served on the staffs of Generals Washington, Lafayette, DeKalb, and Pulaski.

But the mythical yields to the historic record. On Dec. 15, 1779 Captain Verdier of Charleston wrote officially: "I take advantage of the occasion and with much pleasure in my quality of Captain of the Volunteers attached to the suite of Pulaski's Legion, to certify that Mr. Benjamin Nones has served as volunteer in the said company during the siege of Charleston during the Campaign of the same year and the siege of Savannah, and his behavior in all the actions has been marked with all the bravery and courage which a military must show for the defense of the liberty of his Country, and which act gained in his favor the esteem of General Pulaski, as well as that of all the officers who witnessed his conduct. For which reason I have delivered to him the present Certificate, as an eye witness of his good conduct."

After Yorktown fighting virtually ceased. Major Nones settled in Philadelphia and tried business without meeting much success. Active in Masonry and communal affairs, he gained recognition. At home in the Sephardic ritual of Mikveh Israel, Nones served as its president before and after the turn of the century. Official interpreter of French and Spanish for the Board of Health and for the U. S. Government, he earned barely enough to feed his steadily increasing family of 14 children.

On the national level, politics began seething with Thomas Jefferson a candidate for the presidency. The Federalists predicted dire calamity should victory go to Jefferson the agnostic. To the Republicans, the Alien and Sedition Laws stamped the Adams administration as Bourbon despotism. For the conservatives of 1800, the term Democrat had the same connotation as the term Communist in 1950.

It is remarkable how Jew-baiting fits into the pattern of reaction. Certain Federalists resorted to anti-Semitism. Such attacks might have been few. But 3000 Jews scattered in a population of 4,000,000 in 15 states were an inconsequential minority to attack. Some were Federalists, but in general Jews leaned toward the party of Jefferson as the more liberal, progressive, and tolerant.

In one of these anti-Semitic incidents, Benjamin Nones emerges creditably. He was present at a meeting of the Philadelphia Democratic Society, the most influential in the Union. At the close, the chairman asked the audience to pitch in small sums to defray the cost of the hall. Nones pleaded poverty for his inability to contribute. Caleb P. Wayne, the publisher of the *Gazette,* a Federalist organ, seized upon the incident to deride the chairman, the speakers, the audience as the very *refuse* and *filth* of society. His reference to Citizen-N ---- the Jew, intended to be funny, was vulgar, cheap, and shabby.

Benjamin Nones wrote an answer which was earnest, dignified, and masterful. The *Gazette* refused to print the letter even as a paid article. It appeared on August 13, 1800 in the Philadelphia *Aurora* and states in part:

"I am a Jew. I glory in belonging to that persuasion, which even its opponents, whether Christian, or Mohammedan, allow to be of divine origin—of that persuasion on which Christianity itself was originally founded, and must ultimately rest—which has preserved its faith secure and undefiled, for near three thousand years, whose votaries have never murdered each other in religious wars, or cherished the theological hatred so general, so unextinguishable among those who revile them.

"I am a Republican! Thank God I have not been so heedless and so ignorant of what has passed, and is now passing in the political world. I have not been so proud or so prejudiced as to renounce the cause for which I have fought.

"But I am poor; I am so, my family also is large, but soberly and decently brought up. They have not been taught to revile a Christian because his religion is not so old as theirs."

1 8 0 1

GOVERNOR
DAVID EMANUEL

Of Georgia

A NAME will not always denote whether its bearer is Jew or Christian. The Puritans were fond of using names out of the Old Testament. David and Emanuel are surely good Hebrew names, direct from the Bible. But so is Israel Israel, who was a Philadelphia Episcopalian of Anglo-Saxon lineage.

The sixth Governor of Georgia called himself David Emanuel. The evidence is by no means overwhelming that he was of Jewish birth. But one thing is significant, if not conclusive. In the long line of Georgia's Chief Executives, from Oglethorpe to Talmadge, the tradition clings only to David Emanuel that he was Jewish.

Some historians admit it. Others are content with referring to him as a Presbyterian, which in itself does not rule out the possibiliy of birth in another faith. The American Jewish Historical Society became interested, and its curator, the lawyer-historian Leon Huhner, investigated his background. He quotes a letter from Abraham Minis, of the old Jewish family that came over in the second or third immigrant boat to Savannah, Georgia. He states unequivocally that not only was the governor a Jew but the lady he married was a Jewess. The strongest evidence comes from Judge H. D. D. Twiggs of Savannah, whose ancestor General John Twiggs of Revolutionary fame married the sister of David Emanuel. With the authority derived from family traditions, the judge writes: "I do not know where Governor David Emanuel came from. I only know that, beyond a doubt, he was a Jew."

From the best accounts available, David Emanuel was born in Pennsylvania, either in 1742 or 1744. He wandered south as far as Georgia and in his 25th year settled permanently in Burke County. We do not know the extent of his education, but he held the position of Justice of the Peace five years after his arrival. Active in politics, he also became active among the patriotic Colonials intent upon throwing off the yoke of Britain. In the Continental Army, he served as a soldier, a scout, and on the Executive Council.

Burke County became a battleground and fighting intensified the bitterness between the Colonials and the Red Coats, as the British were called. But the bitterest vindictiveness raged between the native Americans on both sides of the struggle. Emanuel almost paid with his life because of this animus.

While scouting, he was captured with two other patriots. The Tories condemned their three fellow Americans to death. A large fire was kindled and the three companions were stripped of their clothes. Two of the prisoners were shot dead. A mulatto, whose reward was the dead scouts' clothes, fired at Emanuel and missed. Quick as a flash of lightning, Emanuel leaped over the fire and made his escape in the dark night. He jumped into the neighboring swamp and sank to his neck. The pursuers passed him by several times, but in the darkness could not detect his head. After several hours he crept out of the swamp and reached the army headquarters of General Twiggs.

This adventure evidently did much to enhance his popularity, for in the same year, with the war still on, he was chosen as magistrate by the General Assembly. In January of the following year, he was appointed Justice for Burke County and in 1783 elected to the State Legislature. In 1784 he was reappointed Justice for Burke County.

Yet for David Emanuel the war went on. He suffered severely after Georgia was overrun by the enemy. Together with thirty other patriot families, he built a cluster of cabins near Augusta. From this refuge they harassed the enemy and became so troublesome that the Tories labeled the village "Rebel Town". We find his brother Levi also active in the struggle for independence. In 1776 Levi Emanuel was commissioned Second Lieutenant by the Council of Safety. Six years later he became sergeant-major in the militia under the command of General Mad Anthony Wayne. Was the original commission issued without authority? Or did the frequent resignations, a common practice in the war for liberty, reduce a commissioned officer to the status of a non-com?

After the war, David Emanuel rose to political importance. He represented Burke County in the General Assembly for a number of years. He became a member of the Constitutional Convention in 1789 and again in 1795. About this time the "Yazoo Frauds" broke into an open scandal. Many of the legislators were involved in the conspiracy that lost a vast land empire to the state of Georgia. Emanuel was one of the three eminent citizens entrusted with the investigation of this betrayal of a public trust. This service brought about his election as President of the State Senate. On March 3rd 1801, David Emanuel was sworn in as the sixth Governor of Georgia.

Some confusion has arisen as to how he became Chief Executive. Several historians maintain that as President of the Senate, he automatically became Governor when his predecessor James Jackson resigned to enter the U. S. Senate. Other authorities claim that Emanuel was elected in 1801. In any case he only held the office for eight months, until his successor was chosen by the General Assembly.

He died in 1808, and is described in Sherwood's *Gazeteer*

"a fine looking man, amiable, of good character and inflexible integrity." Four years later the State of Georgia preserved his name on her map. A vast tract of land within her boundaries is called "Emanuel County".

1802

JACOB I. COHEN

Of Richmond

Pennsylvania at its worst in 1773 was infinitely more inviting than Germany at its best; otherwise there would have been little incentive for Jacob I. Cohen to forsake his Bavarian home town, Oberdorfer. In Lancaster the 29 year old immigrant began trading with the Indians. But as the war moved closer, they became less friendly. Forced gradually out of their hunting grounds by the encroaching colonists, the red men sensed a larger advantage in siding with the British, who at least promised they would confine the white settlements to the east of the Alleghenys.

With few good prospects in sight, Jacob left Lancaster and drifted south to Richmond, still a small town even if it displaced Williamsburg as capital of Virginia. Isaiah Isaacs, the only Jew to settle there, welcomed him and held out expectations for some joint ventures. Cohen however wandered on as far as Charleston. Here he found his co-religionists filled with patriotic fervor. About 27 had enlisted in Capt. Lushington's company of fifty, which caused it to be called the "Jew Company".

Jacob Cohen also joined this brigade and fought in the Battle of Beaufort under General Moultrie. He acquitted himself creditably enough to earn from his commander Richard Lushington the certificate of merit; "Jacob I. Cohen enrolled himself with me on his arrival from the northward here, and has been with me a volunteer on ye expedition to Beaufort, and has in every respect conducted himself as a good soldier and man of courage."

General Lincoln then took over and attempted to retake Savannah. He failed in that "forlorn hope" and had to defend Charleston. With the capture of that important port, the British took Jacob Cohen prisoner and ill-treated him with the other Americans on their prison ship *Torbay*. The prisoners were released on condition that they leave the Charleston vicinity. Jacob found his way to Philadelphia, the national capital and the only Jewish community left intact by the war.

The surrender at Yorktown brought an end to active fighting. In Philadelphia romance came to the 38 year old veteran when he met the widow of Moses Mordecai. She had been Elizabeth Whitlock, an English Christian girl in her teens when she married a man twice her age; she became a good Jewess and followed him to the new world. Jacob determined to marry the widow even if she had three children. Unexpectedly, they tangled with the ancient Levitical law that forbade a priest (Cohen) to marry a proselyte. Either Jacob was not sure of his descent from the Aaronites or did not think it mattered too much. Others took a similar view and synagogue politics boiled the issue into a bitter controversy. The *Adjunta*, or ruling body, wrote to its hazan-rabbi, Gershom M. Seixas, forbidding him or anyone else to perform the ceremony. But love, which according to story tellers laughs at bolts and bars, found a way. They were married. How? We don't know. It is easy to imagine him presenting a ring and saying the 10 word Hebrew formula, followed by a civil ceremony. The marriage proved happy, and Esther (Elizabeth) Cohen remained a great favorite in Jewish circles.

While in Philadelphia, Jacob Cohen had a visit from a member of the Continental Congress who was financially quite embarrassed. Cohen readily advanced £50 to the youthful Representative from Virginia, little dreaming that the borrower, James Madison, would one day become the fourth President of the United States.

Finding his way back to Richmond, Jacob Cohen formed a partnership with his friend, the pioneer Isaiah Isaacs. The firm of Cohen and Isaacs traded in general merchandise and tobacco, the stable commodity that held up best during the war. They had houses, slaves, and *Bird in Hand,* probably the oldest tavern in Richmond. They owned land in about six counties, and took long chances speculating on tracts in the Great Dismal Swamp near Norfolk, thereby following the examples set by the founders of the republic, including George Washington himself.

After the war Congress, in lieu of money, compensated the soldiers with land. A brisk trade arose in these lands as well as with warrants for much larger tracts. When Cohen and Isaacs hired a gaunt, weather beaten frontiersman wearing a coon skin cap and leather jerkin, they had no idea that their agent, a Colonel Daniel Boone, would become immortalized. They advanced him £6, gave him the warrants, with instructions to locate the lands. The Boone receipts for cash and warrants were duly filed. Evidently neither partner was too skilled in written English, for on the back of the Boone paper appears a notation in poorly spelled Yiddish: *Resit fun Kornel Bon far 10,000 agir lanit.* Again they employed Daniel Boone to survey lands in Kentucky several miles south of what is now Cincinnati. Colonel Boone sent in his bill for £22, and judging by the spelling on the accompanying note, the daring trail blazer's English was little better than his employer's Yiddish.

As time went on Cohen prospered and opened a bank. Possessing a feeling of public responsibility, he served a number of terms on the grand and petit jury, and as a magistrate. When

Colonel Bushrod Washington, nephew of the president, moved away in 1795 leaving a vacancy in the city council, the remaining councillors promptly elected Jacob I. Cohen to fill the office.

On Aug. 24, 1789 Jacob Cohen took the lead in organizing the first synagogue in Virginia. The majority of the members were Ashkenazim, yet they followed the pattern set in the other five congregations of the young republic and adopted the Portuguese-Spanish ritual. Beth Shalome started functioning in time for two historic participations. It celebrated the first Thanksgiving Day at the request of the Federal authorities. Jacob Cohen utilized the occasion to compose a prayer for the success of the new government, also paying homage to its first President. This frontier congregation also joined the others in sending a letter expressing their deep veneration and respect to George Washington on his election as President.

When Jacob Cohen died at the age of 79, he freed his slaves, giving a gift of $25 to each. Leaving no children, he devised the estate to the five sons of his younger brother who had moved to Baltimore. He had reason to feel proud of his relatives, the distinguished "Cohens of Baltimore". His nephew and namesake, Jacob I. Cohen, Jr., set up a bank, helped to organize the Philadelphia, Washington, and Baltimore Railroad, and was president of the Baltimore Fire Insurance Company. He expended strenuous efforts in getting the General Assembly to repeal the law that required every public official to take the oath of a Christian. Immediately after repeal of the law he was elected to the City Council of Baltimore.

Mendes I. Cohen defended Fort McHenry in the War of 1812 and was a director of the Baltimore and Ohio Railroad, and a member of the Maryland House of Delegates. The first American to explore the cataracts of the Nile, he brought back a valuable historic collection for Johns Hopkins University.

Joshua I. Cohen, a noted scientist and physician, specialized in eye diseases and served as president of the Medical Faculty of the State University. He founded an eye and ear clinic, and his paper on deafness published in the *American Medical Intelligences* attracted wide attention. A professor of mineralogy and geology at the University of Maryland, he collected rare books in Hebraica and Judaica, and served on the Baltimore City Council.

Mendes Cohen, a noted civil engineer, made his mark in railroading and became president of the Pittsburgh and Connellsville Railroad. Consulting engineer to the City of Baltimore, his suggestions of a modern sewage system were adopted. A man of many interests, including art and history, President Cleveland appointed him on a board to report on a route for the Chesapeake and Delaware Ship Canal. To their Uncle Jacob, the Cohens of Baltimore were ever grateful.

COAT OF ARMS OF GOMEZ FAMILY.

1803

BENJAMIN GOMEZ

Book Dealer and Publisher

IN THE PALACE at Madrid, or the Escorial, King Charles gave his loyal courtier an oblique glance and declared quizzically: "Gomez, the onions are beginning to smell." The jest was warning enough to get his wife and infant son Moses out of Spain. By the 17th century, double-talk had become a fine art, understood particularly by the wary insecure. Mother and child reached France together with a goodly portion of the family substance.

The Inquisition then nabbed Isaac Gomez. His Catholicism had become suspect when the Holy Office began to sniff at the nice fortune he inherited or amassed. For 14 years the secret tribunal could not decide whether its prisoner was a secret Jew or a devout Christian. Possibly the Inquisition released him after squeezing out the remaining treasure. The father finally joined his wife and son at Bordeaux. In gratitude to the King of France, Isaac added Louis to his son's name.

The family tradition goes on to relate how Louis Moses Gomez lived happily in France until the revocation of the Edict of

Nantes denied Huguenots their freedom to worship. The Gomezes took alarm. They had vivid memories of a monolithic state religion that would not suffer any other faith to contaminate the pure air of Catholic Spain. A highly sensitive antenna gave warning that secret Judaism would be tolerated even less than the Protestant dissenters. In short, another Exodus was timely.

The same saga tells that merry King Charles of England graciously permitted Louis Moses to settle in America. Soon thereafter many Gomezes were living on the Caribbean Islands. But a document filed in New York and dated 1705 shows specifically that Queen Anne granted Letters of Denization that gave Louis Moses Gomez and family the wide privileges of a most favored subject in the matter of office holding, land ownership and military rank. It took little time for him to become the leading Jewish merchant in provincial New York.

Louis Moses Gomez brought over and displayed the impressive Coat of Arms granted to his ancestors. Yet aristocratic tradition did not deter his entering trade, which the English gentry scorned. Connections abroad enabled his import-export business to thrive. Into the new primitive world he imported silks, taffetas, wine and chintz, and it was not beneath him to export such plebeian commodities as wheat or limestone. In 1711 he furnished the British troops in Canada with provisions that totaled £354. Nor did he neglect the Indian trade. To attract the profitable fur business, he erected a trading post with thick stone walls near Newburg on the Hudson. The Gomez house in Orange County near a stream long called Jew's Creek still stands as the oldest Jewish residence in all North America.

During the first half of the 18th century the Gomez clan rated as the most prominent family in all the Jewish communities of America. At least seven members were presidents of Shearith Israel at a time when the office of *parnass* represented the highest rank attainable to a people shut out from political and civic honors. But the inevitable decline set in. By the end of the century the Gomez *yichus* (pedigree) had through marriage infiltrated other families. Their loyalty to the American Revolution sapped most of their wealth. Newcomers more successful in business tended to displace the older stock in community leadership.

By 1791 the Gomez affluence had shrunk, perhaps to the ancestral homestead on Maiden Lane. Benjamin Gomez, the great grandson of Louis Moses, at 22 had nothing in particular to do. In older societies the scions of aristocratic forebears generally idled about in genteel poverty, contemptuous of labor, and seeking perhaps to mend their fortune by marrying some heiress even of baser lineage. But the growing democracy in the lusty infant republic set a premium on work and branded idleness as parasitic. It was his taste for reading that led Benjamin Gomez to become the earliest Jewish book dealer in English America.

He set up as bookseller at 32 Maiden Lane and offered a fairly wide selection to a population in which the illiterate outnumbered by far the articulate and polished intelligentsia. Most of the list is forgotten, yet many of his classics stand out as a reminder of the taste and culture prevalent in New York at the close of the 18th century. His advertised stock consisted of histories, essays, medical-scientific works, volumes on the law, novels and romances, travel books, poetry, Bibles, sermons, lectures, and religious books "too tedious for insertion" in the newspaper. Still current among readers are his: Blackstone's *Commentaries*, Vattel's *Law of Nations*, Montesquieu's *Spirit of Laws*, Swift's *Sermons*, Hume's *History of England*, Priestley's *Lectures*, Robertson's *History of India*, and *History of Charles V*, Shakespeare, Richardson's *Clarissa Harlow*, *Arabian Night Entertainments*, Edmund Burke, Fielding's *Tom Jones*, and Sterne's *Complete Works*.

Gomez felt optimistic enough to venture into publishing. In the following year, he brought out a religious work that had already achieved popularity in England and America. *The Christian Economy* was one of those spurious works based on a supposed translation of a Greek manuscript found on the island of Patmos where St. John wrote his Book of Revelation. Its success encouraged Gomez to another attempt. *Female Policy Detected; or the Arts of a Designing Woman Laid Open* is a tavern keeper's advice for female management—full of strained humor, bad taste, and shallow wisdom. Its sale stimulated Gomez into undertaking a number of publications, among them *Captain Cook's Third and Last Voyage* together with a condensed version of *Robinson Crusoe, Pilgrims Progress* by Bunyan, and Goethe's *Sorrows of Werther*.

His most interesting publication was Joseph Priestley's *Letters to the Jews Inviting them to Amicable Discussion of the Evidences of Christianity*. In the same volume Gomez printed the rejoinder by David Levi entitled: *Letters to Dr. Priestley in Answer to Those Addressed to the Jews*. The famous scientist, not content with his great contribution to chemistry, was religious minded and genuinely concerned with the salvation of the Jews.

The forgotten David Levi deserves more than passing notice. In dire poverty, he labored at shoe mending, hat making, and finally as a printer. Through all hardships he studied unremittingly and became the foremost Hebrew scholar in 18th century England. Author and translator, he was the first Jew to write a vindication of Judaism in English. He even had the temerity to answer the attacks on the Old Testament in Thomas Paine's *Age of Reason*. His polemic against Priestley attracted wide attention. Its publication by Gomez was more than justified when it drew the notice of Thomas Jefferson, who wrote to John Adams:

"I have lately been amusing myself with Levi's book in answer to Dr. Priestley. It is a curious and tough work.— Some of his doctrines were new to me.— He avails himself of his advantage over his adversaries by his superior knowledge of Hebrew, speaking in the very language of the divine communication, while they can only fumble on with conflicting and disputed translations. Such is the war of giants. And how can such pigmies as you and I decide between them?"

The success of Gomez induced Naphtali Judah to become the

second Jewish book dealer and publisher. Yet publishing has always been a hazardous game. It is therefore not surprising that Gomez had to take in a full stock of general stationery, so customary among booksellers of the time, to stimulate business. Evidently Judah proved a stiff competitor, for Gomez added lottery tickets as a side line. For a time he devoted all his efforts to his new venture, the "Fortunate Lottery Office". This was a respectable business at a time when governments and most American churches operated games of chance to help meet their annual budgets. But subsequently he went back to book-selling.

Benjamin Gomez kept up the family tradition of communal service. He served in the various offices of Shearith Israel and finally became its *Parnass*.

THE GOMEZ HOME,
OLDEST JEWISH HOUSE IN AMERICA.
BUILT 1718.

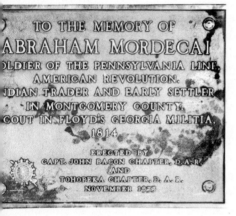

PLACQUE TO MORDECAI ERECTED BY D.A.R.

1804

OLD MORDECAI
Of *Alabama*

MONTGOMERY was formerly the old Indian town of Acochanta, meaning "red earth." While not strictly its founder, Abram Mordecai was the first white settler in the area that is now Alabama's capital and third city. Colonel Albert J. Pickett, the official historian of Alabama, paid a visit to the 92 year old Mordecai living alone in an Indian hut near two others. Strongly impressed, Pickett wrote a full account of the interview, which on Oct. 5, 1847 was published in the *Montgomery Flag and Advertiser*. This article is the source material of the picturesque Jewish adventurer and Indian trader, the first pioneer to plant cotton and set up a gin in Alabama.

Born 1755 in Pennsylvania of a Jewish father and German mother, Abram Mordecai served the Revolutionary cause for three years in the minor campaigns of New Jersey and Delaware. In 1783 he settled in Georgia among the Cassuto Indians and traded merchandise for skins, furs, snakeroot, pinkroot and other medicinal barks. Oil brewed by Indian women from cracked

117

hickory nuts was considered a delicacy by the Spanish, who used it with condiments. He sent as much as 30 gallons to Governor Dufort of New Orleans, then under the rule of Spain.

After French and Spanish occupation ended, Mordecai moved to Alabama in 1789. Other newcomers to the same area were several Tories who found life uncomfortable and unsafe among the victorious patriots. A horse thieving Dutchman came, as well as an English infantryman who had deserted the army and brought along his wife. When he died Milly his widow became a favorite among the Braves and ended up owning a house on the creek with many horses and cattle.

Abram Mordecai got along quite well. His mules and ponies strapped with bundles on the sides and tops of their saddles carried merchandise to and from Pensacola and Augusta. Boats and canoes were used for the trade back and forth between Mobile and New Orleans. In five years he was able to hire some Spanish deserters to build for him a house of mortar in the Spanish style. Like most traders he married a squaw, either for convenience or out of policy, to gain favor with the hostile savages. She bore him children and he became expert in the language, manners and customs of the Indians.

This knowledge enabled him to render great service to many white captives carried away by the Creek Indians from the new settlements, later known as Kentucky. James Seagrave, the government agent for Indian Affairs, employed Mordecai to negotiate with the distant Indian chiefs, who were becoming more and more embittered at the white settlers pressing upon them. With his agreeable manner, remarkable adroitness and knowledge of the language, he was able to ransom the wretched women and children who had ceased to hope that they would ever be released. His name appears often in government reports and correspondence.

With increased prosperity, Mordecai's horizon widened. Hearing of the cotton gin invented by Eli Whitney, he consulted the new agent for Indian Affairs. Colonel Hawkins heartily approved installing the first cotton gin in Alabama, over which he held jurisdiction. He advised setting up the gin house at the juncture of two rivers, so that Indian women could paddle their canoes full of cotton to be exchanged for the articles and provisions they needed. This embankment was the property of the Hickory Creek Indians, so permission had to come from the Chief. It was quite expensive in 1804 to bring Lyon and Arnold from Georgia to build and install the machine. But the investment paid off when Mordecai received in the New Orleans market 33¢ a pound for his ginned cotton, equivalent to about $2.00 in our day. While in the French city, he paid $400 for a fine boat.

The world of Abram Mordecai suddenly crashed. One day in 1805, sixteen braves with hickory poles surrounded the Spanish hacienda. Chief Towerculla (called Capt. Isaacs by the whites) charged that two horses of the paleface had eaten the young corn on the red man's field. Mordecai offered to pay the damage, but the Chief resented the white encroachment and struck him. Mordecai, being physically strong, grabbed the Indian ready to throw him over the ravine, when the Braves overpowered and beat him unmercifully with their staves. They cut off one ear and left him for dead. When he regained consciousness, the expensive gin was destroyed, the valuable boat and all his cotton reduced to ashes. It took months for his powerful physique to recover, and 42 years later Colonel Pickett could still see the knots on his body. A hostile source informed the historian that the real cause of the beating was an affair with a comely married squaw.

The raid ruined Mordecai's economy, and at 50 it was not easy for him to make a fresh start. With the War of 1812, English agents stirred up the Indians, and he fled to Georgia enlisting again for military duty. In 1836 lands were assigned out west for the Creek nation, but Mordecai, now in his eighties, refused to follow his Indian sons to Arkansas. Pickett describes him at 92 as intelligent, pious, not without scholarship, and his deep hazel eyes lighting up in recollection of old occurrences. "Old Mordecai" was held in universal esteem, and the villagers did everything to ease his impoverished, lonely old age.

In 1851 Pickett's *History of Alabama* appeared. The facts of Mordecai's career are substantially as in the newspaper article written four years earlier. But the former tone of respect and admiration gives way to disparagement. Instead of the intelligent, honest, active, remarkably adroit pioneer, of well-formed forehead, hazel-eyed with large expressive mouth and body well knit, frugal and self denying, praying devoutly out of his Bible before eating breakfast, the first settler to plant and gin cotton in the State becomes a strange, dark-eyed Jew, amorous in disposition and married to a squaw darkened with the blood of Ham. One cannot but feel that the historian had given more credence to malicious slander than to his own unbiased impressions.

Notwithstanding the historian's later slurs, the *Montgomery Evening Times* reprinted in 1904 Pickett's original article that appeared in 1847. A special editorial devoted to Montgomery's Jewish founder comments: "No class of our citizens have a better right to share in the pride and glory of Montgomery than those of whose faith the pioneer builder of remote times was an honored and useful type." The appreciative editor advocated a monument on the Court House square to the memory of "Old Mordecai— the noble Jew."

In 1933, the Daughters of the American Revolution erected a marker "To the Memory of Abraham Mordecai, Soldier of the Pennsylvania Line, American Revolution Indian Trader and Early Settler in Montgomery County. Scout in Floyd's Georgia Militia, 1814."

1805

ISAAC MOSES

Merchant and Patriot

Several portraits in oil have preserved the features of Isaac Moses. The painting by John Wesley Jarvis hangs in the Museum of the City of New York. A large, firm nose dominates the face. The closed mouth and strong jaw would suggest decision and force. The features that best indicate the whole man are his expressive eyes, clear, large, steady, yet not without kindness. A sense for elegance pervades the tall, beaver felt hat, the dotted vest, white linen cravat, and velvet black coat. The artists have limned for us a well-to-do merchant at the turn of the 18th century, the beneficiary of an ever expanding industrial Revolution.

Born in Germany at about 1742, Isaac Moses landed in New York at the age of 22. Six years later he married his cousin, daughter of the trader and community leader, Hayman Levy, who gave away with the bride a dower of £1000. But the bridegroom did not do so badly for himself either. He could match the uncle father-in-law by settling a similar sum upon his wife.

During twenty-one years, their union was blest with 10 children, not so large a family by Colonial standards.

Isaac Moses seems to have been endowed with the golden touch. Success began to smile upon him shortly after his arrival; he continued to prosper in spite of disruptions the war brought to business. Uprooted in 1776 when New York was captured by the British, he was soon on the road to affluence in Philadelphia. Before and after Yorktown, he owned in whole or in part a sloop, three brigantines, and four schooners.

An element of luck, perhaps, shaped the conduct of Isaac Moses. Never having lived in England, he was free of the commercial attachments that determined the loyalty of those merchants who became Tories by force of circumstances. He needed only to contrast the barbarous disabilities that obtained in Germany with the freedom and opportunities in the Colonies. No obligation to or sentiment for England made the choice difficult as to whether or not to throw in his lot with the patriots.

But the patriotism of Isaac Moses was not calculated policy. He could have made his peace with the British when they took over New York. Instead he abandoned home, warehouse, and virtually went into exile following such patriots of Shearith Israel Congregation as Samuel Judah, Haym Salomon, Michael Moses Hays, Matathias Gomez, and Gershom Mendes Seixas. Owner of ships and a father of children, he joined the Pennsylvania militia in his 39th year.

Venturing of ships for privateering presented hazards that appealed more to patriotism than to sound business. Many a boat fell captive to British cruisers. This form of legal piracy played a role in winning the war scarcely less important than the battlefield. When we consider the 700 boats captured and the loss of $18,000,000 to British merchants, we can understand the strong petitions of English business to end the war. It was in obedience to the urging of the Continental Congress that Isaac Moses put all his vessels on the high seas to prey on British commerce. With his usual luck he emerged a winner. In 1782 he was able to donate

£112 for building the Mikveh Israel Synagogue in Philadelphia. Two years later he contributed an additional £121 for its upkeep and repair—generous sums for those days.

In privateering ventures Isaac Moses had the cooperation of Robert Morris, who held a partnership in several of his ships. The famous financier of the Revolution evidently had a high opinion of his Jewish associate. In his diary Morris refers to Isaac Moses as "my friend of austere culture and true knowledge," a higher tribute than he ever paid to Haym Salomon, whose contribution to American independence was far greater. It was probably due to experience with vessels that made Isaac Moses a member of the Marine Society of New York.

Risking his fortune in privateering was perhaps his most important war effort. Capturing war material and provisions for the Americans badly in need of supplies had even greater importance than inflicting damage on British commerce. Yet the patriotic deeds for which Isaac Moses is chiefly remembered are his financial acts. During the darkest period of the war, Washington's army was sorely in need of food, clothes, and ammunition. A bank was proposed, probably by Robert Morris, to establish the necessary credits for obtaining the wherewithal to carry on the struggle. In this emergency, Isaac Moses pledged his "property and credit" in the sum of £3000 towards the £300,000 necessary for establishing the bank. He also invested large sums (for those days) in purchasing bills for the support of the French army, and with Haym Salomon was an original subscriber to the Bank of North America. Robert Morris mentions in his diary other services in financing rendered by Isaac Moses during the desperate period in the war to win freedom.

It is curious how social standards change with the generations. In our own day, cafe society or country club Jews shy away from religious or communal responsibility. Yet in the 18th century the elite and fashionable eagerly sought after the honors of the synagogue, which carried leadership in the community. Isaac Moses first received public recognition when 27 years old. For the rest of his life he carried the burdens and duties of Judaism. In 1780 he with his father-in-law brought to Philadelphia the minister Gershom Mendes Seixas, who fled with the Torahs to Stamford, Conn. when the British entered New York. In 1782 he called the meeting that organized Mikveh Israel Congregation and served as its first president. Immediately he took the initiative in acquiring a plot of ground, which within a year supported the first synagogue building erected in Pennsylvania. Returning to New York, he began active participation as a trustee of the synagogue. On four different occasions, he was elected Parnass of Shearith Israel.

In New York, Isaac Moses appears to have sensed the future rise in real estate values. A list of his holdings aggregate the then impressive sum of $160,000. Among his properties listed is a $25,000 estate in the country. This tract of land, known as the Cooper farm, lay between 32nd and 35th Streets from Seventh Ave. to the Hudson River. Had his heirs followed the example of the Astor family and preserved the estate intact, its value today could pay off the national debt of some republics or kingdoms, whose diplomats sit deliberating at the United Nations not too many blocks away.

A top member of the Chamber of Commerce and a founder of the Bank of New York, his repute apparently reached Europe. For in 1805, Isaac Moses received an invitation to attend the ceremony at the coronation of the Emperor Napoleon.

1806

JUDGE MOSES LEVY

Of Philadelphia

I~N~ ~HIS~ ~QUEST~ for an Attorney-General of the United States, Thomas Jefferson wrote his Secretary of the Treasury, Albert Gallatin, "to inquire fully into the legal knowledge, judgment, and moral and social character of Levy." When the President preferred "a good lawyer, and rather that he should be from Pennsylvania" he merely reflected the current faith in the "Philadelphia lawyer", a term that became a popular byword for a sound, ingenious, learned and resourceful attorney.

Gallatin grudgingly admitted the legal ability of Moses Levy, but questioned "if his practice be, as it is presumable, worth six or seven thousand dollars, is it probable that he would give it up for the place of Attorney-General, and exchange Philadelphia for Washington." Moses Levy occupied a top place in the highly distinguished bench and bar of Philadelphia, in 1804 the intellectual and political center of the nation. Washington was as yet but a swamp town on the flats of the Potomac.

The intuitions of Gallatin as to Levy's psychological unfitness for Jefferson's radical Cabinet were confirmed two years later, when the famous Cordwainers Case came up. The attitude of Moses Levy as presiding judge reflects his innate conservatism, his lack of sympathy for the New Deal of Thomas Jefferson. He would have been as out of place as Herbert Brownell in F.D.R.'s Brain Trust. The trial focuses the legal impasse that obstructed the unionizing of labor in the future arsenal of industrial democracy.

While Moses Levy was Recorder (municipal judge) of Philadelphia, eight shoe makers were arrested and charged with (1) demanding $5.00 for making fancy boots, $4.00 for back strap boots, $3.00 for long strap boots, or cossacks, or bootees, a wage higher than the current scale, (2) conspiring to prevent others from working at lower wages than demanded, (3) designing to form a combination to make arbitrary by-laws for governing each other, for exacting "great sums of money", for refusing to work with a master who employed such labor as broke their rules or accepted lower pay.

The Cordwainers Case attracted wide attention as one of the first in America where a court interfered to prevent a strike or form a union. Yet there were also economic, industrial, political and social factors involved. Merchants still accustomed to colonial habits of selling imported goods looked askance at home made wares. The artisan merchant making his article to order for each customer separately resented manufacturing at large for the wholesale trade. This trial marks the slow beginnings of the Industrial Revolution already developing a steady wage earning class that would replace the haphazard, temporary, or seasonal workers drawn from the farms, the fishing boats, the water front. Above all it brought to the surface the inevitable conflict between employers desiring cheap labor and workers demanding higher wages.

The case also had its political repercussions. The monied and propertied Federalists stood by the employers whose rights were consistently upheld by the highest courts of England. The Jeffersonians took the side of Labor. There was also the implied issue whether the English Common Law, brought over by the Colonists, should be the basic law of the land after independence. The Federalists favored adopting the legal system inherited from England. The Democrats opposed being governed by the decisions handed down in the House of Lords.

Judge Levy, caught in the center of a politico-economic storm, could hardly escape the abuse of the losing side. Regardless of personal sympathies, it would have been difficult to go counter to such titans in the law as Blackstone, or Lord Mansfield. After citing these high authorities, he concluded his charge to the jury "that a combination to maintain one another, carrying a particular object, whether true or false, is criminal." The jury found the strikers guilty. This case helped to establish the precedent against trade unions and striking until reversed in 1842 by Chief Justice Shaw of Massachusetts.

The results of the famous trial pleased the powerful, and Moses Levy was made Presiding Judge of the District Court for the City and County of Philadelphia. The first of his stock to rise above Magistrate, he was also the earliest in that long list of Jews to become eminent in the American judiciary. Yet he is forgotten. One is tempted to ask why. There are several reasons. Who was there to preserve his memory? To Jews he was a Christian, and to Christians he remained a Jew, notwithstanding his aloofness from the community. The Federalists regarded him a Jeffersonian, and to the Democrats he was identified with the party of wealth and privilege. Never a member of a synagogue, he nevertheless belongs to American Jewish history.

Named after his grandfather, the New York leading merchant and Parnass of Shearith Israel, Moses Levy was born in Philadelphia in 1757 of a Gentile mother. His father made the social grade when accepted in the fashionable Dancing Assembly. The first student of Jewish origin to graduate from the University of Pennsylvania, he joined the Continental Army and was among the selected soldiers who made the celebrated crossing of the Delaware on Christmas night of 1776 with General Washington. He fought in the battles of Princeton and Trenton. Admitted to the bar in 1778, he became one of those brilliant practitioners who made the Philadelphia lawyer famous in American folklore.

His painted portrait shows the scholarly face and powdered white wig of an 18th century gentleman. It appears that he was baptized in St. Peter's Episcopal Church. Perhaps he was too steeped in the skepticism then in fashion to pay much attention to church or synagogue. The baptism of his two daughters might have been due to the insistence of his Christian wife. In the will, he orders "my body to be buried in a plain decent manner in the yard of St. Peter's Church——near the tomb of my mother and father." Perhaps he was content to live as a lawyer and gentleman, free from close attachment to any faith or creed. Yet in spite of baptism he was not always permitted to forget his origin. During the bitter political election year of 1800, when representing a client who was a Jeffersonian Republican, the ever ranting poisonous journalist, William Cobbett, stooped to write a vicious and vulgar screed attacking Moses Levy as the Jew who talked for money only and not out of any political convictions.

1807

JOHN HAYS

Sheriff and Indian Agent

LOG CABIN COURTHOUSE
OF SHERIFF JOHN HAYS.

W HILE THE Founding Fathers in Philadelphia were framing the Constitution in 1787 for a more perfect union, John Hays in his late teens left the settled security of his native New York for the wilds of the great Northwest Territory. He bypassed what Daniel Boone had called the "Dark and Bloody Ground" of Kentucky, crossed the Ohio and Wabash, and entered a no-man's land through which the red natives roamed in search of good hunting. Straggling Frenchmen in scattered outposts called this wilderness by an Indian name with a Gallic spelling. Forever after this prairie would be known as Illinois.

Young Hays had no difficulty in connecting with a wealthy Canadian house engaged in the Indian trade. On a mission to the headwaters of the Red River "he and two Canadians were caught out in a snowstorm in the prairie and were compelled to lie under the snow for three days and nights, during the storm." In his *Pioneer History of Illinois,* Gov. John Reynolds goes on to say: "They had a scanty supply of dried meat, and thin blankets to cover them. The storm raged with such violence that they were not able to travel in the open prairie, and were forced to remain under the snow to preserve their lives. It snowed in the meantime to a considerable depth. No one who has not experienced the hardships in the Indian trade of the Northwest can realize it. The want of water under the snow was that which incommoded them most."

One may ask pertinently why a lad should quit his native city for the rigors and dangers on the western frontier. Love of adventure could be the answer. Yet the causes might have been more compelling. Actually the Hays closet had a skeleton whose grin was familiar to everyone. When John was but six years old, his father Baruch, or Barrak Anglicized, was one of the 948 signers who pledged loyalty to Britain. A year earlier such a proclamation would have met with general approval. But three months after the Declaration of Independence the Colonials were in no mood to accept the tardy concessions that a panicky George III was eager to grant.

For seven years the Tories of New York basked in the favor of the British. Baruch Hays and two other Tories were able to save the synagogue from desecration or confiscation. But after the return of the Americans, the tables turned suddenly. Many Loyalists left with the English army. If Baruch remained, his lot could not have been pleasant. The 13 year old John must have felt keenly the jeers of the other boys. We can only surmise that he forsook New York at the first opportunity and never returned. He left civilization and traveled on foot, presumably to the edge of the territory northwest of the Ohio claimed by the U. S. government.

The tenderfoot from the East had no difficulty in his adjustment to the backwoodsman's life in the forest, in canoes, on pack horses or rafts. Shortly after the snowstorm, he became agent for Todd and Hay, another commercial partnership with extensive operations in the Northwest. He established headquarters at Cahokia and remained there all his life. But with the death of Todd, the company dissolved. John Hays next proceeded along customary Jewish lines and went into business for himself. Gathering a stock of goods for the Indian trade, he would take his assortment once a year by the river route to Prairie du Chien and come back in the fall with the articles bartered from the Indians. Gradually he prospered and could employ agents and use his own boats.

Living alone in the wilderness could be quite monotonous. Many backwoodsmen or Indian traders lived with squaws. There was hardly a Jewish family within the range of 800 miles. The biographer of Hays informs us that "he married a lady in Vincennes of excellent family, and what is still better, of sound good sense." She was probably French, and their three daughters were no doubt reared in the Christian faith. Yet Hays never appears to have abandoned his Judaism. Gov. Reynolds states: "Mr. Hays possessed a moral and honest character; his morality throughout life was very exemplary. He was not a member of any Christian church, but observed the precepts contained in the word, with due respect and devotion." His granddaughter, Mrs. Eliza Brouillet of Dallas, Texas, wrote in 1904 to the lawyer-historian, Max J. Kohler, that she still had in her possession "a family Hebrew Bible" (probably a prayer book) "and other evidences of her grandfather's Jewish faith" (perhaps a talith and tephilim).

Indian trading began to decline as the influx of white settlers gradually forced the red aborigines beyond the Mississippi to hunt the buffalo and reindeer, the bear or round-horned elk. With the problem of supporting a growing family, Hays turned to farming. He bought land in the Cahokia area and succeeded in agriculture by putting into practice the good sense he used in business. Nor did he give up the trading post, in which he operated the post office as far back as the oldest resident could remember. While not a paid job, the office of postmaster was an accommodation for the settlement, especially to the Canadian pioneers who could never acquire the English language; it was not without benefit to the enterprising trader, who spoke French fluently.

By 1798, the settlement felt a need for orderly government. General Arthur St. Clair, the Federally appointed Governor of the Northwest Territory, selected John Hays as Sheriff of the new country, which the former named St. Clair in honor of himself. For twenty years the latter exercised the duties of the office with diligence and honesty. Then Illinois was organized into a state and admitted into the Union. Thereafter all public officers were elected under the new State Constitution. But Hays did not become a candidate. He grew tired of the post, which he held longer than any sheriff in the territory; besides he had the additional responsibility of a Federal appointment.

A letter written in 1812 to Governor Edwards reveals Hays as intelligent and not without education. Reputation for character, fluency in French, and a first-hand knowledge of the country together with its primitive natives probably induced President Madison in 1814 to nominate him Collector for the Indian Territory. The Senate confirmed the nomination promptly. In 1822 he received the appointment of Indian Agent for the Pottowotomac and Miamis in Northwestern Indiana. The office paid a good salary but kept the aging pioneer away from his home for several years.

Returning to Cahokia, he decided to spend his remaining years in the midst of his family and friends. John Hays died in 1836, leaving a good name and a substantial estate to his three daughters.

HOME OF MOSES MYERS
IN NORFOLK
(SEE FOLLOWING CHAPTER).

1808

MOSES MYERS

Of Norfolk

In 1750 Chaim Mears, fresh from Amsterdam, had difficulty in adjusting himself to the city of New York. He therefore accepted the job of *shohet* for Shearith Israel at the salary of £10 a year, with the tongues of the cattle he slaughtered thrown in as a bonus. In addition, the congregation considered it only fair to pay his ferry charges for crossing the river to the slaughter house. An optimist who believed two could live as cheaply as one, he married the following year and kept an open eye for the main chance. The conquest of French Canada by the British gave him the opportunity. He took the oath under the Naturalization Act, virtually a permit to do business, and Anglicized his name to Haym Myers.

He started trading and seems to have met success immediately. We find him sending goods to Canadian Aaron Hart, the Grand Seigneur of Trois Rivieres. He is in constant communication with that energetic merchant, Samuel Jacobs of Quebec. The recent *shohet* is soon prosperous enough to donate 100 pounds of wax for the candles in the Newport Synagogue—a gesture probably made to ingratiate himself with that prince of merchants, Aaron Lopez. But Haym Myers had to travel constantly from New York to Quebec, to Montreal, and back. Travel and shipping had their hazards. The slow moving sail boats were at the mercy of winds, of weather and of pirates. Travel by land meant facing perils from Indians, highwaymen and rascally employees. Myers decided to concentrate his activities and make his home in Canada.

His son, Moses Myers, mastered early the intricacies and hazards of colonial trading. Living in the newly proclaimed republic during the Revolutionary struggle, he became a partner of Samuel Myers, son of the famous silversmith. Moses looked up to his older associate of the same surname, although not related to him. In Philadelphia, the friends attracted the attention of Isaac Moses, the large scale merchant who left New York at the approach of the British. His experienced eye measured these capable young men as proper associates with whom to form an organization to handle the import-export business made difficult by war conditions.

In the American market the war had created a shortage of manufactured goods. The home commodities of tobacco, rice, cotton, grain and lumber were bringing good prices abroad. The odds against breaking through the British blockade were great but not insuperable. The profits out of a ship that came in were attractive enough to undertake the risk. But the West Indies lay close enough to cut down the hazards of crossing the ocean. A neutral port such as St. Eustatia or St. Thomas would be ideal for the exchange of American products for the finished articles of Europe.

The three formed a partnership. Isaac Moses and Company handled the business at the American end. Samuel and Moses Myers operated out of Amsterdam. For a time this combine came near becoming the largest business concern in all the 13 states, especially after the operations of David Franks began to dwindle as a result of the Tory accusations levelled against him. The extent of their commerce can be gauged from their debts. At the close of the war, the Moses-Myers syndicate owed to American and European creditors something near £160,000, equivalent in our day to about $5,000,000.

Of course they had enough assets. But peace brought on deflation, and goods were dumped on the market at ruinous prices. The young republic found her former allies stiff competitors in business. Britain, smarting from defeat, missed no opportunity to strangle the commerce of the 13 states loosely bound by the tenuous Articles of Confederation. Paper money softened up, yet farmers found taxes even more burdensome than under the royal governors. The States erected against each other tariff barriers of customs and imposts. Freedom seemed drifting towards anarchy, and men talked of drafting George Washington as king over the liberated commonwealth.

There was little chance of recovery in a depression for a business overburdened with debt. The partners tried hard enough. Samuel Myers traveled from Amsterdam to Paris and dined with the intellectual aristocrat, John Adams. But the American diplomat and future President could do nothing for his fellow citizen who needed a loan of at least £40,000. At home, Moses Myers rushed about from state to state trying to collect outstanding accounts. In miserable winter weather he sometimes made 100 miles a day by horse and coach. Yet his efforts proved vain. As usual under such circumstances, the partners fell out and both Myers blamed Isaac Moses for lack of cooperation, if not for greater dereliction.

Nothing could stave off bankruptcy. Assignees were set up in Amsterdam. In New York the trustees appointed were Alexander Hamilton, together with Daniel Ludlow, later the city's largest importer, and Nicholas Low, a real estate speculator in the grand style, who got his start as an Indian trader from the hogshead of rum advanced by Hayman Levy, his employer. The partners, desiring their creditors to receive at least 50 per cent, sold their furniture and silver. Isaac Moses assigned his real estate, valued at £10,000, and his plate that weighed 445 ounces.

The partners separated, each going his way. The bankruptcy did not mar their good name. Every one regarded them victims of critical conditions. Business firms continued eager to extend them further credit. Isaac Moses remained in New York and made another fortune. Samuel Myers settled in Richmond and became a respected citizen.

After much deliberation Moses Myers selected Norfolk. He married Elizabeth Judah of the Montreal family, an attractive widow of 24 years with considerable property of her own. In 1787 he set sail with his bride for their new home. The hold of the schooner contained their furniture and merchandise in the sum of £1000 bought on credit. On arrival he found awaiting him a cargo from Amsterdam worth 15000 florins supplied by his former creditors. With this beginning he made a new start and staged a comeback. Four years later he built a large, magnificent home. Possibly his wife's money went into this Georgian mansion that still stands as a show place and pride for Norfolk.

It took little time for Moses Myers to attain prominence as a merchant and a foremost citizen. Within five years he became the Norfolk superintendent of the Bank of Richmond. At the same time his ship, *The Moses Myers,* was sailing the high seas. Two years later as agent of France, he protests to the Mayor on behalf of the commander of a French ship about some breach of the neutrality law committed by the British. He acts as personal agent for Thomas Jefferson, the Nicholas and other Virginia families. He is a major in the militia and Federal Collector of the Customs. Elected to the Common Council of Norfolk, he becomes its president. In 1802 as representative of Holland (then called the Batavian Republic) he writes a letter to President Jefferson suggesting a friendly reception to Admiral Hartsinck. In 1830 Moses Myers is listed in England among the prominent Jewish office holders in America. They are pointed out as valuable citizens in an appeal for the removal of the archaic disabilities that still prevented Jews from entering the British Parliament without taking the oath of a true Christian.

1809

JACOB HENRY

Legislator

Nᴏʀᴛʜ Cᴀʀᴏʟɪɴᴀ is justly proud of its Mecklenberg Declaration, which proclaimed a free commonwealth a year before the adoption of the far more famous document in Philadelphia on July 4, 1776. Civil and religious liberties were assured for all residents in the state by its new Constitution.

Such a modernism was considered quite a concession to the new spirit, for since 1701 the established church had ruled out such privileges except to its own Episcopalians. Certain Protestant dissenters, after much determined effort, secured toleration for themselves, but agreed with the church in power to exclude Catholics and Jews. Thus Article 32 in the new Constitution simply preserved the status quo when it provided that no person, who denies God, or the Protestant faith, or the divine authority of the Old and New Testament could hold an office of trust or profit. Thus Catholics, Jews, Deists, Unitarians, Quakers, or Atheists could hold no public office in North Carolina.

This religious disability is no indication that North Carolina was steeped in prejudice and bigotry. Far from it. A tolerant, enlightened minority swayed public opinion to the extent that Article 32, though embedded in the Constitution, was regarded a dead letter. Members of dissenting denominations could be elected or appointed to public positions of honor or trust. In fact, a Catholic had already attained high distinction in politics and on the judiciary. William Gaston, probably the ablest personality in the state, gave his name to a county that became rich in textile mills.

In 1808, Jacob Henry represented Carteret County in the state legislature. The following year he was reelected, indicating that anti-Jewish feeling was not present among the voters. But the chain of tolerance snapped at its weakest link. No one had ever questioned the legality of Judge William Gaston serving on the Circuit Court or sitting in the Assembly, of which in 1809 he was a member. But a legislator did challenge the right of the Jewish Representative holding his seat in spite of Article 32 of the State Constitution.

Jacob Henry rose to his own defense and delivered a short oration that for a time stood out as a masterpiece of eloquent diction, integrating constitutional rights and legal reasoning with a plea for tolerance. This speech was printed in many editions of the *American Orator,* an early textbook for students in rhetoric, patriotism, public duties, and private ethics. It closes with:

"The religion I profess inculcates every duty which man owes to his fellow men; it enjoins upon its votaries the practice of every virtue, and the detestation of every vice, it teaches them to hope for the favor of heaven exactly in proportion as their lives have been directed by just, honorable, and beneficent maxims. This, then, gentlemen, is my creed; it was impressed upon my infant mind; it has been the director of my youth, the monitor of my manhood, and will, I trust, be the consolation of my old age. At any rate, Mr. Speaker, I am sure that you cannot see anything in this religion to deprive me of my seat in this House. So far as relates to my life and conduct, the examination of these I submit with cheerfulness to your candid and liberal construction.

What may be the religion of those who made this objection against me, or whether they have any religion or not, I am unable to say. I have never considered it my duty to pry into the belief of other members of this House. If their actions are upright and conduct just, the rest is for their own consideration, not for mine. I do not seek to make converts to my faith, whatever it may be esteemed in the eyes of my officious friend, nor do I exclude anyone from my esteem of friendship because he and I differ in that respect. The same charity, therefore, it is not unreasonable to expect, will be extended to myself, because in all things that relate to the State and to the duties of civil life, I am bound by the same obligations with my fellow citizens, nor does any man subscribe more sincerely than myself to the maxim, 'whatever ye would that men should do unto ye, do ye so even unto them, for such is the Law and the Prophets.'"

The speech impressed the General Assembly. It was reproduced in the newspapers of other states. Liberal forces in the nation condemned the sectarian spirit that insisted on a religious test for public office as a throwback to the fanaticism of an outmoded past.

The Jewish delegate was not unpopular in the House; he even had friends among the top leaders of the state. But an issue that stirs up religious emotions is seldom settled through appeals to sentiment. Besides, there were few Jews living in North Carolina, and expelling a Jewish legislator would hardly cause a ripple in the Protestant constituencies of the various counties.

Yet certain powerful forces lined up behind Jacob Henry. Some were liberals of the civilized minority who resented the blot upon the fair escutcheon of their state. Others consisted of such groups as Quakers, Deists, Unitarians, who might be legally, if not actually disqualified for public office. But the Catholic element knew that the constitutional arguments used to oust Jacob Henry could be used against them with telling political effect.

The two most prominent figures in the state's public life were, perhaps, William Gaston and his brother-in-law Judge John Louis

Taylor, highly regarded as a jurist and Grand Master in Free-masonry. Both sensed the latent dangers to free government in the dismissal of Jacob Henry for religious reasons. Too adroit politically to rely on appeals to reason or tolerance, they, as skil-ful lawyers, employed legalistic arguments as a basis for future interpretation in the event of a constitutional test in the State or Federal Supreme Court.

The exact language in Article 32, they held, limited the denial of public office only *in the Civil Department within the State.* The General Assembly is no Civil Department but stands above any department in the State. Furthermore neither Catholics nor Jews actually *deny* the truth of the Protestant faith. They may have doubts; but denial is a public overt act, something more positive and articulate than secret opinion or mental reservation. These arguments coming from eminent jurists convinced the legislators. Jacob Henry was permitted to retain his seat.

Who was this Jacob Henry? Was he the son of Joel and Amelia Henry of Beaufort, N. C.? He was an active Mason yet not a member of any synagogue nor known to be identified with the flourishing communities in Charleston, Savannah, or Richmond. The date of his birth or death is unknown. His very victory was more personal than substantive. In principle, it actually riveted more firmly the denial of public office on religious grounds. In 1835, a state convention changed in Article 32 the word Protestant to Christian, thus excluding only Jews and atheists from holding office. Only in 1868, after the gigantic blood bath of the great Civil War, did a convention remove all Jewish disabilities in North Carolina.

1810

JACOB MORDECAI

Schoolmaster

THE FATHER of Jacob Mordecai left Germany for England and there married Elizabeth Whitlock, who changed her Christian name to Esther when she became a Jewess. The couple immigrated to New York and later moved to Philadelphia, where in 1762 Jacob was born. Sent to a school run by an English naval officer, the lad was swept away by the martial spirit that was in the air prior to the Revolution. His shirt was dyed to match the school uniform. A sergeant at 12, he marched with his drilled company of boys as an escort of honor that accompanied the First Continental Congress to its opening session.

In his teens Jacob received some basic training in the business outfit of David Franks. This tycoon of Philadelphia, in spite of assimilatory propensities, often would open his countinghouse to the bright Jewish lads, who ultimately rivaled and even surpassed him in business. Jacob was even welcomed in the fashionable Franks' mansion. There he watched a certain Major Andre paint a miniature of witty and beautiful Rebecca Franks; this

British officer was later to be hanged as a spy for talking treason with Benedict Arnold.

But neither the swank nor the fashion in the Franks' menage impressed the Mordecais. Jacob's father had signed the agreement refusing to buy British imports; his family never deviated from its patriotic loyalty to the cause of Independence. The Franks household sided with the British and deserted Judaism. Jacob Mordecai remained all his life a steadfast follower of the Torah.

Before the war ended his father died. His English mother, the former Elizabeth Whitlock, remarried Jacob I. Cohen of Richmond. After the war Jacob Mordecai, 23 years old, married Judith Myers and followed his mother south. He tried Richmond and Petersburg, then found himself in the peaceful, friendly town of Warrenton in North Carolina. As a country merchant he did well, trading in cotton, tobacco, cereals, as well as in the staples of general merchandise. Judith gave birth to six boys and died. The widower, still young, married her half-sister Rebecca Myers, who not only mothered the orphans of her sister but presented her husband with seven girls.

Bad business came on at a critical moment when Jacob over-speculated in tobacco. He gave up store-keeping and got a job at the Warrenton Academy, of which he operated the steward's house and ran the mess hall. The work was neither congenial nor profitable, and he resigned after two years. Yet the experience proved valuable. He had mastered the practical details of conducting a boarding school.

Home folks, aware of his fondness for reading books, had come to the conclusion that Jacob Mordecai was more the intellectual than a business man. He spoke well, exuded charm, and had a way with women. His refined and gifted family displayed similar tastes for things intellectual. Friends agreed among themselves that the Mordecai family was eminently qualified to operate a boarding school for girls. Leading citizens urged the project as an asset to their town and locality.

Jacob Mordecai re-rented the home he had occupied during

prosperity. The adjoining storeroom was fitted up for classrooms. The Warrenton Female Seminary advertised tuition, board with room for $105 per year; with extra charges for drawing, music, books, quills, ink and paper. More applications came in than anticipated. The quarters proved too small. The next year saw the purchase of a bigger plot of ground on which stood an unfinished building that had to be enlarged with additions.

Before the era of public schools, girls were generally denied elementary education. Colleges were closed to women. The Warrenton Female Seminary consequently grew in fame and reputation. The annual student body averaged 80 girls per year. Applicants had to be rejected. It became necessary to advertise that the Seminary was filled to capacity. The people of Fayetteville wanted the academy moved to their city because it offered larger opportunities for expansion. But Mordecai was content to let well enough alone. He could operate a smaller institution efficiently, with the teaching staff confined chiefly to members of his family. He would be independent in the selection of students and maintain high standards of scholarship and character. After 10 years of successful management, Mordecai closed the school. His earnings enabled him to retire on a farm near Richmond.

Mordecai's academy is not without significance. It marks the new liberalism displacing old prejudices, at least among the intelligent. In the Europe of 1810, it was inconceivable for Christian girls to attend a school operated by professing Jews. Parents still believed their children would be slaughtered and their blood used in baking matzos for Passover. Even in England Jews could not serve in Parliament without taking the Christian oath. It was not until 1868 that North Carolina abolished all religious disabilities.

The school also earned a minor place in what is now called public relations. In North Carolina, as elsewhere, inherited prejudices had distorted the popular estimate of Jews. But in the Seminary young girls could form independent impressions not easily effaced. When they became grandmothers they could recall the gifted and attractive Mordecai family; the pretty, brilliant Ellen

who recorded life in Warrenton in her "History of Hastings";
Samuel, later a successful cotton broker and author of *Virginia,
Especially Richmond in Bygone Days;* Rachel who carried on a
correspondence with Maria Edgeworth, the widely read novelist
of England; the handsome Alfred, a West Point graduate, who
made a distinguished career in the U. S. Army.

The Mordecai with the largest measure of personal magnetism
was, perhaps, Jacob himself. Rebecca Gratz records her delight
"with the patriarchal manner and wisdom of his conversation."
A single incident reveals the respectful affection the Mordecais
inspired. A former student had married John Y. Mason, subsequently appointed Ambassador to France. She came to say farewell to "Mother Rebecca", now aged and worn. Mrs. Mason
knelt and begged a blessing. The silver-haired old lady pronounced the priestly benediction of the Old Testament that be-
gins: "The Lord bless and keep you."

1811

NAPHTALI PHILLIPS

Lived Almost 100 Years

O<small>N HOLIDAYS</small> the numerous progeny of Jonas Phillips, who had 21 children, would gather around the family table at Philadelphia, chatting excitedly about current events. No autos, no movies or television to draw them away, the boys would listen open-mouthed to their older brothers expounding of the battles, the sieges, the great soldiers of the Revolution. Hero worship of General Washington bordered on idolatry.

Their brother Naphtali came in for special envy. When only 15, he marched in the procession celebrating Pennsylvania's ratification of the Constitution, on July 4, 1788. And at 16 he joined the cavalcade that accompanied George Washington from Philadelphia all the way to New York and watched him being inaugurated as first President under the new Constitution that created the Federal Republic. It was a matter of deep regret that no member of the family could tell of his impressions on July 4, 1776 when the Liberty Bell rang out the great news that the Declaration of Independence was signed. Although Jonas Phillips did business in Philadelphia, the family apparently lived then in New York, and Naphtali was but three years old.

Father Jonas might often have talked of the consternation at the news of Washington's defeat on Long Island, his retreat to Manhattan, then his decision to withdraw the army into New Jersey. Patriots simply would not live under British rule. Like Isaac Moses, Jonas Phillips might have waited for the Sabbath to be over, and leaving his goods on the shelves, crowded his wife and dozen children into a large wagon covered with a tarpaulin. His horse would also plod wearily over the rain-soaked roads. Finally they would reach Philadelphia and remain there.

Abandoning his stock of merchandise to the enemy did not prevent Jonas Phillips from doing business in Philadelphia even during the British occupation. Relatives probably helped. The fluctuations of prices in war times enabled a shrewd or lucky speculator to get on his feet quickly. Jonas needed success to feed many mouths. It might seem that Naphtali would follow his father's example and also go into business. But the younger generation, pervaded by a new spirit brought into being by war and freedom, no longer felt the urgency for making money as their only source of security in a hostile world. A learned profession or mental work, though less remunerative, became preferable to trading. Naphtali Phillips got a job with Claypole's *American Advertiser* and learned the newspaper business.

Newspaper work brought Naphtali into contact with the departments of the Federal Government, which had its capital in Philadelphia. He was able to see the advance copy of Washington's Farewell Address sent in September, 1796 to the daily for publication. Immediately he grasped its importance, evaluated its significance. He stood near the press and took away the *first* copy printed in the *Advertiser*. Half a century later, New York City projected a monument to George Washington on Fifth Ave. and 64th Street. Phillips presented his copy, and it was placed in the cornerstone. But this memorial was never completed. Congress proposed to honor the First President with a pile of stone that would rise 555 feet. As other cities or states sent their local rock, New York presented its cornerstone already dedicated for the purpose. Washington's Farewell Address, the gift of Naphtali Phillips, is cemented in the tall obelisk that overlooks the National Capital.

When the Federal Government moved to the banks of the Potomac, Philadelphia went dead, so to speak. The city lost its preeminent place as the intellectual, as well as the political, capital of the nation. Many residents forsook what became "the sleepy city". Naphtali had married Rachel, the daughter of Moses Seixas, head of the Newport congregation, who had written the letter of congratulation to President Washington and received the now famous reply. The couple decided to leave. Maybe the young wife could not adjust to the home town of her husband since childhood. Possibly Naphtali was influenced by his father. Jonas Phillips willed to be buried in New York on account of differences with the powers of Mikveh Israel, which he had helped to build, and to which he had devoted years of faithful service. In 1801 the married couple moved to New York and remained there until Rachel Hannah died in 1822 of yellow fever, and Naphtali expired of senility in his 98th year.

Naphtali Phillips became owner and editor of the *National Advocate,* a leading newspaper in New York during the early years of the century. This position gave him standing in the affairs of the Democratic Party in New York. He held a post in the Custom House until the middle of the century when his eyesight began to fail. For 70 years he continued as an active, influential member of the Tammany Society and died its oldest member.

The painted portrait of Naphtali Phillips reveals a well groomed, clean shaven, elderly gentleman of the Van Buren era. His white scarf contrasts sharply with the black cape thrown over dark formal clothes. The gold-headed cane suggests fashion rather than a support. A well formed head, bald and towering over a pair of thoughtful eyes, together with a firm mouth and compressed lips, slightly curling upward into a faint smile, give the impression of a generous, intelligent, well integrated personality.

One would hardly look for meticulous piety in a well adjusted American of the third generation, without memories of ghetto religiosity. Yet Naphtali observed Orthodox rites with no less scruple than his devout father. After all day services on Yom Kippur, when every worshipper rushed home to break the 24 hour fast, he would remain to read a portion of the prayers for the following morning, a practice followed only by the ultra pious. While traveling, he carried along the utensils for cooking food according to *Kosher* laws and experienced neither difficulty nor embarrassment in having Christians conform respectfully to his wishes. Traveling on a boat, he found the cabin stuffy. On deck in the presence of other passengers, he set his *tephilim* (phylacteries) for the morning prayer. When his son suggested that he better go below, Naphtali answered with the assurance of the secure: "Young man, if you are ashamed of your religion, I am not."

Needless to mention, Naphtali Phillips served Shearith Israel with fidelity. Clerk and trustee of the Congregation, he was elected Parnass 14 times. Anxious lest the story of Jewish settlement in New York or the affairs of the Spanish-Portuguese Synagogue be forgotten, he wrote a historic sketch, recording all the facts he could gather from the oral testimony of old residents that he could recall. Since its publication much data inaccessible to him has come to light. Nevertheless, his document is important. The material may sometimes be faulty or incorrect, yet it reveals attitudes prevailing in his own day and time.

Naphtali Phillips has the rare distinction of voting for every President from George Washington to Ulysses S. Grant. Another distinction was the honor associated with his burial. During a period of three centuries he remains the only layman whose funeral was held in the vestibule of Shearith Israel.

1812

CAPTAIN
MORDECAI MYERS

Assimilationist

Gentiles seldom understand the Jewish taboo against inter-marriage. Of course, there is the obvious objection that the Christian spouse generally alienates the other mate from Judaism. But the non-Jew is confused when those who have shed orthodoxy, or even their ancestral faith, continue to draw the line at mixed marriages, even if solemnized outside of church portals. The life of Mordecai Myers may serve as a case history that explains this baffling attitude.

In 1776 Mordecai Myers was born in Newport. Nothing is known of his parents, not even their names. The son seemed anxious to obliterate all memory of his Jewish antecedents. In his *Reminiscences 1780-1814,* written when 77 years old, he fails to mention the names of either parent. His own name Mordecai is contracted to the lone initial *M* on the title page. Yet up to his 38th year he remained active in synagogues, loyal to Judaism, with his friendships or associations largely, if not exclusively, Jewish.

His parents lived in Newport until the British evacuated the city. Then they followed the army to New York, where in 1781 the elder Myers died. Evidently he had been a Tory and aroused the ire of the patriots. After the treaty of peace, the widow and her children departed for Nova Scotia, the refuge of colonials loyal to England. The family seemed quite chummy with the other Tories. Yet in 1787 the widow managed to bring back her children to New York. Mordecai was ever fond of relating the big thrill of his boyhood when he witnessed General Washington take the oath as first President of the U. S. A.

Mordecai's education was slight, judging from the wretched spelling in a letter that has come down. Yet he appears alert, energetic, and expresses himself with clarity. He has the normal ambition of Jewish lads to go into business for himself. Apparently opportunities were not too good in New York. He tried storekeeping with a partner at Richmond. Soldiering had a strong appeal, so he joined a military company under the command of Col. John Marshall, later the Chief Justice of the U. S. Supreme Court. He also devoted time to congregational matters and lent a hand in building Beth Shalome Synagogue. But meeting scant success in business, he returned to his home town.

In New York the pattern of his life continued typically Jewish. On attaining the age for admission, he joined the Masonic order, which had for Jews an attraction hardly less than their religion. Mordecai "went through the chairs" and remained steadfast throughout his long life, even during that dangerous period after the killing of Morgan at Batavia when popular feeling against Masons rose to frenzy. He became a member of the Manumission Society for the freeing and aiding of slaves.

His abundant energies also found an outlet in politics. A member of Tammany when the Wigwam was a progressive society largely made up of artisans and workers disfranchised for not owning land, he took an active part in the campaign that defeated the Federalists, composed in his own words of "rich merchants and traders, who boasted of having all the wealth, talent, and respectability of the American People." A Jeffersonian Democrat, a humanitarian and Mason, Mordecai Myers reflected the progressive liberalism that imbued Jews but recently emancipated from religious intolerance.

The only deviation from the pattern was his penchant for military service. In New York he increased his competence by joining Captain Swarthwort's artillery company. Commissioned an officer, he studied military tactics for two years. His training came into demand as the War of 1812 approached. Rendering service in raising volunteers for that unpopular war, Myers was made a Captain in the U. S. Infantry and ordered to report for duty.

In the war, Captain Myers reached his apogee. Never before nor after did he experience a deeper fulfillment for his capacities, for his ego, for his sense of belonging. He writes to Naphtali Phillips from Cantonment Williamswell: "It is a fine thing to abandon the persute of welth. I never ware hapy in Persute of Riches and now that I have abandoned it I am much more contented. My situation is not unpleasant for when with the regt I am considered in a favorable light by my superior officers and treated with respect by my Equals and Inferiors. I have a compy that both respect and fear me. I keep but little compy, give my whole attention to duty.— I have the sick, the invalids and convalesents of three regts to superintend besides there protection, and the genl police of the whole, ordering of Courts Martal aproving of sentences &c one third of my compy are continually on duty. I have enough to do but am content."

In action the Captain acquitted himself creditably enough. The high command had assembled a fleet at Sacketts Harbor on Lake Ontario for the invasion of Canada. A storm scattered the flotilla and sank 15 boats. The islands and shore were strewn with wreckage. During the fierce winds Capt. Myers volunteered and was sent to the rescue. "He found two schooners lying on the sides, the sails flopping, and the sea breaking over them.— The hatches were open and the vessels were half filled with water." At great risk and exertion, he succeeded in saving about

200 soldiers, mostly dead drunk with liquor from the hospital supplies. About 50 men had perished.

Far more bloody, if not more dangerous, was the battle at Chrysler's Farm. During the murderous fire, 23 out of 89 in Myers' company were killed. Both sides were relieved by the oncoming darkness, and the Americans claimed victory when the British withdrew. While leading his men in assailing the enemy behind a stone wall, Capt. Myers suffered a bullet wound near his shoulder. Dr. Mann, a noted physician, considered the injuries dangerous and took him to his home ten miles away.

The wounded officer convalesced four months and met romance. The daughter of Judge William Bailey of Plattsburg was visiting her uncle. The 17 year old girl, uncommonly pretty, if the painter was not too flattering, nursed the 38 year old soldier with flashing dark eyes and handsome in his high stiff collar and golden fringed epaulettes. They fell in love and were married the following year. Subsequently the captain was mustered out on half pay. The life of Myers, who now abandoned the name Mordecai for the initial "M", altered radically. He no longer knew the people of his origin.

What caused the change can only be surmised. Perhaps he was overawed by his in-laws. His wife's uncle had been a U. S. Senator, and her aunt was married to James Kent, the famous Chancellor. Her brother Theodorus would soon be an Admiral. Before the war, Mordecai was flattered when appointed on a committee of Shearith Israel. He no doubt cherished secret ambition to be some day its parnass. After the war he was quietly dropped from the membership role.

The erstwhile captain lived 95 years. In 1831 he represented a New York district in the State Assembly. Later he moved to Schenectady and served as its mayor. For the benefit of their children, the family name was hyphenated into Bailey-Myers, which a century later still appeared in the social register. The sword, the Masonic regalia, and other relics of M. Myers are on display at the National Museum in Washington.

His granddaughter Cassie Mason Myers Julien published for private circulation her *Biographical Sketches of Bailey-Myers-Mason Families 1776-1905*. This expensive folio bound in green leather, containing two portrait paintings of M. Myers, can be seen in the Genealogical Division of the New York Public Library. The reader of M. Myers' *Reminiscences,* or of his granddaughter's biographical sketches, will never ascertain from them whether the founder of the socially prominent Myers-Bailey-Mason family was ethnically Magyar, Ostrogoth, or Mongol.

HARMON HENDRICKS

And His Copper Rolling M

THE SETTLEMENT of Jews in the English colonies might be attributed to Oliver Cromwell. He looked wryly at the Dutch whose wealth exceeded the economic power of England. Some credited the Jewish colony of Amsterdam with initiating and directing the Netherlands' far flung trading empire. Before political economy became a science, such exaggeration could not easily be checked. The Puritan dictator came to a simple conclusion: if Jews could enrich Holland, then why not have them in London?

A conference disclosed that English merchants objected to the coming of such skilful competitors. The clergy clung to their ancient prejudices. But strangely, the lawyers for once displayed a liberal attitude. Eminent jurists could find nothing in the English Constitution that prohibited Jews from residing in Britain, notwithstanding the expulsion in 1290. Cromwell took the hint and refrained from applying to Parliament. He gave the nod, and Jews came in quietly. When the Royalists regained power they repealed the Puritan laws. As regards Jews, there were no statutes to repeal. They traded and worshipped and remained.

154

Following the trend, Haim Hendricks left Amsterdam for London. His son Uriah migrated to New York in 1755 and did well enough in seven years to marry the daughter of wealthy and socially prominent Mordecai Gomez. Their eight children became ancestors of a family that spread over many states. Besides operating a general store which offered numerous articles of merchandise unknown even by name today, he became an "ironmonger" and opened a metal business that remained with his descendants for 175 years.

As tensions began to mount and lead to war, the sympathies of Uriah Hendricks continued with the Mother Country. Born in England, he considered separation from the Mother Country unnecessary. Besides he might have felt a loyal attachment to Cromwell's land which treated his coreligionists better than they were treated anywhere in Europe, excepting Holland. His Tory affiliations came in handy during the British occupation. He, Barrak Hays and Alexander Zuntz, the Hessian commissary, no doubt prevailed upon the British authorities to spare the synagogue from military seizure, something many churches were unable to do. When two British soldiers broke into the building and destroyed several Torah scrolls (the one on ivory rollers belonging to Uriah) they were flogged with such severity that one of them died. Yet Uriah Hendricks did not exasperate the patriotic group. With the advent of peace, we hear of no ill feeling against him. He remained in the city and died in 1798 of yellow fever.

His son Harmon, born in New York in 1771, suffered no such conflicting loyalties. His deep patriotism became manifest in the War of 1812. The unpopular second round with Britain, considered unnecessary by many, failed to evoke much jingoism. Cautiously the U. S. Treasury attempted to float bonds. Of the $16,000,000 issued only a fourth were subscribed. And Harmon Hendricks became one of the largest subscribers when he purchased a $40,000 block.

For years Harmon Hendricks and his partner brother-in-law

Solomon I. Isaacs did a substantial business with Boston's firm, Paul Revere and Son. The hero of the midnight ride, that sank deep into the national folklore, was an artist and inventor, a skilful engraver, a gold and silversmith, craftsman, gunmaker, a caster of bells and cannon, a maker of gunpowder. The first to roll sheet-iron in America, he also laid the foundations for the vast copper rolling industry. Hendricks and Isaacs acted as Paul Revere's New York agents and supplied his mills and foundry with much of their required metal, some of which went into the famous warship "Constitution" and the first steamship launched successfully by Robert Fulton.

War created the usual shortage and demand. Rolled copper sheets from the Revere mill could not reach New York. The British blockade also prevented the shipping of metal from European ports and made it difficult for Hendricks to supply his Boston customer. Demand increased to the extent that Hendricks and Isaacs deemed it advisable to set up their own copper rolling factory at Belleville, New Jersey. While not initiators, they were pioneers in the production of copper sheeting and exercised an influence in the development of the copper industry in the United States. This plant with its increase and growth continued in business until 1939, when the Hendricks Company sold out to the Andrew Jergens Company.

By the standards of his time, Harmon Hendricks was a wealthy man. Yet he is remembered more for character, service, leadership, and honorable dealing. His name appears often in the records of Shearith Israel, which he served as Parnass and in other capacities. Excepting Judah Touro, he is the first American in Jewish life to attain the status of philanthropist. His approach was that of the aristocrat, who demands correctness of manner and form as well as responsibility in leadership. He showed little patience with the slovenly attitude that hardly differentiated between a gift and a loan.

In his make-up there was lacking that narrow acerbity that keeps men petty. While Parnass of Shearith Israel, a group

seceded to form another congregation. Such a step usually promotes acrimony. Yet Harmon Hendricks was the speaker who
dedicated the newly formed B'nai Jeshurun. To this competitive
Synagogue, he even advanced $5000 on a mortgage for five years
and charged 1% interest per annum. When payment came around
he accepted $4850 and cancelled the debt.

Impatient of laxity, he conducted business or congregational
matters with rigid precision. The sexton once came to collect dues
and was ready to accept two cents less than the stipulated amount.
For such laxness, Hendricks rebuked him roundly; this time it
might be only two cents, next time $2, and later $200 will be
short. In all charities he stood in the forefront. He attempted
to reduce the burdensome cost of kosher products, yet furnish
the poor with wholesome meat. Because Moses Levi Maduro
Peixotto, minister of Shearith Israel, expressed the wish to lie in
the old cemetery on Chatham Square, Hendricks paid the fee of
$250 imposed by the city to prevent further interments in the
built-up area.

The strict punctilio of Hendricks came in for a humorous test.
The congregation needed funds and borrowed $1000 from him.
The interest he refused to accept was credited as his donation.
A month later, the bequest of $10,000 came in from Abraham
Touro of Newport. The trustees promptly paid back the borrowed sum and deducted 11 months interest. Hendricks returned
the money with the request that they send the sum he advanced.
He rejected the subtle logic of the trustees: (1) that the year's
interest had been paid since it was credited as his donation;
(2) that he could immediately lend out the money and charge
interest; (3) that surely he did not want double interest on his
principal.

The correspondence with Paul Revere preserved in the Massachusetts Historical Society attests to the character of Harmon
Hendricks for honest dealing. In his *The Old Merchants of New
York City* published in 1863, Walter Barrett eulogized the "great
copper merchant of former years" and says:

"No man stood higher in his community while he lived, and no man has left a memory more revered than Harmon Hendricks. When he died, the synagogue which he attended lost one of its best friends, and the rising generation of that numerous family could not have a better example."

PHINEAS J. HORWITZ.

1814

JONATHAN HORWITZ

And the First American Hebrew Bible

THE TITLE "People of the Book" carries with it a responsibility and obligation. The "Book of Books" had to be studied, cherished and made available by its Jewish creators. For about two millennia the Torah had been transcribed by hand and carried over land and sea to countries far and near.

To no other people did Gutenberg's invention in 1450 bring a greater boon. Almost immediately Hebrew presses were set up in Italy. Soncino's Hebrew type has never been surpassed for beauty. The printing of Hebrew books followed in Spain, Portugal, Turkey, Holland, Germany, and by the 18th century Amsterdam had become a center for Jewish publications. Here Van der Hooght's Hebrew Bible with its Latin introduction was printed; it enjoyed a large circulation among Christian scholars.

In 1812 Jonathan Horwitz arrived in New York. From Amsterdam he brought along Hebrew type together with his manuscript of a Hebrew grammar almost completed. Rumors had reached the Amsterdam publishers of a good market for the Scriptures in Hebrew in the growing young republic. Institutions of higher learning, especially in Puritan New England, had been teaching Hebrew for about a century. Clergymen and lay scholars were prospective purchasers.

The Rev. Dr. James P. Wilson in his introduction to a reprint of Parkhurst's *Hebrew Grammar* informed the public: "Mr. Horwitz, a learned foreigner now in America, permits me to say that he has also an English-Hebrew grammar; which is nearly ready for the press. The highest expectations may be entertained by the critical Hebrew scholar, from his uncommon proficiency in oriental learning."

Before venturing on a grammar, Horwitz thought it feasible to utilize his type for a Bible. This would be a sure fire hit, for no one in America had yet printed Holy Writ in Hebrew. He traveled throughout New England soliciting subscribers, and met with some success. Harvard College and Andover Theological Institution ordered 40 copies each. While in the midst of his efforts, he read in New York's *Commercial Advertiser* that the publishers Whiting and Watson were preparing an American edition of Van der Hooght's Hebrew Bible. This was disconcerting, for the Reverend Doctors S. M. Mathews and J. M. Mason would supervise and direct the publication. These professors at theological seminaries had access to learned institutions and were influential with educated circles. Moreover two similar publications were in the offing; one by a missionary society and another by Benjamin Boothroyd. Besides, the second war with Britain made it difficult, if not impossible, to obtain suitable paper for a two-volume de luxe edition.

It is therefore not surprising that Horwitz became discouraged. A recent arrival and alone, he felt too weak financially for the undertaking. It would seem likely that he would seek a Jewish partner. But the expensive kind of Bible he projected had little prospect of sale among Jews; they no doubt had an abundance of *tanachs* and prayer books brought over from Europe. Besides the synagogues had no difficulty importing the handwritten scrolls, or the religious literature that was printed extensively in the German ghettos, in Amsterdam, and even by the presses of Warsaw, Prague, Wilna, and Cracow.

Yet Horwitz was determined to see his project through. He sold his Hebrew type to the printer William Fry and the list of subscriptions to Thomas Dobson, a book dealer. Both operated in Philadelphia, so the printing went through without a hitch. Its publication was announced in the Philadelphia press in the spring of 1813 and by 1814 the first complete Hebrew Bible in the U. S. A. was issued. Horwitz possibly worked in the printing shop; certainly he planned the format, proofread and corrected the galleys. In a letter to Rev. John Wright, author of *Early American Bibles,* the eminent Philadelphian, Rabbi Sabato Morais of Mikveh Israel stated: "The edition is good, and I think as correct as others. The marginal annotations are helpful and copious."

While working in the printing shop, Horwitz was studying in the medical school of the University of Pennsylvania and completed the required two year medical course. On presenting his thesis on colic, the University conferred upon him the degree of M. D. in 1815, and later appointed him on its faculty of medicine. Dr. Horwitz then married Miss Debbie Andrews, daughter of Joseph Andrews, formerly a *shohet* in New York. He settled in Baltimore, but continued to maintain relations with the Jewish community of Philadelphia where he served as official doctor for the United Hebrew Beneficent Society.

Practice of medicine did not hamper other scholarly pursuits. The critical attacks of scientists upon the account of Creation in Genesis drew his fire. In 1839 Dr. J. Horwitz published *A Defence of the Cosmogony of Moses.* The book attempts to refute the scientific new arguments explaining the origin of the universe as inconsistent with the Old Testament. He examined Dr. Buckland's treatise concerning the Mosaic history of the origin of the world in the light of latest geological discoveries. He also reviewed and analyzed the essay of J. G. Morris on "Geology and Revelation," published in 1838 by the American Museum.

At the outbreak of the Mexican War, the President called for 50,000 volunteers. Dr. Jonas Horwitz, as he now called himself, enlisted as surgeon to the Jewish company of volunteers from Baltimore. This mass enlistment by immigrants elicited favorable comment. The New York *Herald* of July, 1846 quotes from a Baltimore paper: "The next in order is the 'Hebrew Volunteers' who although composed principally of foreigners, have nonetheless evinced a love and devotion for the institutions of their adopted country by the organization of a military corps to act in concert with the native militia in defense of these institutions; and although professing a religion opposite to the gentleman whom they have chosen their commander, they have still more strongly evinced a love for the honor, glory, and perpetuity of the independence of their country." Dr. Jonas Horwitz served for the duration, returned home, and died in 1852.

His son Phineas Jonathan Horwitz had a distinguished career. Born in 1822, he studied at the University of Maryland and the Jefferson College of Philadelphia. Following his father's example, the younger Dr. Horwitz enlisted during the Mexican War. He was commended by Commodore of the Squadron, M. C. Perry, and placed in charge of the temporary naval hospital at Tobasco, Mexico—still hardly 26 years old. For the next 12 years he served at sea and saw duty on the Brazilian and African stations.

In 1859 Dr. Phineas J. Horwitz became Assistant to the U. S. Bureau of Medicine and Surgery and served in that capacity throughout the Civil War. His official biography states: "The whole system of tabulating the casualties of the war, of indexing the books of reference, reports of survey, certificates of disability and diseases was designed and carried forward by Dr. Horwitz, so that there was probably no case of injury, disease, or disability that occurred during the doctor's connection with the Bureau that will not be found in its appropriate place in the Surgeon General's office; the immense number of pension cases accruing during the war were all examined, adjusted, and prepared by the doctor, and every official letter that left the Bureau was written by him."

The efficient discharge of duty earned him a unanimous vote of commendation from Congress. In 1865 he was promoted Chief of the Bureau; he became Medical Director in 1873, and retired with the medical rank of captain. He projected the Naval Hospital in Philadelphia and was instrumental in its construction. His picture hangs in the Surgeon General's office of the Brooklyn Navy Yard.

JOSHUA MONTEFIORE

Adventurous Author

GRAVESTONE OF MONTEFIORE
IN ST. ALBANS, VERMONT.

THE NAME Montefiore is highly honored in Jewry. This notable
family has produced a number of distinguished persons. Its most
eminent personage, Sir Moses, rates highest among the numerous
leader-philanthropists who guided the insecure destiny of Jews
during centuries of oppression and abuse. Without mandate to
act as defender, intercessor, advocate or spokesman, Sir Moses
Montefiore exercised his self appointed *shtadlanuth* by universal
consent. A *hof-jude* in the best, if not literal, sense, he ranks as
the *shtadlan* par excellence.

Finding his surname in a small town of Vermont might cause
surprise. But more surprising was the discovery that several Christian residents of St. Albans claim descent from an uncle of
Sir Moses. They can present absolute proof that the first Jewish
settler in the state, Joshua Montefiore, was their ancestor. He was
one of the many Jews who, detached from their moorings, found
oblivion in obscure graves, forgotten except by the original genetic
strain which they forsook.

Joshua Montefiore, a maverick who acted up in queer contrast to the staid mores of his conventional herd, was born in 1762 in London. His father came over from Italy during the 18th century when the Disraelis, the Ottolengues, the Supinos decided that Protestant England offered the tolerance denied in the land inhabited by their ancient families for centuries. According to Joshua's own boasting, he was the first Jew to study at Oxford and hold a commission in the British army. These claims cannot be verified, though he was admitted to the bar—no easy attainment for a non-Christian in the "enlightened' era of George III.

A lawyer and notary in 1785, Joshua felt confident enough to marry Esther Supino, a daughter of the distinguished family that claimed descent from the nobility of ancient Jerusalem. Yet two years later he was in Jamaica applying for admission to practice law. Evidently he considered the London certificate an open sesame in any British possession. He had yet to learn that the Englishman, a liberal gentleman at home, could be clannish, arrogant, or snobbish in Bombay, Trinidad, Mombassa, or Quebec. The 60 lawyers of Kingston objected; they even cited a local ordinance of 1711 that no Jew, Mulatto, Indian or Negro could officiate as clerk in any public office on the island. He sailed back to England.

Opportunity for adventure came. An English group wished to demonstrate that colonization in the tropics could succeed without slave labor. They selected the isle of Bulama, off Sierra Leone on the West African coast. Joshua joined the colonists, who were outfitted and supplied in two ships. The experiment proved a failure. Hostility of the natives, bad leadership, and dissension among the untrained, ill prepared settlers doomed the project from the outset.

On his return Joshua published a 63 page account of the expedition, in which he appears as military chief. He does not hesitate to lay the blame of the debacle upon the heads of those who refused to heed his advice or follow his leadership. He left the island and spent some time adventuring among the "Indian" natives of Sierra Leone. He regarded himself as a returning hero, whom the king honors with an audience. George III was impressed and offered him a knighthood. Just why so high a distinction was declined, he did not explain. Instead he accepted a captaincy in the army; but the military have no record of this commission.

In his biography of Sir Moses Montefiore, Lucien Wolf writes that the eminent philanthropist in his old age "still retains a vivid recollection of his dashing 'Uncle Josh', whose laced red coat and pigtail, and cocked hat and sword, together with his fund of tremendous anecdotes rendered him a huge favorite with his nephews." One might get an impression that Joshua was a mere fabricator of tall tales, a picaresque adventurer without substance or quality. Such an estimate would be quite unfair, for in Montefiore a roving disposition and taste for adventure united with some genuine capacities. Almost a character out of the Gothic novel, he expressed some phases of the romantic movement reflected in the literature that produced a Roderick Random, a Tom Jones, Byron's Don Juan, or Casanova's Memoirs.

Printer's ink ran in the Montefiore blood. Joshua could express in effective English a variety of facts gathered and stored away in a retentive memory. Compilations rather than original investigations, his books served a useful purpose for people in need of practical information. His *Commercial and Notarial Precedents,* dedicated to Chief Justice Lord Ellenborough, enjoyed a large circulation in England. Of the three American editions, the last was printed 20 years after his death.

It is difficult to trace Montefiore's peregrinations. In 1803 he appears in Philadelphia, where the first American edition of his *Commercial and Notarial Precedents* was published and favorably reviewed in the local press. According to his own statements he took part in the British attack upon Martinique and Guadalupe in 1809 as an officer of the York Light Infantry. Two years later he was editing and publishing in New York his "Men and Measures", a political weekly subsidized by the British government. Living at the same time in Philadelphia, he dedicated to the Chief Justice of Pennsylvania *The American Trader's Compendium—Containing the Laws, Customs, and Regulations of the United States Relative to Commerce, Including the Most Useful Precedents adapted to General Business.*

It would appear that he travelled about considerably, soliciting subscriptions for his forthcoming books. This authorized practice for writers in his day fitted in with his propensity for roaming. Subscribers from Halifax, N. S. to Savannah, Ga. would signify his presence. He also engaged in law practice. Yet his importance as an author cannot be ignored. Neither original nor profound, some of his 10 books nevertheless enjoyed wide popularity. They supplied useful information, especially along legal and commercial lines not easily available to laymen before the extensive use of. cyclopedias or year books.

The lack of Jewish association is quite puzzling in a Montefiore. Outside of a few subscribers, he appears to have had no American Jewish contacts. Yet he lived in Philadelphia and in New York, the important centers with synagogues in his own Sephardic tradition, modelled after Bevis Marks in London. When 73 years of age, he married a young Catholic woman, apparently the maid of his deceased wife. In 1835, the same year, he moved to Vermont and bought a farm near St. Albans. His remarkable vitality is attested by the birth of eight children in eight years. When he died at 81, the youngest was six weeks old.

The children were reared in the Protestant faith. Yet he never forsook his own religion. When about to die, he assembled the family and offered objections to a Christian burial. From memory, he dictated a translation of the Hebrew service to be read at his funeral. He was laid to rest in a solitary grave on his own farm. Three miles from St. Albans, about 300 feet from the highway, a stone slab bears the inscription, almost effaced, of the birthplace and life span of Joshua Montefiore, which the natives pronounce *Mounty four.*

1816

SAMUEL NOAH

Class of 1807
U. S. Military Academy

The name of Samuel Noah would never be known had not a Jewish historian by chance thumbed through the pages of *Biographical Sketches of the Deceased Graduates of the United States Military Academy*. His attention was arrested by the title over a sketch: *Samuel Noah, Class of 1807*. The surname Noah holds a highly honorable place in the annals of American Jewry. The story of the first Jew to graduate from West Point may have its significance. But far more arresting is his relationship to Mordecai M. Noah, the most colorful leader, perhaps, in all American Jewish history.

Since there are no other data in existence, it might be of interest to quote verbatim the complete record of this wayward, errant character as written down by General George W. Cullum, the author of those biographies.

"Samuel Noah, who was born July 19th, 1779, in the City of London, died March 10th, 1871, at Mount Pulaski, Logan County, Illinois, at the advanced age of nearly 92, he having been for several years the senior surviving graduate of the United States Military Academy. He was of Jewish descent, and was a cousin of Mordecai M. Noah, formerly Consul to Tunis and for many years the editor of various New York journals.

"When twenty years old he emigrated to this country, and after a residence of several years in New York City, solicited a midshipman's appointment, but not succeeding, accepted May 5th, 1805, that of a Cadet in the First Regiment of Artillery. Being intelligent and a good penman, he was often selected as amanuensis to the Superintendent of the Military Academy and frequently acted as Judge Advocate or Recorder of Courts at West Point. Upon graduation, December 9, 1807, preferring the Infantry arm, he was promoted an Ensign in the Second Regiment, which, after a tedious journey, he joined at Cantonment, Columbia Springs, in the rear of Fort Adams, Miss. Here he devoted his leisure hours to the study of the early campaigns of Napoleon, who was then the military prodigy of the world; but this fascinating occupation was soon interrupted by his having to watch smugglers on the Florida frontier and march from one unhealthy camp to another in the Gulf States. During these migrations he met Captain Winfield Scott just after his duel near Natchez with Dr. Upshur (brother of the Secretary of State blown up on board the *Princetown*), Lieutenant James Gibson, subsequently killed at the sortie from Fort Erie, General James Wilkinson, Captain Edmund P. Gaines, General Wade Hampton, and other since famous officers of whom he had many anecdotes to relate. Wearied finally with slow promotion, and disgusted that ignorant civilians were appointed to rank him, he resigned March 13, 1811, his commission of First Lieutenant in the Army.

"Soon after this period, a Mexican deputation from the Junta of Coohuila, General Bernado Guiteres and Captain Manshac, arrived at Natchitoches, where Lieutenant Magee, a graduate of 1809, was stationed, and offered him the command with the rank of Colonel of the combined forces there assembled of Mexicans and Anglo-Americans. After Magee assumed the command, Noah, allured by visions of a golden future, joined as First Lieutenant this little undisciplined Falstaffian regiment on the Brazos River, while on its march to Fort Bahia, which it entered November 14, 1812; but no sooner was the fort in possession of the Patriot Army than the Spanish Royalists besieged it with a force of five times the strength of the garrison. In this struggle poor Colonel Magee sickened and died, and was buried with the honors of war during the enemy's cannonade, a six-pounder ball lodging close to his grave. After the siege was raised, March 28, 1813, and the Patriots re-enforced, this little army, with Noah in command of its rear guard, pursued and routed the Royalists April 4, 1813, in the sharp combat near San Antonio, and three days later entered the capitol of Texas, Salcido, the Governor surrendering at discretion with his entire force.

"Informed soon after of the United States' declaration of war against Great Britain, Noah, true to the flag of his adopted country, left Texas, and escaping through many perils by flood and field, reached the city of Washington, where he was most sadly disappointed in not being recommissioned by President Madison in the United States Army. Nothing daunted, however, he proceeded to New York, and volunteered his services as a private soldier with Captain Benjamin Dunning's Company for the defence of Brooklyn, then being fortified by General Joseph G. Swift, to repel an anticipated descent of the British on Long Island at Sag Harbor. His services here and at Harlem Heights, to the close of the war, in aid of the militia force, were most zealous and untiring, his military education, practical knowledge, and quick intelligence proving powerful auxiliaries to his patriotic devotion to duty. After the termination of Noah's military career, he taught school near Goshen, New York, till 1820; then for two years was in England, being present at the trial of Queen Caroline and the Coronation of George the Fourth; resumed school teaching, and was employed in various academies in Virginia till May 24, 1848, and subsequently resided with a faithful friend at Mount Pulaski, Logan County, Ills., where he died. The romantic record of Samuel Noah's early life is full of wild adventure and thrilling incidents; his after history was a curious medley, almost the very counterpart of the vicissitudes to which Gil Blas was exposed; and his long declining years were an old age of poverty, with little relief even from sources upon which he confidently counted to ease his weary journey to the grave."

The story of Samuel Noah reveals his knack for missing the bus. He had two opportunities that came knocking for fame, for distinction, for at least economic security in old age. He resigned from the army in 1811 for no good reason. A year later, a commissioned West Pointer should have gone far in the war with Britain.

But in leaving Texas he sacrificed a bright future. Among the very first Americans who came into that vast domain, still under Spanish rule, he could only benefit by the cataclysmic changes that led to independence. A trained soldier and seasoned veteran, he might have ranked with General Sam Houston. But even as a settler he would have become the influential pioneer and leading citizen in the Republic and subsequent State of Texas.

It is hardly conceivable that he knew nothing of his kinship with the most influential families in American Jewry. Apparently he made no effort to identify himself with the Noah-Hart-Philips-Hays-Seixas clan. Consequently Samuel Noah paid the price for his dis-identification with a lonely, neglected, impoverished old age.

1817

REBECCA GRATZ

Scott's Heroine

W<small>ASHINGTON</small> I<small>RVING'S</small> <small>FIANCÉE</small>, the 18 year old Matilda Hoffman, died of tuberculosis. The creator of Rip Van Winkle hoped to find solace in travel. European scenes and personalities might soften his grief. At Abbotsford he called upon Sir Walter Scott. The author of Waverly Novels was touched by the pathos of the lovely young girl wasting to a shadow. Scott became intrigued with the story of her friend Rebecca Gratz, the beautiful, gentle, cultured Jewess who refused to marry the Christian she loved.

Scott never knew Jews and indulged in the prejudices of the day. Imbued with the unpleasant things current about them, he was surprised to learn of the high esteem in which Philadelphia held the Gratz family, of the merchant prince Michael Gratz who had the vision to assist in colonizing parts of that vast domain located in Pennsylvania and Kentucky, even in far away Indiana and Illinois. It was his daugther who had nursed Matilda in her final illness, disregarding all danger of contagion. Washington Irving just could not express sufficient admiration for the

172

remarkable personality of Rebecca Gratz. Her nobility of character, lofty spiritual qualities, rare understanding, and self-sacrificing generosity recalled a heroine of the Old Testament.

In addition she possessed striking beauty—and even more important, an irresistible charm. Her portraits painted by Thomas Sully reveal dark lustrous eyes, a firm yet sensitive mouth, a high intellectual forehead over a faintly aquiline nose, denoting strength of character. Too beautiful to escape romance, she was too genuine and loyal to benefit by the love she inspired. Rebecca refused to marry outside her faith; even though the man she loved was the eligible and literary son of Dr. John Ewing, noted clergyman, educator, and Provost of the University of Pennsylvania.

Scott was mulling over his next novel—over armored knights and tournaments, worldly churchmen and besieged castles, cruel Normans and submerged Saxons, a trial by combat in behalf of a beautiful maid charged with witchcraft. A sudden inspiration struck him. Why not follow the example of Shakespeare and make Irving's fascinating Jewess a heroine in his romantic tale. Two years later appeared the romance *Ivanhoe*. Scott sent a first copy to Washington Irving with the note, "How do you like your Rebecca? Does the Rebecca I have pictured here compare well with the pattern given?"

Born in 1781, the year Washington's cannon were booming in Yorktown, Rebecca Gratz lived to 88, long enough to see the Union restored after the surrender of Lee at Appomattox. As a little girl she listened to people talking about the new Constitution that was being drafted and saw the founders of the Republic walking the streets of Philadelphia. Her completely integrated family circle moved among the elite. Some had married Christians, with whom she remained most intimate. She always expressed a broad view for the religion of others. All the more wonder why she rejected the ardent love and marriage that Samuel Ewing offered. Instead she remained a lifelong spinster. One can only wonder whether it was attachment to Judaism or a congenital coolness of temperament and emotion that chose a career of good works in preference to wedded life. Perhaps she had reasons to fear the psychological and emotional pitfalls inherent in a mixed marriage.

Yet it is disappointing to see a gifted woman, blessed with all the physical and spiritual graces, living on the periphery of life. A goodly portion of her great store of affection she lavished upon the nine children of her sister Rachel, who died prematurely. She raised them with a mother's tenderness; but they were not *her* children even when she called them her own. It was a distinct loss that such qualities of mind and heart could not pass on to her own posterity.

Socially Rebecca's life appeared full and satisfying. Her spacious home on Chestnut St. was a polished and distinguished salon. Washington Irving continued to be a house guest whenever in the city. The artist Sully, the tragedian Cooper, the painter Malbone, the novelist Paulding, as well as Prince Joachim Murat and other Bonapartist exiles, were frequent callers. The great English actress Fanny Kemble, a raging storm of emotions, found soothing refuge in Rebecca's steadying influence. Montgomery Blair, subsequently to become Postmaster General in Lincoln's Cabinet, found pleasure in the cultivated circle. Rebecca was guest of honor at a magnificent dinner given by Henry Clay, the "Great Compromiser," during her visit in Kentucky.

Her public activities were largely charitable, yet she never aimed to shine in executive limelight. In 1801 when a lovely debutante, she became a member, then secretary of the nonsectarian Female Association for the Relief of Women and Children. A charter member of the Philadelphia Orphan Asylum, she kept its records for almost fifty years. Her organizational experience became valuable in the fields of Jewish philanthropy. In 1819 she participated in organizing the Female Hebrew Benevolent Society, the oldest Jewish charitable institution in continuous existence in America. She helped found other organizations, among them the Jewish Foster Home.

A pioneer in the modern religious instruction of American Jewish youth, Rebecca Gratz was a founder of the Hebrew Sunday School Society of Philadelphia. For 20 years she was concerned with religious training not only for the children of Mikveh Israel, her synagogue, but for all the Jewish children of the city. Under her direction, the first Jewish Sunday School in the U. S. opened in 1838. She composed a prayer for its service and remained the active, energetic head until her 83rd year. The idea took root, especially in Reform Judaism, and spread to every American city that has a Jewish community.

Rebecca Gratz was conventional in social conduct, orthodox in religion, conservative in thought, philanthropic in action. The stirrings of Reform Judaism left her cold; propaganda for abolition of slavery evoked little response. No revolutionary passions consumed her; no crusading impulses disturbed the calm of her virtuous existence. Yet she had a good mind. Her well written letters, unaffected in their pre-Victorian diction, reveal insight, wide reading, tender sentiments, critical evaluations, and beneficent instincts. A lady primarily, she had the virtues and limitations of a benevolent, idealistic *grand dame*. Her useful life cannot be measured by accomplishments; her fame rests on a kindly, gracious, soulful, charming personality.

1818

JOSEPH SAMUEL
CHRISTIAN
FREDERICK FREY

Missionary

IN MODERN TIMES a distinction is often made between convert
and apostate. A convert might be a well-intentioned Jew who is
attracted to another religion. Some have been known to remain
sympathetic, and even helpful, to their birth stock. Disraeli is a
shining example.

Yet in the main, the convert harbors antagonism towards his
origins; the resentment probably stems from a sense of guilt in
having deserted a helpless minority to join its detractors or per-
secutors. He compensates by salving his conscience; he determines
to rescue the exposed kindred; he would secure their well being
by bringing them under the protective wing of the dominant
religion. But when his efforts meet scorn or ridicule, he turns
vindictive and outdoes the anti-Semites themselves in vilifying his
brethren. Then he lives up to the expected role of apostate,
renegade, or *meshumed*.

Jews feel instinctively that an element of the meshumed lies
imbedded in most converts. But the human being is not all black

176

or white. There are borderline cases that do not fit into either
genus. The missionary Rev. Frey perhaps belongs to the doubtful
category.

Joseph Samuel was born in a Bavarian town in 1771, to a poor
melamed who could not make a living teaching, nor at anything
else. His mother, following the tradition of such a life, supported
the family by petty trading. She displayed enterprise in supplying
grain and provisions for a Prussian army division. Her son apparently inherited his father's ineptness for business and after trying to assist by working elsewhere, gave up and returned home.
He claims to have received a good Jewish education and at the
age of 18 taught Hebrew in Hesse. At 21 he could perform as
hazan; later he received proper credentials as a qualified *shohet*
for slaughtering cattle and fowl in the ritual manner. His learning, in spite of later boasting, could not have been deep. In the
first discussion with a plausible Christian, he succumbed. It is
difficult to see the overwhelming argument for Christianity that
moved him so profoundly in Chapter 31, Verses 31-35, of Jere-
miah. After chastising Israel for breaking the first covenant, the
prophet goes on: "After those days, saith the Lord, I will write my
law in their inward parts, and write it in their hearts; and will
be their God, and they shall be my people."

Joseph Samuel, son of Levi, seemed to have been conditioned
for apostasy. His mother's brother had been baptized, and the
Hebrew School (heder) boys taunted him to follow in his uncle's
footsteps. After meeting with the Christian he traveled on, probably seeking an opening in his overcrowded profession. In Rostock
he went looking for the friendly traveler, who was out of town.
It was on the Sabbath, and significantly Samuel violated Talmudic law by writing him a note. Then he proceeded to the
synagogue. The authorities informed him that no Jew could
remain over night without the magistrate's consent, and then only
after paying a specified sum. But Joseph's plea proved stronger
than the law itself. He had come to take instructions in the Christian religion. That was different. Immediately he was taken to

the clergy. Obviously he could no longer make his living as *hazan-shohet*. An apprenticeship with a shoemaker solved the problem. In 1798 he was baptized and given the name Joseph Samuel Christian Frederick Frey.

The world being open to a Christian, there was no point in remaining a shoemaker. He went to Berlin and entered a missionary seminary. The following year the school sent him to the *London Missionary Society,* which had a project in Africa. The Society, quite avid about converting Jews, and with little understanding of psychology, was convinced that their German would be ideally equipped for communicating the glad tidings of salvation to his own obstinate brothers in the flesh.

For six years Frey worked with the London Missionary Society. When it ceased functioning, he associated with the *London Society for Promoting Christianity among the Jews,* which he helped to organize. By 1815 its affairs became so tangled that the Episcopalians had to take over. Frey had traveled all over England and succeeded in raising money. But his efforts in converting Jews proved disappointing. Complaints against him came from Jews and Christians. The new directors terminated Frey's connection. Meanwhile he had married in England a converted Jewess and was father of four children. The missionary business in England seemed on the decline. America now attracted him, even if its Jewish population was numerically insignificant. In 1816 he sailed with his family to New York.

He came at the right time. In the U. S. A. the desire for converting Jews amounted almost to an obsession. To this end, more than a score of societies dedicated their efforts, and they received support from the highly prominent Adamses of Massachusetts and the Clintons of New York. Dr. Elias Boudinot, a former President of the Continental Congress and founder of the American Bible Society, headed one of these organizations. But neither directors nor officers, however influential, could instil life in the society by merely calling meetings. Its resolutions could be adequately implemented only by paid officials, whose livelihood depends on vigilant attention to detail.

Missionary Frey's coming proved a godsend. Armed with letters of recommendation, he received encouragement from clergy and laity. Soon he stood on firmer ground when ordained a minister. His prestige increased on being given a pulpit in the Congregational Church. By the end of 1816, he was largely instrumental in forming *The American Society for Evangelizing the Jews*. Frey then applied to the New York Legislature for incorporation. The lawmakers objected to the word "Evangelizing" as unconstitutional. He gladly accepted the corporate name changed to *The American Society for Meliorating the Condition of the Jews*.

As preacher and author, Rev. Frey might have earned his place in W. B. Sprague's "Annals of the American Pulpit". Yet his fame arose because of his activities in the missionary society. In the capacity of fund raiser, he traveled the length and breadth of the country and preached 5147 sermons. His coming to cities or villages was hailed as an event. At a time when the minister received the highest accolades in public life, he became one of the best known preachers in America.

The place of an apostate in Jewish annals might be questioned. But history has a way of utilizing trivial circumstances which seem unrelated. Frey, without intending or knowing, actually rendered a service to the people he forsook. It was a romantic, sentimental age. The historical and Gothic novels stimulated interest in stone castles and armored knights, in the bizarre, the strange, the spectacular of the antique forgotten past.

Rural America, with a Bible in every home, read daily of the Chosen People. Yet very few had ever set eyes on a living Jew. Rev. Frey's appearance excited wonder and curiosity. In the isolated communities he seemed an apparition out of the Old Testament. His emotional eloquence, foreign and piquant, stirred a sympathetic response, not only to himself but for all other Jews.

He knew how to play up his conversion and shrewdly guessed that maligning his people would also blacken himself, something Jewish missionaries often forgot. Joseph Samuel Christian Frederick Frey could hardly know that he was creating a legend, the archetype image of a Jew who would linger in American consciousness for several decades. Unknowingly this turncoat implanted in the public a kind feeling towards the incoming emigrants escaping German intolerance and the refugees fleeing from Russian pogroms.

As a missionary Frey was unsuccessful. He died a lonely man in the summer of 1850 in Pontiac, Michigan, at the age of 79; and for all the attention he attracted in England and America he hardly received a four line obituary in the American press.

1819

SHEFTALL SHEFTALL

Of Savannah

In 1762, Mordecai Sheftall named his newly born son Sheftall Sheftall. This was unusual, if not odd, at a time when Jews preserved in their children the memory of departed parents or grandparents. Conformity becomes a habit with insecure minorities. They ask for nothing better than to pass in the crowd unnoticed and unmolested.

And yet Mordecai was formal in religion and conventional in society. This double use of a patronymic might on the contrary indicate assurance, perhaps arising out of social and material well being. After all, he was born in Savannah two years after the founding of Georgia by Oglethorpe. His father Benjamin stood well enough with Christians to be one of the five incorporators of the Union Society, an organization for philanthropy without sectarian bias, unusual in mid 18th century. Possibly economics might explain this unconventional departure in a conventional age. Mordecai already owned 1000 acres and nine slaves; if not affluent, he was at least a substantial business man.

Sheftall Sheftall received his business training quite early. At 15, he was a competent merchant. Experience and self reliance came in handy when his father was appointed Deputy Commissary General of Issues to the Continental troops in Georgia and South Carolina. Fifteen year old Sheftall held down the job of Assistant Commissary of Issues and became deputy to his father. But he could not swim, and lack of this skill cost him his liberty. For when the British closed in on all sides and attacked Savannah, the patriots could not hold out. Both Count Pulaski, the Polish combatant for American independence and Sergeant Jasper, hero of the Battle of Ft. Moultrie, fell mortally wounded. Every one who could fled. Mordecai was able to ford Musgrove Creek but would not abandon his son. Consequently both were captured.

Father and son endured a stretch on a prison ship; then on parole they served time with other prisoners at Sunbury, Georgia. The British withdrew and left all Continentals to the mercy of their fellow Americans loyal to England. But the patriots knew that these Tories would make short shrift of all Rebels. They managed to escape. About to reach Charleston on a brigantine, the Sheftalls were retaken by a British frigate and sent to Antigua, an island in the West Indies. Again Sheftall and his father were put on parole and permitted to sail for Philadelphia. Six months later when exchanged for English prisoners, they were released of the honorable promise not to fight for the duration.

Sheftall had already lived through more adventures than most men experience in a lifetime. No one considered him a mere lad of eighteen. He tried to help his father by pestering the bureaucrats for the money advanced to the government. Alexander Hamilton, who was only five years his senior and Secretary of the Treasury, listened respectfully but would do nothing. Of course, the Treasury was quite empty.

Officialdom evidently felt like doing something for the matured boy whose story was more than of common interest. Hamilton himself might have dropped a hint. One day Sheftall felt more than gratified; he was thrilled. The all powerful Board of

War offered an assignment which would have flattered a far older veteran. Sheftall was commissioned Flag Master of the sloop "Carolina Packet" to carry money and provisions for hungry American prisoners in Charleston. For a deed of mercy to soldiers without food, the enemy issued a permit that would carry the boat under a flag of truce through the British blockade.

The voyage went along smoothly except for the desertion of a sailor on reaching port. Sir Henry Clinton had limited the crew to six seamen. Sheftall had to write Gen. Moultrie, himself a captive, to furnish the "Carolina Packet" with an additional crew member; there were not enough men to haul in the anchor and hoist the sails for the return voyage. The General was also requested to notify the Board of War that the delay was no fault of the Flag Master. On his return to Philadelphia, Sheftall could report his delivery of £1367, 18 shillings and one pence, besides flour and provisions for the starving prisoners of war and needy civilians of Charleston.

The trip to South Carolina's capital was highly gratifying to the young Flag Master. To the Jews of Savannah, Charleston was a business metropolis, their social and religious center. A trip to that city was an event and especially pleasing to Sheftall who could preen himself in the new clothes his father bought for $12,800 in paper bills. The girls, especially Joshua Hart's giddy daughter, would now take notice of the young hero, commander of a boat in charge of a government mission. But far more important was meeting his mother and his siblings who fled for refuge before the British captured Savannah. Frances Sheftall with her four children and Negro slaves had managed to survive the cannonading and the smallpox. Now in dire need, she battled for hard money, the only exchange accepted.

After the Peace Treaty, the Sheftalls returned to Savannah to take up where they left off. But merchandising no longer appealed to young Sheftall. He had seen something of the world and found mere money making not wholly satisfying. His days of adventure, of danger, of fighting, of flight, of sailing the blue seas were over. He studied law and entered the sedentary calling of law practice. Like many Jews of the time, he joined the Masonic order, which during the 18th century commanded the reverence of a religion. Sheftall stood high in public estimation and was made honorary president of the Georgia Historical Society. In 1819 when James Monroe visited Savannah, Sheftall Sheftall was among the prominent citizens selected by the mayor and aldermen to dine with the President of the United States.

Sheftall Sheftall lived to the ripe age of 86. As he advanced in years the Revolutionary period of his youthful days loomed in his consciousness as the heroic age. Approaching the mid point of the 19th century, his soul and spirit remained anchored in the 18th century. He refused to change his clothes to conform with advancing styles. Up to 1848 he walked about in knickerbockers and hose, wearing the three-cornered hat of the Washington era, in proud disregard of the good-natured banter that named him Cocked Hat Sheftall.

ROAD SIGN IN FLORIDA.

1 8 2 0

MOSES
ELIAS LEVY

Dreamer of
A Zion in Florida

IN THE *Florida Historical Quarterly* can be found the highly interesting story of a Jewish pioneer. This colorful personality, a man of parts, of imagination and adventure, was the father of David L. Yulee, the first U. S. Senator from Florida. In fact, the father emerges the bigger man, morally and spiritually. But his bold pioneering is obscured by the political career of his son during the stormy period of the American Civil War.

Moses Elias Levy, born in Morocco about 1782, was descended from the exiles who left Spain in 1492. His father seems to have held a high position in the Sultan's palace. Unlucky enough to discover a plot by the Crown Prince to dethrone the ruler, he was indiscreet enough to mention the incident. The "Emperor" of Morocco could not see the joke and put his son in jail. Before imposing a severer penalty, the old ruler obliged his boy by dying. The son succeeded as Sultan. Suddenly "Grand Vizier" Levy found it expedient to become travel minded; he took a cruise to Egypt and died at Cairo.

At 19, Moses Levy found employment on a sailboat. He disembarked at the Island of St. Thomas and decided to enter business. Quickly he prospered in lumber. Business took him to Cuba. The vast domain of Florida was then governed out of Havana by a Spanish intendant. Moses thought he might as well take a look at the Florida backwoods, neglected for centuries by the proud, sleepy grandees of Spain, who did not know what to do with a paradise.

The vast forests and fertile soil intrigued the young business man. But every Jew seems to have a Messianic complex submerged in his subconscious. What a splendid land for Jewish colonization! A Zion in the Florida wilderness! Levy didn't confine his Zionist dream to the visionary stage. He purchased 52,900 acres for $40,000, acquired more land later, and sailed for England in search of colonists. In London he negotiated with Frederick S. Warburg, probably of the noted banking family. Warburg was engaged in purveying Jewish as well as Gentile settlers for the new world. Levy also spent time furthering his project in the flourishing communities of Charleston, Philadelphia, and especially in New York where he planned a Hebrew agricultural school in 1821.

When he got back to St. Augustine, he heard excited talk about the U. S. preparing to purchase Florida from Spain. At the same time, the Spanish King granted a prominent resident of St. Augustine 289,000 acres in Alachua—but with the string attached that 200 Spanish families must settle on the domain within three years. Levy ascertained that the Arrendondo grant had better soil for colonization than his own land. In a trade, he exchanged part of his purchase with Don Fernando de le Moza Arrendondo. Either he didn't know or disregarded the limitation placed in the deed by the King. When he woke up, time was running against him. He dispatched an urgent plea to Warburg for immediate settlers, Jewish or Christian.

Moses Levy was destined to suffer keen disappointments. Colonists were not rushing to his Florida paradise. This is not surprising when we consider that the young American Republic, stretching from the Atlantic to the Rockies with a population of 10,000,000, was also bidding for immigrants. Another bitter pill was the vice of Negro bondage. While in England, Levy attacked the evils of chattel slavery in a pamphlet which attracted wide attention. He even debated this question in London public forums. Now he was caught in the vicious system; either utilize slaves, or lose his investment and the prospects of colonization. And since free labor was unavailable, he had no choice.

As a colonizer, he showed considerable energy and ability. To provide stable and profitable crops for settlers, he brought various seeds and fruit trees from Cuba. There is even a legend that Moses Elias Levy was the first planter to import sugar cane into the U. S. But he was beset with many difficulties. His farm houses were burned by Indians during the Seminole wars and his men attacked and scalped. Then he became involved in a flock of lawsuits arising out of the clouded title in the Arrendondo tract. It is from the depositions in these cases that Leon Huhner was able to piece together the meager data for his biographical sketch.

The Zionist dream in Florida did not materialize; nor did the colonization scheme succeed. To be sure, Levy had vast tracts of acreage with high potential value. But he was weighted down with litigation. By 1840 he found himself in the usual situation of big farmers: land poor. His lawyer had to obtain a loan to defray the costs of the numerous lawsuits. Finally, the courts cleared up the legal mess, and he ended his days in comfort.

Through the mist of a century, Moses Elias Levy emerges a picturesque pioneer attempting to colonize Florida, even during its Spanish occupation. The times were not favorable and he met the fate of most colonizers. Yet the man had vision and daring, a driving ambition to do big things, with a strong sense of obligation to his persecuted co-religionists. George R. Fairbanks, a prominent attorney, wrote: "Moses E. Levy was a man universally respected in St. Augustine. His probity, large intelligence, and benevolence were recognized by all. He was just and generous in his business transactions. I held him in the highest regard and veneration."

Yet there is something tragic about the lonely seer and man of action who watched a great scheme fritter away. Actually his idea of colonizing Florida was no pipe dream. The feverish Florida land boom of the 1920s but re-echoed his promotions and boostings in the 1820 decade. The phenomenal development of Florida is the culmination of the vision he caught a century earlier.

Moses Levy came too early and consequently is but a forerunner. His sons could have carried on his life work without sacrifice to their political or material ambitions. And here perhaps lies the crux of his frustration. We do not know what caused the family split. His daughters married and lived at St. Thomas in the Virgin Islands. His two sons remained distant, if not hostile. It must have been a cruel blow to the proud Jew and sensitive parent to hear that his 35 year old son, the first senator from Florida, abandoned the honorable family name of Levy for the strange exotic Yulee. Intermarriage and conversion widened the breach.

In 1845 the Florida Legislature added Yulee to the name of Senator David Levy. In the same year, a large tract of land on the Gulf Coast was named Levy County. The law makers probably intended to honor the Jewish Senator from Florida. Yet they preferred to retain the old patronymic—probably in subconscious tribute to the vision, energy, drive and sacrifice of Moses Elias Levy.

1821

CAPTAIN
JACOB de la MOTTA

Surgeon and Scientist

On July 2, 1816 Gershom Mendes Seixas died in New York. Orthodox law requires the body to be interred the same day. For so distinguished a patriot as the minister of Shearith Israel it was no easy matter to deliver a fitting panegyric on short notice. Yet a speaker was found in the stranger, Capt. Jacob de la Motta of Charleston. The eulogy delivered the following morning by the 27 year old military surgeon has been preserved in a pamphlet of 11 pages.

The captain no doubt heard about the Reverend Seixas from his father. In fact, the elder de la Motta was better qualified to eulogize a fellow patriot of his own generation. Emanuel de la Motta, a veteran of the War for Independence, became prominent in Freemasonry. In 1801 he was one of nine who founded in Charleston the Supreme Council of Scottish Rite Masonry. The Council, probably anticipating the coming sectionalism, decided to divide the Ancient and Accepted Scottish Rite into Northern and Southern jurisdictions. Emanuel was sent as Special Deputy-

Representative of the Charleston Council to organize a jurisdiction in New York. A controversy was precipitated by a rival Masonic lodge, which Emanuel claimed had been organized illegally. In the heat of conflict, his authority was challenged on the ground that as a Jew he could not hold the high office because of the ritual. The Sovereign Grand Inspector of the 33rd Degree and Illustrious Treasurer-General of the H Empire in the Sublime Grand Lodge of Perfection had to prove that as one of four Jews out of the nine who organized the Supreme Council, he took good care to modify the ritual so that he could take the higher degrees without violating his Judaism. While the controversy was raging Emanuel de la Motta no doubt met Rev. Seixas, who probably gave him strong moral support.

In selecting the eulogist, the Trustees recognized his calibre. When 21, Jacob de la Motta had already published as a medical dissertation the pamphlet entitled, *An Investigation of the Properties and Effects of the Spiraea Trifoliata of Linnaeus, or Indian Physic.* Two years later he abandoned science for the Army, thus following the example of his father who enlisted during the Revolution. Throughout the War of 1812, he served as a surgeon in the South Carolina Second Artillery, holding the rank of Captain. In 1818 he was surgeon in the Third Brigade of the New York State Infantry. Yet on Jan. 1st, 1820, he addressed the Georgia Medical Society *On the causes of the mortality among strangers, during the late summer and fall,* which was later published.

On leaving the Army, the Captain settled in Charleston and practiced medicine. Yet he kept up intimate relations with his birthplace Savannah. In the summer of 1820 he was called to address Congregation Mikveh Israel of Savannah in commemoration of its establishment. This oration marks the greatest literary effort of Jacob de la Motta. Couched in the florid, sentimental prose then current, it reveals the fervent gratitude of Jews living under the free institutions of America in contrast to the conditions of "their brethren in foreign lands, writhing under the shackles of odious persecution and wild fanaticism." But Jews earned their freedom. "Resolving to separate from the standard of tyranny, they united with free men for the general good; contended for the independence of the states, and none were found more zealous, more active, more brave, and more patient amidst the sufferings that the fortune of war, the cravings of hunger, and the merciless beast had daily subjected them."

The reactions of two former Presidents to this discourse are significant. James Madison wrote to Dr. de la Motta: "And it is particularly pleasing to observe in the citizenship of such as have been most distrusted and oppressed elsewhere, a happy illustration of the safety and success of this experiment of a just and benignant policy. . . . The account you give of the Jews of your congregation brings them fully within the scope of these observations." The letter of Thomas Jefferson states: "It excites in him the gratifying reflection that his country has been the first to prove to the world two truths, the most salutary to human society, that man can govern himself, and that religious freedom is the most effectual anodyne against religious dissension; the maxim of civil government being reversed in that of religion, where its true form is 'divided we stand, united we fall.'" Both great men were happy to witness the success of their experiment.

Having studied medicine under Dr. Benjamin Rush in Philadelphia, Jacob de la Motta practiced with success in Charleston. The attending physician at the City Dispensary, he served as secretary of the Medical Society for many years. In 1836 he was elected a corresponding member of the Royal Academy of Medicine in Paris. In the days before modern pharmacy, doctors had to fill their own prescriptions. Dr. de la Motta therefore acquired the "Apothecaries Hall", perhaps the oldest drugstore in all America, started supposedly in 1780. It was still the age of signs rather than street numbers, and over the door hung a large golden bowl, which the Negroes christened "de big yaller bucket". The equipment, the brass scales, the interior woodwork of this old pharmacy can still be seen at the Charleston Museum, on corner Rutledge Ave. and Calhoun Street.

A good physician who stood high in the profession, Dr. de la Motta nevertheless did not avoid politics. He rendered public service in accepting two city appointments: Commissioner of the Charleston Alms House and Assistant Commissioner of Health. He was an active Whig in the national election of 1840 and President William Henry Harrison appointed him Receiver-General of his district.

The interests of Dr. de la Motta reached beyond medicine or politics. Science had a particular attraction. He lectured "On the Natural History and Product of the Silk Worm," and "On the Philosophy of Botany." These essays and other articles were printed in the *Charleston Courier*. For eight years he was secretary of the Literary and Philosophical Society. In Freemasonry, he followed in his father's footsteps. He "went through the chairs" and served as Worshipful Master of Friendship Lodge. He enjoyed the high Masonic distinction of Lieutenant Grand Commander on the Supreme Council of the Scottish Rite. Shortly before his premature death, he was acting Grand Commander— a post he might have attained had he lived longer.

In the last two decades of his life, the Charleston Congregation was agitated by the first Reform movement in American Judaism. One would expect Jacob de la Motta, with his scientific perspective, to join the Reformers, who constituted the progressives of the day. But the Doctor had a penchant for fundamentalism, both substantive and ritualist. He would often be the cantor at services in Charleston and Savannah. When Reform won over the Sephardic bastion in Kahal Kodesh Beth Elohim, the Orthodox withdrew and formed Shearith Israel. For two years Dr. de la Motta was President and Hazan of the secessionist synagogue. But he ran into domestic trouble. The women in the family favored Reform. The feud must have waxed bitter. The mother-in-law never forgave him. He died at 56, and the old lady spitefully added a codicil to her will, leaving an extra bequest for her daughter "in consequence of the inadequate support left by Dr. de la Motta for his family."

1822

ISRAEL BAER KURSHEEDT

Erudite Layman

Τ<small>HE MOST</small> learned of American Jews in the early 19th century, Israel Baer of Kurcheidt, never wielded the influence his knowledge or character denoted. He always reflected a condition or illustrated a situation. Lesser men presided where his authority should have directed. His very surname Kursheedt (the spelling changed for American ears) indicated the prevailing habit of European Jews to adopt the name of their city, town or village.

Born in 1766, he studied at the Frankfort Yeshiva conducted by the eminent Rabbi Nathan Adler. When war broke out with the new French Republic, Israel Baer demonstrated the swift transformations demanded for Jewish survival through the centuries. The student turned into trader and contracted to deliver provisions for Prussian forces. The war with France soon ended and the purveyor was out of business. He decided to leave for England. Enroute at Hamburg he heard of an American boat in the harbor. Immediately his imagination took fire. The heroic struggle that established Independence had impressed Europe deeply. Why not cross the sea to the infant republic where the first President was relinquishing his office—something a European ruler never did willingly.

After a perilous journey of 70 days in the small skiff, he reached Boston to find that the only Jew, Moses Michael Hays, had a family but no synagogue. Israel Baer felt a necessity for Jewish society. Of course, he heard of the famed congregation at Newport; but it had declined sadly since its heyday under the benign leadership of Aaron Lopez. He had to be content with New York, even if its Jewry in 1796 lacked the distinction of the community in the national capital of Philadelphia, or in far away Charleston.

The Reverend Gershom Seixas welcomed the Ashkenazi *lamdan,* to whom he could turn for advice or information. The Hazan of Shearith Israel freely acknowledged the superiority of the newcomer in Jewish lore. Their relations were permanently cemented when the bachelor of 38 years married his 26 year old daughter Sarah Abigail. The congregation showed respect in bestowing upon the learned newcomer its highest honor: *Parnass* of the Spanish Portuguese Synagogue. Yet this elevation of a foreign Ashkenazi or his adoption by the Seixas family hardly concealed the fast ebbing of Sephardic "tolerance" as the 18th century receded.

Economic conditions in New York were not too encouraging before DeWitt Clinton approved of the canal that connected the Great Lakes with the Hudson River. In fact, it was difficult to earn a living there. Kursheedt held on until 1812, then decided to try Richmond. He moved the family by stagecoach and shipped his Hebrew library and Masonic paraphernalia by water. As a result of war with England, the ship carrying his property was captured. Some years later he was amazed when a boat brought ashore his Hebrew books and Masonic regalia. He always felt it to be the kind act of some Masonic brother, whether Jew or Christian he could only guess.

For 12 years Israel Kursheedt remained in Richmond. He helped reorganize the congregation and enlarge the Beth Shalome Synagogue. Throughout his residence he officiated as Reader and took an active part in all communal matters. Meanwhile New York grew and the community increased. Sarah Abigail probably longed for the city of her birth. The Kursheedt family left Richmond in 1824, the year Isaac Lesser arrived.

Until 1825, Shearith Israel remained the only synagogue in New York. For a century the Ashkenazim had outnumbered the Portuguese element, but the ritual continued rigidly Sephardic. Old-timers insisted on the status quo, while the more recent arrivals longed for the accustomed *nusach* of Central and East Europe. A group of Ashkenazim petitioned for holding separate services that would not conflict with the established worship. This request was turned down in the same spirit that the Charleston *junta* rejected the more radical, yet reasonable, demands for reform submitted by Isaac Harby. The petitioners seceded and formed Congregation B'nai Jeshurun.

I. B. Kursheedt joined the seceders, although personal necessity did not compel him. His wife and children had their roots deep in the aristocratic old families and he was not subjected to Sephardic hauteur. He evidently deemed the secession justified on more counts than the mere right to pray in the accustomed tradition. The erudite Talmudist could hardly fail to recognize abuses in the rigidity of a leadership that overlooked progress or, sometimes, fairness in maintaining a strait-jacket mold over a community that was increasing beyond the capacity of a single congregation. He probably sensed the irritation against autocratic rule by the Parnass, the inequalities of a stratified society, the sanctions employed against secular intransigeance.

There being no ordained or qualified rabbis in the New World, Kursheedt was the acknowledged authority on religion. Questions regarding interpretation of ritual law were submitted to him. No one disputed or rejected his lay decisions. Every one knew that he never passed judgment on any issue unless certain of its correct interpretation. Each doubtful case he referred to the Rabbinate of Europe. His reputation for scholarship even reached the Gentile world. While a resident of Richmond he visited

Thomas Jefferson and was no doubt put on his mettle to satisfy the voracious curiosity of the Sage of Monticello.

Scholar rather than dynamic leader, Kursheedt lived in retired modesty. Lack of ambition held him from starting institutions needed in the young community. Yet when called he never refused active cooperation for a worthy cause. Among the first to engage in extra-synagogue activity, he served as president of the Hebrew Mutual Benefit Society. More significant was his work in establishing the Hebrath Terumath Hakodesh. This organization for the relief of the poor in Palestine had more importance than mere charity. There were poor in need of help everywhere. Before the dawn of Zionism, he saw the necessity of uninterrupted residence in the Holy Land until the day when Jews would demand their ancient homeland from the world.

Kursheedt's last public act demonstrated the clarity of his judgment despite his 74 years. In 1840 Victorian optimism about the progress of enlightenment received a rude jolt when a French monk disappeared in Damascus. Reactionary forces resurrected the 13th century libel that Jews murdered for ritual purposes. Medieval practices such as arrest and torture of adults and children were revived. Liberals were bewildered and did nothing. European emancipation, outside of England, had not yet progressed sufficiently for Jews to take any initiative.

In New York the Damascus Affair came up for consideration at Shearith Israel. The oldest and leading synagogue in America was unable to meet the issue and refused to take action. Individuals took the matter in hand, and a self-styled *Committee of Israelites of the City of New York* held a protest mass meeting, with Israel B. Kursheedt as chairman and colorful Mordecai M. Noah the principal speaker. A letter signed by Kursheedt requested President Martin Van Buren to intercede in behalf of the imprisoned Jews in Syria. The communities in Philadelphia and San Francisco followed the pattern set by the New York meeting and letter. This action set the precedent for American Jews to assist their persecuted co-religionists anywhere in the world.

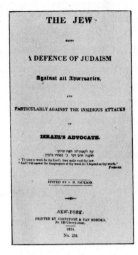

1823

SOLOMON H. JACKSON

Opponent of Missionaries

FIRST AMERICAN JEWISH PERIODICAL
EDITED AND PUBLISHED BY JACKSON.

ATTEMPTS at converting Jews have made bizarre history. Paul the Apostle, recalling his experiences as Saul of Tarsus, shrank from the task and turned his superb talents in the direction of Gentiles. Yet Christians have never ceased trying. They employed strange and often diverse methods, from revolting cruelty to extreme kindness, from fanatical monks inciting blood-thirsty mobs to gentle nuns giving sanctuary to victims fleeing the gas chambers.

A curious lack of psychological awareness characterized this zeal to Christianize. Even the infallible wisdom of the Popes did not perceive the incongruity of packing Jews in a church and forcing them to hear the rants and threats of a priest, who never disguised hatred or contempt for the stiff-necked deicides he was expected to persuade into the religion of humility and love. As late as 1858 an infant, secretly baptized by its nurse, was torn from the arms of its parents; to get back the child they would be forced to give up Judaism.

While the Protestant churches might not be charged specifically with such flagrant outrages, their early attitude towards Jews differed little from the official attitude of Rome. But with the decline of faith in the 18th century, the century of reason and enlightenment, vast changes were perceptible. To convert became the voluntary task of missionary societies. They began to understand that conversion of Jews involved more than mere church attendance. The convert often found himself in a vacuum, as it were, rejected by Jews and not accepted by Christians. Another discovery pointed to a relationship between economics and evangelizing. As religious fervor declined, the rich or ambitious found their way to the baptismal font without the aid of missionaries. To the impoverished, on the other hand, the prospect of earning a living was often a far greater inducement than salvation.

Thus with the increase of converts, problems of adjustment became manifest. The grooves of hatred formed by caste, religion, rank, or money ran deeply in a society emerging from feudalism. The new Christians married among themselves and constituted a new class that evoked old hates under new names. It became apparent that conversion did not banish inherited phobias.

Meanwhile the young American Republic grew steadily in size and population, in strength and prestige. Over in Europe stories were afloat of a new order which encouraged the living together in amity of various sects, creeds, national or racial stocks. Here, the missionaries concluded, is the ideal land for Jewish converts. Coming in with Christian names, they could easily be absorbed into the welter of immigrants, among natives without the tradition of inveterate hates or blood vendettas.

American attempts to proselytize Jews stemmed from the Puritans of Colonial times. Missionizing increased until 20 societies are said to have functioned in New York alone during the first quarter of the 19th century. A member of Boston's Female Society for Promoting Christianity, Hannah Adams of the noted Presidential family, wrote her *History of the Jews,* the first publication in English that told what happened *after the Destruction of Jerusalem*. This book, with inaccurate additions made for missionary purposes, was used by the more prominent missionizing societies in England for propagating Christianity among Jews.

American and European missionaries exchanged views. The suggestion came from Europe that Jewish converts, or would-be converts, should be transported to the U.S.A. Under the energetic lead of the apostate Rev. Joseph S. C. F. Frey, the American Society for Meliorating the Condition of Jews was organized. Prominent personalities such as John Quincy Adams and DeWitt Clinton interested themselves in this organization that had more than 200 local chapters throughout the land. An ambitious scheme to acquire thousands of acres was projected for a Hebrew-Christian settlement. Rev. Frey traveled in all the states, preached in churches and solicited funds. An aggressive periodical under the misleading name of *Israel's Advocate* propagandized the conversion of all Jews. Seemingly a full scale campaign was on.

In the past Jews did not dare to fight back. Nor could a population of less than 6000 scattered in all states be equipped for such a fight. Synagogues, without ordained or qualified rabbis, constituted the sole organizations in the era when the Monroe Doctrine was formulated. Yet an individual did come forth as a champion. Solomon Henry Jackson, born in England and related to Mordecai M. Noah, had received a good Jewish and secular education. He came in 1787, settled in Pike County, Pennsylvania, and married the daughter of a Presbyterian minister. Such a step usually marks the end of Jewish affiliations. The children are either baptized or marry into the Christian faith. But the Jacksons were exceptional.

Strange under the circumstances, Jackson reared his five children in the Jewish religion. Four of them married Jews when he moved to New York after his wife's death. Eliza married Dr. Peter Donovan, and he subsequently embraced Judaism and joined one of the most Orthodox congregations in the city.

Solomon Jackson operated a printing business and wrote English with style. He evidently had reason to be annoyed with missionaries. Without help he began publishing the first Jewish periodical in the Western Hemisphere. For two years he edited *The Jew; Being a Defense of Judaism Against All Adversaries and Particularly Against the Insidious Attacks of Israel's Advocate.*

The valiant fight of Solomon Jackson reads somewhat like the public religious disputations in the Middle Ages. He denied the claims and pretensions of *Israel's Advocate.* His polemics contradicted the editorials, the pamphlets, the preachments of the missionaries. He reiterated the Jewish arguments against Christianity and cited in support the Hebrew Prophets by chapter, line and verse. His editorials scored the methods used by the American Society for Meliorating the Condition of Jews. In short, he utilized every weapon of his arsenal to confute, to demolish and to defeat his opponents.

After 1825, *The Jew* ceased to appear. This raises a negative presumption as to its original necessity. The sum total of missionary activities in the U. S. among Jews showed such meager results that, one by one, the societies folded up. All the efforts of Dr. Peter Wilson, a Columbia professor and authority on Josephus, scarcely netted a single convert. The years of labor by the apostate Frey could not even produce one. The 400 acre farm in Westchester, 35 miles out of New York, operated for a "Hebrew-Christian settlement" by the Society for Meliorating the Condition of the Jews, was abandoned after a brief trial. The four converts imported from Europe refused to cooperate and charged the management with discrimination and exploitation. The conversions of American Jews were voluntary and resulted from intermarriage and the desire to integrate completely into the society of the dominant majority.

The activities of Solomon Jackson continued chiefly in communal affairs. Besides serving as one time secretary in Shearith Israel, he translated the prayer-book and published an English Hebrew *sidur* 60 years after Isaac Pinto first rendered the Sephardic ritual in English. A decade later he printed the first

American bi-lingual edition of the Passover service in English and Hebrew. In 1837, during the worst of all American economic depressions, he served as president of the Association Zeire Hazon (Tender Sheep). This society aimed at settling the Jewish immigrants, coming out of Germany in ever increasing numbers, on agricultural colonies in the Far West, on the fertile soil which a benign government was giving away gratis.

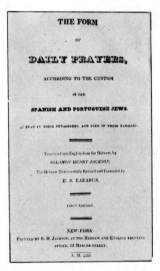

PRAYERBOOK TRANSLATED AND
PRINTED BY SOLOMON H. JACKSON.

1824

ISAAC HARBY

*The First Reformer
in American Judaism*

IN CHARLESTON there occurred something that was almost without precedent. A lay group initiated the first reform of Judaism in America. It happened in 1824 before the synagogue had an ordained rabbi, before the South Carolina metropolis possessed any scholar steeped in Jewish learning. The leader of the Reformers, Isaac Harby, was a playwright and schoolteacher, a critic and journalist.

Isaac Harby was a born writer. At 17, he revealed the talent of a youthful prodigy in composing a tragedy in five acts. Years later another play, "Alberti", was considered good enough for entertaining President Monroe on a visit to Charleston. But writing plays could hardly support the large families that were being raised in the Republic's early days. His family budget had to be supplemented with the income of a private school. Harby offered to slave owners' sons arithmetic, penmanship, grammar, elocution, geography—and to more advanced students Latin,

202

Greek, geometry and composition. Virtue and patriotism, honor and morality were instilled gratuitously as useful to youth when they became men.

The urge for creative writing prompted Harby to reject the rewards of schoolteaching. Instead, he became successively the publisher or editor of several newspapers in Charleston. His political editorials attracted attention for their fearlessness, patriotism and grasp of public affairs. In a trenchant essay he advocated Andrew Jackson for the Presidency. A master of rhetoric, he could use satire, humor and righteous indignation with telling effect, yet preserve candor and calm reasoning. His friend, the novelist William Gilmore Simms, said that "he wrote essays and orations with spirit, grace and effect."

Charleston was in the midst of its Golden Age. A century of plantation agriculture worked by slaves had bred a landed aristocracy of wealth and leisure. They cultivated courtly manners and gracious living, taste and refinement. They boasted of a theatre and library, yet enjoyed horse races and cock fights, suppers and cotillions. Van Wyck Brooks devotes a whole chapter on the Charleston of this era in his *World of Washington Irving.* Yet among the writers, poets, essayists, editors and cultured lawyers of Charleston he left out Isaac Harby, Penina Moise and Jacob Newton Cardozo, a trio of Jewish literati who should have been included.

The environment exercised a strong influence upon the integrated Jews, especially those of Portuguese stock. They adopted the mores, even the duelling code of the upper class, with whom they had contacts in business, in politics, in the professions. Educated Jews had friendships in the literary circle. They yearned for acceptance in this society, yet were unwilling to sacrifice their religion. Unconscious of secret assimilationist complexes, they were anxious to uphold the honor and dignity of Judaism and eager to render it comprehensible and attractive. In the words of Isaac Harby, they aimed at "order and decency in worship, harmony and beauty in chanting, the inculcation of morality and charitable sentiment upon individuals, and the promotion of piety towards the Deity."

A memorial bearing 47 signatures, drafted by Isaac Harby and Abraham Moise, was presented to the officers of Beth Elohim Congregation. In respectful language the document requested shortening the long repetitious service, the rendition in English of important parts of the ritual and a regular Sabbath discourse that would interpret the ancestral faith. The petition was tabled without discussion; the *adjunta* disdained even to reply. There was nothing left to do but organize the first "Reformed Society of Israelites" on the American continent.

The mild reforms demanded by the Charleston group have long since been adopted by Orthodoxy. It would therefore seem that the inflexible leadership of Beth Elohim is open to the charge of Bourbonism, which never concedes an inch no matter how intelligent the request or necessary the change. But before condemning, several things must be considered. The authority vested in the Synagogue for centuries never tolerated an infraction of its rigid discipline. The rebel would immediately feel social pressure, the denial of religious privileges, the scorn of the communal leadership. Such was the established practice in the Bevis Marks Synagogue of London, which caused Disraeli's father to withdraw from the congregation. The haughty Sephardim refused to brook changes in the Orthodoxy that had served the Golden Age of Spanish Jewry and for which their ancestors had suffered martyrdom at the stake.

Developments soon demonstrated that reform meant more than harmless changes in the ritual. The new prayerbook confirmed the intuitive fears of the Orthodox. Harby's knowledge of the reforms in Germany caused, perhaps, the deletion from the Sidur of the Messiah, of any return to Zion, of any reference to the resurrection of the dead, to the revival of sacrifices in the restored Temple. The intention of breaking away from the authority of the Talmud became quite apparent.

The breach widened. A growing bitterness prevented reconciliation and the Reformers felt the arrows of hostility directed at them. Isaac Harby found it difficult, perhaps impossible, to earn a living for the support of his nine motherless children. Animosity probably hastened his decision to leave Charleston for New York and start life again at forty. He opened a school, wrote excellent articles for the New York press and died in the same year.

To the Reformers in Charleston, the loss of Isaac Harby proved a disaster. The group held together for several years and even gathered donations for building a temple. But the inspiring force was no longer alive. There was no lack of intelligence, character or education among them, yet spiritual direction was missing. In 1833 a reconciliation was effected on the terms of the Orthodox, and the Synagogue welcomed its dissenting members. Apparently, the breach was healed. Yet the spirit of Reform continued to seethe beneath the surface. Within a decade, the Reformers captured Beth Elohim, and this time the Orthodox seceded. Controversies lasted another decade, but Reform became permanently intrenched in the citadel of Sephardic Orthodoxy.

While it cannot be claimed that Isaac Harby inaugurated the Reform Movement in the U. S. A., he was, nevertheless, its pioneer and the forerunner of Isaac M. Wise, Max Lilienthal and David Einhorn, his superiors in Jewish learning. His movement may not have spread out of Charleston, yet the fact remains that Beth Elohim was the first Reform Temple in the Western Hemisphere. Its existence served as an example and influence to the others that sprang up in Baltimore, Philadelphia, New York and Cincinnati.

Isaac Harby's niche in history is due to his initiation of Reform in American Judaism. Yet it must be insisted upon that he also deserves a place in American letters. As a critic he ranks higher than as a journalist or playwright. He would probably have made a lasting contribution to American literature had he lived longer than forty years. His wide range reveals a scholarship ranging from Homer to Sir Walter Scott. His varied critical observations cover Shakespeare, the drama, the discovery of printing, the value of the classics in university education, actors and acting. The *London Times* considered Isaac Harby the finest dramatic critic in America. The *New York Mirror,* the leading literary paper in 1828, declared editorially:

"The death of this accomplished scholar and able writer has awakened great and merited regret in the circle of his friends and admirers. Possessing vast acquirements in classical learning, endowed with a chaste and refined sensibility and gifted with a lively and active imagination, he was highly successful in his literary pursuits. As a critic he was considered unrivaled in this country."

THE CHARLESTON SYNAGOGUE
WHICH ISAAC HARBY ATTEMPTED TO REFORM.

1825

MORDECAI MANUEL
NOAH

"Governor and Judge of Israel"

In Mordecai Manuel Noah, patriotism for the young Republic and loyalty to ancient Judaism were twin passions that blended into synthetic harmony. Born in 1785, he listened to first hand accounts of suffering and victory from the veterans of the Revolution. In his native Philadelphia, he could watch Congress deliberating through the administrations of the first and second President. His grandfather Jonas Phillips would point out the venerable figures of Franklin and Washington walking the streets of the then national capital. Voracious reading in the libraries of America's intellectual center supplemented an inadequate education and prepared the boy for his future roles as orator, playwright, editor, judge, politician and office holder.

As a young man he displayed capacity, for in his 26th year he was offered a consulship at Riga. But with Napoleon preparing to invade Russia, there was no point in accepting. Instead he went to Charleston, where his mother was buried. Philadelphia was on the decline since the national capital had moved to the muddy flats on the Potomac. Charleston seemed to offer a better opportunity to study law and enter politics, especially since it contained the leading Jewish community in the 17 states of the Republic. Here he quickly made sufficient impact to draw three challenges on the Field of Honor. In a duel he wounded his opponent and was thereafter known as the *Major*. His speech making and journalism must have been valued at Washington. He soon received the appointment of U. S. Consul at Tunis.

While the War of 1812 was on, he boarded a ship at Charleston, but was captured by a British frigate almost within sight of the Spanish coast. War feeling was evidently not too bitter. The American Consul was allowed freedom of movement in London and later permitted to reach his destination. After romanticizing in France and Spain, the Major presented his credentials to the Bey of Tunis. It was a trying assignment to a den of thieves. The pirate state lived by plunder on the high seas. The Powers in Europe found it cheaper to pay for protection than clean out the water rats. The Moslem robber chieftain neither feared nor respected the new Republic separated by 3000 miles of ocean.

Our Consul thought he was doing a splendid job when he learned that the U. S. Treasury refused to honor his draft for money paid to release American captives. Then Commodore Stephen Decatur brought him a dispatch from the Secretary of State, James Monroe, that the President had revoked his commission on the ground that his *religion* formed an obstacle to the exercise of consular functions. This was not true. The Bey knew nothing of Noah's religion; besides in those days the African Moslem states were accustomed to have Jewish agents represent them at home and in Europe. Enemies were evidently doing some knifing.

Returning to New York, he began a career remarkable for its versatility. But first of all, he demanded an inquiry and received vindication from his Government. Editor of influential newspapers, he had a gift for polemics, for controversy, and even vituperation, that made him respected at a time when gunplay was not rare in politics. His friendship was appreciated by Andrew Jackson, Martin Van Buren, John C. Calhoun and many leading Democrats in the nation. Politics and journalism went hand in hand. Elected Sheriff, he later became Grand Sachem of Tammany Hall. Appointed Surveyor of the Port of New York, he also served a term as Judge of the Court of General Sessions. His political life would have satisfied the ambition of many an office holder.

But he was also a litterateur, far better known than young Edgar Allan Poe, whom he helped and encouraged. Historians of the American theatre give Mordecai M. Noah a leading place among the early successful dramatists. In the florid, romantic vogue of the day, his plays abound in fervent propaganda for the young Republic. As a founder of New York University, his interest in education is attested. He supported the idea of a Jewish Hospital, and a year after his death such an institution was founded by Sampson Simson, an institution which ultimately became Mount Sinai Hospital.

At dawn of September 15, 1825, booming cannon awoke the 2500 dwellers of Buffalo, N. Y. By 10:00 A.M. the militia in uniform, Masons in regalia, Indians with feathered headgear, state officials and curious civilians were parading towards St. Paul's Episcopal Church. The central figure in this procession was clothed in austere black, draped over with a mantle of crimson silk, trimmed in white ermine. As "Governor and Judge of Israel" Major Noah thus marched into Jewish history. On the communion table of the church lay a rectangular stone engraved:

Shema Yisroel Adonoi Elohenu Adonoi Echad
ARARAT
A City of Refuge for the Jews
Founded by Mordecai Manuel Noah

After the Episcopal service, the self-appointed Messiah mounted the rostrum and announced his mission to establish a Jewish state within the Federal Union. Noah's Ararat was not intended to supplant the Zion of Holy Writ; it would become a temporary haven of the persecuted until the time for the fulfillment of Prophecy. In some mysterious way the 50 square miles of Grand Island in the Niagara River, close to the Falls, would sustain millions until the sounding of the great Shofar of Redemption.

All this might smack of the eccentric, the poseur, the self-seeking charlatan. But it also foreshadows the most trenchant movement in the long Jewish saga. It reveals that the first important political figure of American Jewry, a patriot intoxicated with the constant daydream of 4th of July rhapsody, felt the pressing need for a Jewish homeland. In the melodramatic and bizarre ceremonial, he stated in essence the gist of Zionism. He anticipated another self-appointed Redeemer, the far abler, nobler and more romantic Theodore Herzl, whose daydream became Medinat Israel.

JOSEPH JONAS

*Founder of
the Cincinnati Community*

Iɴ ᴛʜᴇ English town of Exeter, Joseph Jonas was growing dis-
satisfied. By 1816 he had reached the age of 24 and got nowhere
with his trade at watchmaking. There were simply too many
watchmakers for repairing the few clocks that only a small part
of the population could afford.

With little work and abundant time, he read copiously, especially about the lands overseas. Fascinated by descriptions of the
Ohio valley, he was particularly intrigued with Cincinnati, a
name appropriate for the town of rugged backwoodsmen, types
similar to the old Roman who left his oxen standing at the plow
when his country called. Almost two years had elapsed since
Britain signed a treaty that ended the second war with her
former colonies. Believing that anti-English feeling had calmed
down, Joseph embarked on a ship for the U. S. A.

From New York he proceeded to Philadelphia and met with
old residents who used many persuasive arguments that he remain. The larger cities on the seaboard offered better opportuni-

ties to a watchmaker and silversmith than the unsettled hinterland. The venerable Parnass of Mikveh Israel, Levi Phillips, warned: "In the wilds of America, and entirely amongst Gentiles, you will forget your religion and your God." He did not speak idly, for many pioneers who ventured into the backwood lands were lost through intermarriage and assimilation.

Starting out on January 2, 1817, Joseph Jonas reached Pittsburgh only to find the Ohio frozen and blocked to navigation. There was no difficulty in obtaining profitable work for a skilled handicraftsman. He could easily have stayed on, but the city of his quest beckoned. He left as soon as the ice cracked on the river and reached Cincinnati on March 8, 1817.

His reception came as a pleasing surprise. The rustic settlers outside the city were mainly native Americans of pioneer stock who had left their homes on the eastern seaboard in search of more fertile land. Hard-muscled farmers, they felled the trees, cleared the soil of stumps and built block houses of rough-hewn timber. Working from sunrise to sunset, they had little time for reading other than a daily passage of Scripture. Except the Bible, they had few, if any, books in their log cabins.

These honest provincials, simple but sound, frugal yet hospitable, conceived of Jews as bearded patriarchs with flowing raiment, staff in hand and sandals on their feet. Jonas wrote in later years: "Many persons of the Nazarene faith, residing from fifty to one hundred miles from the city, hearing that there were Jews living in Cincinnati, came into town for the special purpose of viewing and conversing with some of the children of Israel, 'the holy people of God,' as they termed us." Their reactions were, most probably, summed up by the old Quaker woman, who seeing Joseph Jonas for the first time exclaimed: "Art thou a Jew? Thou art one of God's chosen people! Wilt thou let me examine thee?" She inspected him from head to foot, front and back, and finally added with evident disappointment: "Well, thou art no different to other people."

Success in business, the respect of fellow citizens, the friendship of Christian townsmen, an office in the Royal Arch Chapter of Masons were not sufficient to offset the lonely feeling of being the only Jew in Cincinnati. He longed in his own words: "that he might be a nucleus around which the first congregation might be formed to worship the God of Israel in the great western territory." A year later David Israel of Portsmouth, England, passed through to join his brother Phineas Israel, who had settled in Brookville, Ohio, and was called, or actually adopted, the surname Johnson. Jonas pleaded with his English *landsman* to remain in the growing city. But David had to see his brother first.

Urging and letter writing evidently brought results. In 1819 Lewis Cohen of London, Barnet Levi of Liverpool, and Jonas Levy of Exeter arrived. The High Holidays were approaching, and Joseph sent to Brookville for David Israel, who by now had also added Johnson to his Hebrew names. The five pioneers celebrated the first New Year and Atonement service in the Northwest—quite a departure from the required quorum of ten males, insisted on by the strict Talmudic code. But Jonas, sensible and not without scholarship, reasoned that a service with an incomplete *minyan* was better than none at all.

Towards the end of the year, Joseph's heart was gladdened at the coming of his brother Abraham and his sister Sarah with her husband. After several more arrivals, the tiny community took form and had no further problems with a *minyan*. Joseph and Abraham Jonas became established. They married sisters who were daughters of Gershom Mendes Seixas, the patriotic New York minister during the Revolution. Both marriages were not blessed with long life. Abraham's wife lived but 20 years, and Joseph's died in her 26th year. Abraham Jonas left Cincinnati, settled in Kentucky, then in Quincy, Illinois. He became prominent politically, a lawyer, postmaster, and died a friend of President Lincoln.

The first community asset, a burial ground, was acquired as the result of a dying request. In 1821, Benjamin Leib, or Lape, Anglicized, asked that several of the Jewish newcomers be called to his bedside. He had married a Christian and had remained unknown as a Jew. Now he wanted a Jewish burial in a Jewish cemetery. His wishes were fulfilled. In 1824 when the group had increased to 20 residents, the Kahal Kodesh Benei Israel, the oldest congregation in the central Northwest, was organized. Six years later it was incorporated by the Ohio General Assembly.

The growing community worshipped in a hired hall. The need of a synagogue became imperative. Joseph Jonas and two committeemen were delegated to raise money and proceed with construction. The cost exceeded the resources of an immigrant congregation. Jonas had to solicit funds from individuals and communities. His letter to Charleston declares that no congregation existed within 500 miles and, if Cincinnati had a synagogue, worshippers from New Orleans would travel by water to attend holiday services. Charleston sent $100; Jacob I. Cohen of Baltimore gave $150; fifty-two Christian fellow citizens donated $25 each; Harmon Hendricks of New York forwarded $100; individuals of Philadelphia collected $470; from Portsmouth, England, came currency equivalent to $71.55; a resident of Barbados, W. I., mailed $50.

In his four articles in Isaac Leeser's monthly, *The Occident,* Joseph Jonas lingers in detail over the architecture and ornamentation of the completed synagogue. The ceremonial of dedication moved him profoundly. The 33 by 80 foot structure could not contain the assembled crowd. Admission of Christians had to be limited to the clergy and the families of generous donors. It was a day of consecration and triumph for the pioneer, who lived to deliver the concluding address as founder and Parnass.

To the religious yearnings and communal responsibility of Joseph Jonas might be added a love of learning and flair for literary expression. His magazine essay on "The Jews of Ohio" has preserved a valuable record of Jewish pioneering in the middle Northwest. But he worked at a more ambitious task. For years he had been reading and accumulating material for a book that would (1) refute the conclusions of Ernest Renan about ancient Israel, (2) review the "higher criticisms" leveled at the Book of Genesis, (3) discuss the Biblical prophecies, past, present, and future. Some excerpts appeared in the *Israelite* published by Isaac M. Wise, but the work itself remains in manuscript.

When Andrew Jackson ran for President in 1828, Jonas was his first supporter. His interest in politics continued and in 1860 Joseph Jonas was elected to the Ohio Senate as a Democrat. His known sympathies for the South probably made his position difficult in the mounting bitterness of the Civil War. When his second wife died in 1867, he went to live with his daughter in Alabama. He died outside of Mobile and was buried on his 77th birthday. He did not live to see his nephew Benjamin F. Jonas elected U. S. Senator from Louisiana.

SOLOMON ETTING

Civil Rights Champion

Cᴇᴄɪʟ Cᴀʟᴠᴇʀᴛ, the First Lord Baltimore, achieved eternal fame by establishing the Colony of Maryland for Catholics under heavy disabilities in 17th century England. But a paper charter is seldom protection against a fanatic majority. Soon the Protestants predominated, and the disenfranchised "Papists" fled to Virginia. The help of Oliver Cromwell enabled Lord Baltimore in 1649 to enact his Edict of Toleration for all Christians, excepting Quakers.

Nine years later, the arrest of "Ye Jew Doctor" Jacob Lumbrozo demonstrated that toleration had less meaning in Maryland than even in Europe. The Portuguese doctor, landowner, and trader had settled in the colony and seemed quite popular, his roguish tendencies notwithstanding. Visiting a Quaker, perhaps to honor the host's guest, also a Quaker and a missionary to boot, he foolishly became involved in a religious discussion, seldom wise and never profitable, particularly at a time when Protestants and Catholics had just ended a bloody religious war which lasted

30 years in Europe. Lumbrozo answered the missionary quite frankly that Jews did not accept the divinity of Jesus, something Europe had tolerated with bad grace for 1300 years. This statement was enough to hang "Ye Jew Doctor". Clapped into jail and awaiting trial, he was one morning amazed and delighted to hear that the new English dictator, Richard Cromwell, had granted amnesty to all political and religious offenders.

Until the Revolution, a Maryland statute provided that any one denying "our Saviour Jesus Christ to be the Son of God, or deny the Trinity" shall for the first offense be fined and have his tongue bored; for the second, his face shall be branded with a hot iron; and hanged for the third transgression. This statute was not repealed until 1776, and William Pinckney tried to pass a liberal law in keeping with the times. The legislators considered it a great concession to permit every one the free practice of his religion. It also seemed the essence of liberalism to require the oath of a true Christian of any one holding a public office.

Jews were not eager to rush into a State in which the grooves of bigotry ran deeply. Yet as the 18th century was drawing to a close, Solomon Etting and Barnard Gratz moved to Baltimore. Born in the new world, Etting had been in partnership with his father-in-law Joseph Simon, the Indian trader of Lancaster. After his wife's death, he married the daughter of Barnard Gratz and was thus through both wives both uncle and cousin to Rebecca Gratz. Immediately, the newcomers began to agitate the repeal of the oath designed to keep Jews out of every public office, from Governor to garbage collector.

In 1797, a petition to the General Assembly signed by Etting, Gratz, and others urged that Jews be given the same rights as other citizens to hold public office. The matter was referred to a committee of three, who considered the request reasonable but informed the petitioners that a constitutional matter being involved, it was too late in the session to make the change. For five years nothing was done. Yet the absurdity of the situation became more apparent when Pres. Jefferson appointed Reuben

Etting, brother of Solomon, the U. S. Marshal for Maryland. But no one could hold the meanest constable job in the state without affirming the faith of a Christian. Another petition introduced in 1802 was shelved. It came up the following year and was refused by 38 votes against 17. In 1804, after a full discussion of the removal of Jewish disabilities, with many speakers taking part, the bill was defeated 39 to 24 in the Lower House.

For a dozen years no public action was attempted. Solomon Etting was no doubt disheartened but did not give up the fight. Much pioneer work had to be done. Assistance came unexpectedly with the arrival of the Cohen family from Richmond. Jacob I. Cohen, Jr. opened a bank that established a reputation for honorable dealing. He became a valuable co-leader with Etting and wrote every petition from 1816 to 1826. Important also in the fight for Jewish civil rights was the rise of Baltimore's Jewish community in prosperity and influence.

No opportunity was neglected to enlist the aid of influential Christians. Thos. Brackenridge, General Winder, E. S. Thomas, Col. W. G. D. Worthington, and John V. L. MacMahon showed sympathy and made strong speeches. But the most ardent champion was Thomas Kennedy whose devotion to religious liberty caused him to be denounced in his home constituency as a "Judas Iscariot, the one half Jew, and the other half, not Christian."

In the General Assembly, each year from 1818 to 1826 legislation kept being introduced. Jewish emancipation became a state wide issue between the city and the rural section. In Baltimore, a legislator opposing the "Jew Bill" could not be elected, while rustics, who had never seen Jews, defeated in 1822 sixteen members who voted for it. Thomas Kennedy was defeated in 1821 and 1823. Newspapers and magazines in other states denounced the intolerance in Maryland. In 1822 the Bill passed both houses, but the Constitution required its publication and confirmation the following year. In the next session, the Senate confirmed it, but the House refused the necessary vote. The Senate in 1825 passed a similar measure, and on the last day of the session the House voted 26 to 25 in its favor. At the 1826 session both Houses finally confirmed "the Act for the Relief of the Jews of Maryland."

Throughout the 19th century the Etting family was conspicuous in civic, cultural, military and commercial affairs. Reuben Etting, organizer and captain of the Independent Blues, fought with distinction in the defense of Baltimore during the War of 1812. While yet a second-class citizen of Maryland, Solomon Etting corresponded with Robert Fulton about building a steamboat to be presented to the Federal government. The termination of the war with England made this project seem unnecessary. His activities ranged from assisting in the installation of the first water works for the city to helping establish the public school system. One of the founders of the Baltimore and Ohio Railroad, he served on its first board of directors.

The Christian voters of Baltimore evidently appreciated the 30 year sustained effort to end the Jewish disabilities for public office. In the same year of the "emancipation" they elected Solomon Etting and Jacob I. Cohen, Jr. to the City Council. Later Etting was selected as president of that body. It is gratifying to remember that he was also mindful of the social and political disabilities of others. Solomon Etting was active as a director of the Maryland Colonization Society to Improve the Condition of Negroes.

1828

SAMUEL B. H. JUDAH

Playwright

B Y THE END of 1822, Samuel Benjamin Helbert Judah, hardly out of his teens, reached the apogee of his life. Never again would the 23 year old author enjoy the plaudits and prestige that followed the successful production of three plays. He published his conventional melodramas during a period when he was comfortably situated and even resurrected a poem written when he was sixteen.

The Byronic mood of this dramatic poem, *Odofriede; the Outcast,* was suggested by a quotation from Milton, printed on the title page:

> *"Such are those thick and gloomy shadows damp*
> *Oft seen by charnel vaults and sepulchres*
> *Lingering and sitting by a new made grave."*

Judah sent "Odofriede" to Thomas Jefferson. The great Democrat thanked his young correspondent and regretted that "the chill of 80 winters has so completely extinguished his sensibility to the beauties of poetry, so as to leave him no longer competent either to enjoy or judge them."

A promising future, it would seem, awaited the young poet and dramatist. His plays were by no stretch of the imagination dramas in the classic tradition. Yet if judged by the brash taste of the raw society in the infant Republic, just beginning to articulate its native ethos, they were not bad—that is, no worse than the average contemporary performance in the New York playhouses.

His first effort, *The Mountain Torrent,* something of a musical comedy with its songs and choruses, had a fairly successful run at the Park Theatre. *The Tale of Lexington,* in spite of its sudden descents from heroics to bathos, does somehow retain the high patriotism of the Revolutionary era. *The Rose of Arragon,* his greatest success, has all the elements of the florid play as conceived in the midst of the Romantic movement, and is considered by the Cambridge History of American Literature a good example of the Gothic melodrama.

All in all, these compositions were no mean accomplishments for a youth in his early twenties. Life and experience still lay ahead of him. And it takes years of effort to master the technique of the drama, possibly the most difficult literary art form. But suddenly he kicked into the fire, as it were, his career, his future, his talents, as well as the good will of his fellow townsmen.

In 1823 appeared anonymously the booklet, *Gotham and the Gothamites,* a medley of scurrilous insults against 103 prominent residents of New York City. According to Charles P. Daly, author of *The Settlement of the Jews in North America,* those maligned consisted of "public officials, politicians, merchants of the highest integrity, eminent lawyers, editors, clergymen, booksellers and publishers, literary men, professors in colleges, actors, theatrical managers, prominent military men, scholars, and artists." Although not specifically named, each could easily be identified by the first initial of his Christian or surname, followed by asterisks in lieu of the letters omitted. Judge Daly could 70 years later trace 98 out of the 103 lampooned.

To make sure that his pasquinades would not be overlooked, the author wrote unsigned letters calling the attention of the traduced to their treatment in the book. One of these letters came to Col. W. L. Stone, editor of the *Commercial Advertiser*. He compared the handwriting with another paper in his possession and identified the author as Samuel Judah. Stone took up the matter with the District Attorney, who filed a criminal libel suit. The case, after several postponements, came up for trial. It took but five minutes for the jury to bring in a verdict of guilty. After hearing from Benjamin S. Judah that his son was too ill for a jail sentence, the judge imposed the then stiff fine of $400. But Samuel Judah either would not or could not pay the fine. He was jailed. After six weeks' incarceration, the prison doctor certified that Judah, because of a pulmonary infection, could not live in jail, especially during the heat of summer. The Governor pardoned him.

It is somehow significant that Samuel Judah, in his time of trouble, could get no moral or financial support of any member in the Jewish community, with the possible exception of his father. Yet the Judah clan, rooted in America for a century, were numerous and widespread, reaching from Montreal to Georgia. The Connecticut branch was already absorbed into the Christian majority. Generally Jews helped a co-religionist in distress. But in this instance they had good cause to feel mortified. A minority feels insecure when one of its members creates a public scandal. A vicious attack upon prominent citizens was certainly not conducive to promote good relations with their Gentile neighbors.

But embarrassment gave way to anger when the venomous screed pilloried in rhymed verse and explanatory prose the prominent leader and spokesman of New York Jewry. Mordecai M. Noah, the playwright and journalist, is addressed:

> *"Thou bloated impudence; still turn thy pains*
> *To letters nature unknown, and art forgot*

Without a character, a form or plot.
New loads of words thou mayst together lay
And swear, though damned, it is a play."

These rhymed couplets are "explained in a commentary by "Terentius Phologombos"; and lest the unwary fail to recognize the person harpooned, footnotes elucidate the commentary. The *bête noire,* who seemed to gall Judah most, was Mordecai M. Noah. Jealousy and hatred creep through the malevolent diatribes heaped upon the successful editor, dramatist, orator, politician, leader, and office holder, who is referred to in the footnotes as "a pertinacious scribbler of uninspired garbage—a writer of linsey-woolsey paragraphs and still-born lumps of stupidity—a smirking, wriggling, smiling thing who says his plays were not hissed, which was because his audiences were unable to hiss and could only gape—who denies the worth he cannot equal and never blushes except when, unawares, he stumbles upon a truth."

The conviction virtually closed the literary career of Samuel Judah. He could never again show his face, figuratively speaking, in the theatre. The frustrated litterateur decided to become a lawyer. While reading law in an office, as was then the custom, he was admitted to the bar. Judge Daly wonders how any attorney could sign a certificate vouching for his character. The jurist and historian, friendly enough to Jews, cannot conceal aversion for Samuel Judah, who sometimes appeared before him in court. He probably exaggerates when he represents Judah as altogether without ability as a lawyer or poet. A gentleman and scholar of the Victorian era, the Judge could never forgive the youthful indiscretions in *Gotham and the Gothamites,* patently an imitation of the satire in Swift's *Tale of a Tub,* or Pope's *Dunciad.* The impartial jurist accepts uncritically the estimate of a lawyer, perhaps an enemy, who disparages Judah as "acute, cunning, technical, and not very reliable," a shyster who could only succeed in collecting claims at a time when the prison was open to defaulting debtors.

In 1827, Judah attempted a literary comeback with the *Buccaneers,* a voluminous historical romance from the time of the settlement of New Amsterdam to the era of Captain Kid the Pirate, using his familiar nom de plume, *Terentius Phologombos.* Even this work had to be censored by having five pages cut from the book to make it acceptable. It was followed by *The Maid of Midian,* "a tragedy in four acts founded on the massacre of the Midian captives by order of Moses." The play was never produced, nor did his name appear on its title page when published in Philadelphia. His attitude towards the Bible was in the 1830s no doubt considered sacrilegious. Bitterness towards religion, after the tradition of Thomas Paine, became an obsession. In his ballad, *The Battles of Joshua,* also published in Philadelphia anonymously, he vents his spleen upon Joshua for cruelties towards the vanquished. Nor does he abstain from snide innuendoes against the Hebrews in making slaves of the Gibeonites for the work they never do.

Samuel B. H. Judah is forgotten, except for the antiquarian book collector, so that the date or place of his death remains unknown. One cannot help feeling that he was an eccentric with a gift not adapted to his time. In a literary age where libel and blackguardism were not infrequent, Judah took advantages that did not square with his ability. In modern times, psychiatry, instead of prison, might have afforded him relief.

1829

SAMPSON SIMSON

Founder of Mt. Sinai Hospital

THE ECCENTRIC, yet practical, Sampson Simson belongs to the category of "firsts" who blaze trails. In the first year of the 19th century, he was the first Jew to graduate from Columbia College and the first of his school to deliver a commencement oration in Hebrew. The Holy Tongue did not sound strange in an era that considered it good form for a student to read his graduating address in Latin or Greek. Sampson also can rank as the first alumnus to make a contribution to his Columbia Alma Mater. Moreover he was the first Jewish lawyer to pass the New York bar.

His father, Solomon Simson, an important exporter and importer before, during, and after the Revolution, left him well provided, so he had no need to practice. To keep occupied, Sampson read law at the office of Aaron Burr, former U. S. Vice-President and perhaps the ablest lawyer in the city after killing Alexander Hamilton, his rival, in a duel. While studying, he worked as confidential clerk to Burr. Sampson then had desk space in the office of the prominent Riker law firm. His practice was slight, confined chiefly to personal affairs, benevolent and religious matters.

His father died in 1801, and for about a dozen years Sampson, a rich man's son, dawdled about doing nothing in particular. He had neither his grandfather's scholarly interests, his father's capacity for business, nor his uncle's daring originality or superb abilities. In 1802 an ensign, the following year a lieutenant, and later a captain in the militia, he was, apparently, not called for active duty in the War of 1812. His chief interest centered in Shearith Israel, until inveigled into a controversy that almost split the congregation.

The laws of Kashruth have always demanded a meticulous compliance with their burdensome regulations. Cattle could only be slaughtered by the shohet, qualified by learning, skill, and, above all, piety—a combination not always obtainable in the New World. The unscrupulous butcher in cahoots with the shohet could sell *trefa* meat if camouflaged under a kosher seal. To guard against frauds, the City Council passed an ordinance prohibiting the sale of kosher sealed beef unless the animal had been killed by a shohet authorized by Shearith Israel.

This regulation by the city was not altogether unjust. Supervision had to be exercised by some authority conversant with ritual law, and Shearith Israel was the only synagogue that functioned in the small New York community. A dissenting group, probably nursing grievances, seized the opportunity to raise an issue of principle. Jacob Abrahams, a shohet of dubious integrity, helped to foment discord. Sampson Simson headed a committee and petitioned the Common Council to annul the *kosher* law. The City Fathers, not eager to become embroiled in a synagogue schism involving religion and "conscience", promptly repealed the law.

The action of Sampson and his committee created strong resentment. Normally a Sephardic congregation that patterned its conduct upon the model of Bevis Marks Synagogue in London imposed disciplinary sanctions. Nothing was done beyond engag-

ing a new shohet. Evidently the petitioners were too prominent
or represented a faction ready to secede—as actually happened
a decade later when a discontented group formed the B'nai Jeshurun Congregation. Beneath the surface lurked the not too concealed rift between the Sephardim and Ashkenazim, the old
families and newcomers, the English speaking versus German
or Polish minorities.

While the intransigeance of Sampson did not bring retaliation,
it nevertheless could not enhance his popularity in Shearith Israel.
We do not know which side the unpredictable Simson would
have chosen in the secession that brought B'nai Jeshurun into
existence. We do know that he withdrew from active participation in religious or communal affairs. An unfortunate incident
might have brought on his withdrawal. Some one attacked him
at night and caused injuries that confined him to bed for months.
On recovery, he remained on his barony at Yonkers, which extended from Palisade Avenue to Saw Mill River. Here he lived in
the manner of a country gentleman, satisfied with the devotion
of his sister and her two children.

For a whole generation he remained in virtual retirement but
not isolated from the life of the immediate vicinity. Interested in
prison reform, he followed closely the politics of Westchester
County. An admirer of Andrew Jackson, he treasured the cane
received as a gift from the President. His practical sense found
interest in the new machinery, in improved technique and methods of agriculture. He contributed his share to the religious and
charitable activities of Yonkers. Always a member of Shearith
Israel, he remained content to criticize its policies and management at a distance. He would speak reverently about the eminent
men of his youth but did nothing to preserve their memory in
writing. Devout in worship, he would rise early for his daily
prayers. Matzos were baked upon the estate, under his personal
supervision.

He revealed his eccentricity by continuing to wear outmoded
clothes, including the breeches, stockings, and silver buckles of

the 18th century. He never married. His stiff formality and humorless inflexibility might have been corrected by the gentle yet critical railleries of a sensible wife. Cultivating good penmanship, he signed his name with the grand flourish of a John Hancock. He could speak harshly to people he disliked, but was always considerate to Negroes. Impatient of criticism and autocratic, he nevertheless remained fundamentally the benevolent philanthropist.

Wearying finally of isolation, especially after the death of his sister and her children, he was again induced to engage in communal affairs. Like Rip Van Winkle, he looked with surprise at a changed world. Gone were the days when New York looked to Charleston for a shohet. A number of institutions, religious and secular, had sprung up, and a new generation no longer emphasized religion as the central element in life. Fraternal, benevolent, social, and educational activities were seeking qualified leadership. Sampson saw his place in the city of many facets. He contributed to churches, Protestant and Catholic, and donated $3000 of the $4500 required for a new synagogue on Allen Street, the Beth Hamidrash Hagodol for immigrants out of Central and Eastern Europe.

Sampson Simson entertained notions which people waved aside as Utopian. His overall interest became focused on Jerusalem. Some intuition, confused and misty, germinated in his subconscious about the significance of Palestine. The only practical approach to Palestinian Jewry was to relieve their appalling poverty. Influenced perhaps by the benefactions of Montefiore and Judah Touro, he communicated with Warder Cresson, the Quaker proselyte who demonstrated the feasibility of agriculture as a solution for the pauperized Jews of the Holy City.

He founded the North American Relief Society for Indigent Jews in Jerusalem, and willed $50,000 for teaching Palestinian Jews "arts, sciences, and mechanical and agricultural vocations." His intent was clear but not the provision in his will that devised the sum "to any responsible corporation in the city whose per-

manent fund is established by its charter for the purpose of meliorating the condition of Jews in Jerusalem." Such language offered endless arguments to lawyers hired by relatives to contest
the bequest. The money ultimately went to a grand-nephew who
left the Jewish fold. Yet a great benefit did accrue. Litigation went
on for years, until a young lawyer from Syracuse was retained by
organizations concerned with Palestinian relief. The lawyer, Louis
Marshall, studied Jewish needs and problems, remained in New
York City, and later became the unofficial leader of American
Jewry.

But the permanent achievement of Sampson Simson consisted
in his organizing the first Jewish hospital in New York. Serious
problems then beset the Jewish sick. Medical science did not yet
discover that germs carry and spread disease. Poverty stricken immigrants lived in squalid cellars or basements, and many would
die victims of contagious or foul air. Those who did get into hospitals, such as they were, often met ridicule while praying with
tephilim or refusing to eat anything not kosher. But worst of all,
missionaries or zealous nuns would sometimes baptize the sick
too feeble to object. The church then insisted on Christian burial
for their converts.

There was much talk but no action about a Jewish hospital.
Mordecai M. Noah delivered an eloquent speech and died before
his words were implemented. Without notice or warning, Sampson Simson assembled a group and organized the Jew's Hospital
in the City of New York. He conveyed his two lots on 28th Street
near 8th Avenue and received $1034 from a charity ball given by
young people at the swanky Niblo's Garden. Opposition groups
were aghast at the unorthodox methods of a benevolent visionary
with fantastic ideas. But the hospital became a *fait accompli* with
the receipt of $20,000 from Judah Touro's estate in New Orleans.
Following the Civil War, the name was changed to Mt. Sinai
Hospital. After a century of healing and scientific research, the
institution launched by Sampson Simson ranks as one of the great
medical centers in the world.

1830

BENJAMIN GRATZ

*Railroad Organizer
and President*

THE UNCLE of Justice Brandeis lamented in 1892 that "the arrival of Jews in Kentucky, from its earliest settlement to as late as 1836, marks only so many ends of Judaism. There is no frequenter of the synagogue who lived in Kentucky or whose ancestors lived there before 1838. Whoever came, came singly, found no one to pray with, and, what is more, no one to mate with. Intermarriage of the newcomers with daughters of the land followed naturally, and the descendants of the early Jewish settlers of Kentucky are known only by their Jewish family names and their oriental features."

The words of Lewis N. Dembitz sum up succinctly the private life of Benjamin Gratz. A descendant of America's foremost colonial Jewish family, he was the youngest son of the old pioneer Michael Gratz. The Gratzes could boast a heritage from the top intellectual and spiritual leadership of Polish Jewry during the heyday of its power in the 16th century. Benjamin Gratz graduated from the University of Pennsylvania in 1811 and delivered the outstanding oration at the commencement exercises. He hardly began his legal studies when the War of 1812 drew him in as a volunteer. Mustered out a lieutenant, he resumed reading law and was admitted to the Philadelphia Bar.

In the competitive field of "Philadelphia lawyers" Benjamin opened an office. Prospects should have been good in his native city. His family played a prominent part in its commercial, civic and social life. Like his brothers he became active in local politics. The business started by his father and uncle had descended to his brothers Hyman and Simon Gratz. His sister, the celebrated Rebecca, then at the height of her beauty and charm, moved in the so-called best society. Before becoming engulfed in the exacting details of a busy practice, the family thought Benjamin should visit Indiana and Kentucky to examine the status of large tracts of land acquired years earlier by their father, their uncle Barnard, or their grandfather Joseph Simon of Lancaster.

Benjamin established contact with a friend, who had settled in Kentucky as far back as 1808. Salomon, a firm believer in assimilation, had married a Christian and lived in the stone mansion he built at Harrodsburg. When the newly chartered Bank of the United States opened a branch at Lexington, Salomon was appointed cashier, an important position in the chain of banks backed by the power and prestige of the Federal Government. Still hankering for some association with the Philadelphia group of his youth, Salomon offered Benjamin a job in the bank.

Knowledge of finance and experience in banking might go well with law practice. But Benjamin, still under the spell of Judaism practiced in his family circle, demurred on the ground of violating the Sabbath; the problems involved in praying with phylacteries or in general observance offered obstacles. The highly empiric Salomon advised him "to put his *tephilim* together with the Sabbath in his *talith* bag and throw the entire package behind him."

The Vincennes of 1820 was quite a muddy village when it rained, and here Benjamin spent his first year "out West". This Indiana frontier outpost inhabited by French and French-Indians was nevertheless a center of administration, the place for untangling the snarls incidental to acquiring land in a semi-primitive world. He then proceeded to Lexington, the boom town which already manufactured rope and hemp that grew in the surrounding country and was sold by the Gratzes in Philadelphia. This town promised to expand into a metropolis, until the newly invented steamboat shifted the commercial axis to the banks of the Ohio.

Benjamin Gratz might have spent a year in Lexington and then returned to the affectionate family awaiting him in Philadelphia. But he chanced to lift his eyes and see "a daughter of the land" He fell in love with Maria Gist, a girl of unusual charm and culture, whose father was a colonel in the Revolutionary Army and whose grandfather was a close friend of George Washington. They made a striking couple. Benjamin was a man of real ability and exceptionally handsome, judging from the picture painted by Sully. They married and Benjamin remained in Lexington for the rest of his 65 years.

In Lexington, Benjamin displayed the public spirit which he absorbed in Philadelphia. He became a member of the first city council and a director of the Bank of Kentucky and the Northern Bank of Kentucky when both institutions were organized. He was elected a trustee of Transylvania University, the important academy of learning for the entire region. In fact there was hardly a movement of public welfare in which he did not play a leading part.

The contributions of Benjamin Gratz to the upbuilding of his adopted Kentucky were in a sense the result of ancestral speculations. In the 18th century, his father Michael, his uncle Barnard, his grandfather Joseph Simon, the founder of Aaronsburg, Aaron Levy, and tycoon David Franks of Philadelphia formed the Illinois and Wabash Company. This syndicate acquired large tracts from the Indians, who probably sensed their hunting grounds were vanishing with the rapid encroachments of white settlements. This group, in concert with some of the eminent figures of the Colonial epoch, had negotiated with the Indian chiefs another gigantic deal, which the British Crown refused to confirm. Among their agents, George Croghan and Daniel Boone have become famous.

But the Colonial generation had passed from the scene. Benjamin seemed the only person capable of salvaging anything out of the wreckage of buried claims. We do not know the extent of his success. A wealth of detail lies hidden in the archives of Virginia, Illinois, Kentucky, Western Pennsylvania, and West Virginia. We can only surmise. Benjamin was an organizer of the Lexington and Ohio Railroad and its second president. It would seem that some connection existed between the successful launching of the second oldest railroad in the U.S.A. and the land claims or legal rights of the Illinois and Wabash Company.

An eminent citizen of Kentucky, Benjamin Gratz was a neighbor and friend of Henry Clay. In fact Clay's grandson subsequently married Gratz's daughter. This intimacy came in handy on one occasion when the great compromiser was asked to explain his anti-Jewish slur on the Senate floor against "a small man with red hair . . . flitting about between the House of Representatives and the Treasury Department . . . Moses Myers, the Jew." Henry Clay wrote of "the friendship of many Jews, among them one of the Gratzes of Lexington, formerly of Philadelphia, stands in the most intimate and friendly relations to me." One of Henry Clay's pallbearers, Gratz was also a member of the association that erected the Lexington monument to Kentucky's greatest son.

Besides his Kentucky friends, Gratz had many friends among the prominent men of the nation. In Lexington he publicly welcomed William Henry Harrison, when he ran for the Presidency. He was among the staunchest supporters of the Union. He freed his slaves and used his considerable influence to hold Kentucky within the Federal column. His youngest son Cary was killed in battle at the beginning of the war.

In matters of Judaism he followed the advice of his friend Salomon, but only in part. He did put the Sabbath and *Tephillim* in the *talith* bag, but did not throw it behind him. He stored it in the attic to be taken out on rare occasions. When the small Jewish group in Lexington could hold services occasionally he was generally present, probably to say *Kaddish* for his father and mother. He wished to lie in the parental burial plot, but Mikveh Israel refused permission. Reform Rabbi Isaac M. Wise officiated at the funeral and remarked dryly that he and the 92 year old corpse of Benjamin Gratz were the only Jews present.

1831

LEVI CHARLES HARBY

*Captain in
the U.S. Marine Service*

S PANISH JEWS had a penchant for ancestry. Every one attempted
to connect with the ancient nobility of old Jerusalem; the more
eminent even traced their lineage to the Royal House of David.
Even intelligent and scholarly Isaac Harby could not resist the
trend; he preserved the legend that his warrior ancestor, Isaac
ben Solomon, bore the nickname *herab*—hence the family name
Harby, literally "my sword" in Hebrew.

He went on to state that his ancient forbears who survived the
destruction of the Temple made their peace with Titus and so-
journed in various lands within the Roman Diaspora. For centuries they lived in Spain, then in Portugal. The Inquisition forced
their migration to Northern Africa; there notwithstanding Moslem bigotry, they could at least practice their religion. About the
middle of the 18th century, Isaac Harbie served Morocco's "Emperor" (the title adopted by the Sultan) in the capacity of lapidary,
which today means simply jeweler. A sultan's palace is seldom
free of intrigue. And although Isaac had the ruler's confidence,

he nevertheless found it expedient to leave quite suddenly. Garroting was a favorite pastime in Mohammedan courts.

Isaac Harbie fled to England and drowned his troubles by marrying a young woman from Italy. Their son Solomon changed the spelling of his surname to Harby and decided to live in the New World. He landed in British Jamaica while the American Revolution was still on and in 1781 managed to reach Charleston. Solomon Harby married Rebecca the daughter of Myer Moses who had contributed money and supplies quite liberally to win the war of liberation. Their first born, Isaac Harby, became the critic, playwright, journalist and classical scholar, who attempted the first reform of American Judaism.

In the 19th century's first quarter, Charleston contained the largest and best integrated community in American Jewry. The reasons are not too obscure. The port of a rich hinterland, this city enjoyed prosperity. But it also had a tradition of religious tolerance that attracted Huguenots from France and Nonconformists from the British Isles and possessions. Jews began to infiltrate, and by 1750 Kahal Kodesh Beth Elohim was formed. A goodly portion of the congregation served the patriot cause during the Revolution. By the War of 1812, the majority were native born who had absorbed English culture and American folkways. Confined no longer exclusively to trading, the community could point to its lawyers and teachers, to its doctors and journalists as well as merchants and planters. There were three painters and an architect in this Americanized congregation.

Levi Myers, the third child of Solomon and Rebecca Harby, was born in 1793. Like Uriah P. Levy, he set his heart on a career in the U. S. Navy but appears to have escaped the harrassments, the annoyances, and the court-martials experienced by his co-religionist. At the start he avoided the error Uriah Levy made in taking the short cut towards a commission. Levi Charles Harby, as he was subsequently known, enlisted in 1807 as a midshipman. Serving in the War of 1812, his vessel was captured; he was imprisoned for 18 months at Dartmoor, the notorious British prison that foreshadowed the modern concentration camp. A Jewish baker sold bread daily to the prisoners. One day Harby refused to buy, evidently because he was out of cash. The baker insisted on giving him a loaf. On breaking the bread, he found a newspaper account of the American victory at New Orleans. This was a signal for Levi Charles to make his escape.

On his return, Harby regained his position in the Navy. The peace with Britain that followed enabled the U. S. Navy to punish the Moslem pirates who preyed upon American shipping. The Mohammedan corsairs, sent out of the Barbary ports in North Africa, and encouraged by Britain to stifle the commerce of her rivals, continued a menace on the high seas well into the 19th century. It appears that Harby commanded a vessel in the expedition against the pirates of Tripoli. On December 4, 1827 he resigned his commission, yet seems to have taken part in the Seminole War in Florida, but in what capacity the record fails to disclose. One source states that he fought for the independence of Bolivia, or in the struggles that followed.

When Texas began her war for independence, a number of American volunteers flocked to her aid, among them Levi Charles Harby. Evidently he saw the coming struggle for Texan independence and had to resign his commission to fight Mexico, then on friendly terms—at least on the surface—with the U.S. government. Evidently he retained the good will of the Brass Hats, for subsequently he was commissioned a Captain in the U.S. Revenue Marine Service, under the Treasury Department and given command of a ship. This friendly act of the Marine authorities stood out in marked contrast to the treatment of Uriah P. Levy, who begged of and pleaded with the Navy for active combat duty, and was refused.

A sea faring officer constantly on the move would hardly take time off to marry. The 45 year old Captain had perhaps given up the idea, but on meeting Leonore Rebecca de Lyon of Savannah he succumbed. The disparity of age between the 14 year old girl and the middle-aged bachelor proved no impediment. They married and appear to have lived happily ever after. Yet one must consider the problem that faced the small group of Sephardim, who were rapidly becoming extinct. This exclusive society was permeated with bachelors and spinsters. Selection of mates became more and more difficult in the haughty circle that was decaying for want of fresh blood. The Harby of Portuguese-Moroccan descent met his *yiches* in the daughter of Levi S. de Lyon, Judge of the County Court of Chatham County, Georgia, and Rebecca de la Motta. In their shrinking community it was not often that a couple could find mutual attraction together with parity of pedigree. As the 19th century reached its middle, the Spanish Sephardim would not think of marrying into any group of Ashkenazim, whether German, Polish, Hungarian, or Lithuanian. Consequently they were doomed to oblivion.

The Harby couple appear to have settled in Texas, and as the Civil War approached, the Captain reached his 68th year. Obviously too old for active service, he evidently resigned from Marine Service. But the Confederacy had need of all the trained officers available. His 52 years of experience were too valuable to pass unnoticed. Given command of a company of volunteers on the boat Neptune in the Confederate fleet at Sabine Pass, Captain Harby rendered good service to the cause he believed in and distinguished himself at the Battle of Galveston.

Faithful at all times to his religion, he received support from his wife, whose devotion to Judaism matched his. She was a Hebrew scholar and taught in the first Jewish Sunday School in Texas. She was also a founder of the Ladies Hebrew Benevolent Society of Galveston. When Capt. Levi Charles Harby died in 1870, his last words were: "There is no God but Israel's God."

1832

BERNARD HART

New York
Stock Exchange Official

Mulling over the past and peering into the future, Bernard Hart had cause to feel grateful. In two years he would pass the Biblical three score and ten, and his health was excellent. He might even reach the optimistic four score, reckoned by the Psalmist as more than adequate for the span of life. And why not? Harking back 37 years, he recalled the yellow fever which ravaged New York in 1795. He had rendered aid to many of the stricken, yet remained free of infection throughout that highly disastrous epidemic. The doctors marvelled at the power of resistance in his strong constitution.

Next to the blessing of health, he mused on, comes prosperity and a good name, which the Proverbs rank even above riches. He had both, else the Stock Exchange would not in the year previous have elected him secretary. Several Christian brokers might envy him that distinction, judging by the black looks he sometimes received. Yet he was successful. Perhaps the reputation of a relative, dead now for six years, may have been a contributing factor. He took pride in his distant kinsman, Ephraim Hart, one of the 24 organizers who met in 1792 under the buttonwood tree and formed the first Board of Stock Brokers, out of which the New York Stock Exchange evolved.

Thinking of Ephraim brought to mind his son, Dr. Joel Hart, who had just returned after an absence of 15 years. Joel had been a good scholar and studied medicine at the Royal College of Surgery in London. He was a practicing physician and in 1806 became one of the co-founders of the Medical Society of the County of New York. In 1817 President James Madison appointed him Consul to Perth, Scotland. At the time, the family might have wondered whether this appointment came as amends for the shabby treatment accorded by the Administration to Joel's first cousin, Mordecai M. Noah, who was summarily dismissed from his consulship at Tunis. Joel resigned his position after 14 years and spent a year in Rome hobnobbing with the American circle of artistic-bohemian expatriates. He now returned to the United States to resume his old career.

Of course, the 48 year old Dr. Joel Hart was a credit to the community and was respected. But Bernard's own son Emanuel, just turned 23, he thought, showed far greater promise. After all, Joel proved but a dilettante, shuttling from medicine to politics, not knowing which way to turn. Emanuel had helped in the election of President Andrew Jackson and was an up-and-coming figure. Of his six sons and four daughters, Emanuel would claim the greatest distinction. Already Tammany Hall slated him for a minor office.

The serenity of his pleasant day dreams became overcast. The mood changed as an old shadow intruded. Was it his Christian son Henry? But why did that figure depress him? Did the son of Catherine Brett resent his Jewish father? Bernard Hart had no bad conscience when thinking of his first wife. He probably met her during the yellow fever plague. They married in 1799 and Henry was born the following year. One day Catherine declared the marriage a mistake. She would give him his freedom. How could she support herself and baby? Why, her own Protestant people, who had opposed the marriage, would now take her back.

Bernard Hart never quite understood what caused the change. He was satisfied there was no one else, for Catherine, an attractive young woman, never remarried. Yet they remained on friendly terms. She accepted the support he gave and would consult him on family or personal problems. Six years after the separation, Bernard in all probability asked her opinion about the marriage he contemplated with Rebecca, daughter of Benjamin Mendes Seixas and niece of the famous rabbi. Catherine might have urged him to marry and even gave her blessings.

Their son Henry attended Union College at Schenectady, passed all examinations, yet failed to receive any degree. It seems that a bill of $90 remained unpaid. This appears strange, for Bernard would undoubtedly have paid the bill on presentation. According to the writer Clement Shorter, Henry Hart was alienated from his father and never entered his house. He possessed a good education, knew two classical and three modern languages, lectured, taught, translated, yet never got anywhere. He moved from place to place and had difficulty making ends meet. Brought up in the Dutch Reformed Church, his mother an Episcopalian, Henry became a Catholic. He married at 30, and on one occasion took his little son Francis, the future Bret Harte, to the New York Stock Exchange and pointed out the boy's grandfather. But Henry did not speak to him, and the grandson never saw his grandfather again. Yet after Henry's death, Bernard helped with the support of his widow and children.

But in Emanuel B. Hart, the father felt all his hopes fulfilled. From city alderman in 1845, he went to the Democratic State Convention as delegate, then in 1849 was elected Chairman of the Tammany General Committee. Fatherly pride reached its summit when Emanuel was in 1851 elected to Congress by a large majority. Bernard Hart did not live to see his son Surveyor of the Port, selected by President Buchanan, then reappointed at the request of Abraham Lincoln. For the rest of a long life Emanuel continued in public service. In 1860 he was sent by the Treasury Department to investigate revenue frauds in Europe. His report brought about important reforms. He served as a Presidential elector, a Commissioner of Immigration, as disbursing agent of New York's Custom House. For years President of Mt. Sinai Hospital, he was Treasurer of the Hebrew Relief Society and at the same time head of the Home for the Aged and Infirm.

While Emanuel B. Hart was building up a solid reputation in public office, in communal and administrative service, a young writer out of San Francisco was making the name Bret Harte talked about throughout the land. His poems helped to sustain the morale in the North during those dark hours when the sledge hammer blows of Lee and Jackson threatened to shatter the Union. His short story, *The Luck of Roaring Camp,* introduced the local color of the mining camp, the quaint rough dialect, the picturesque ruggedness of the Wild West during and after the California gold rush; it created a new vogue in American fiction. Immediately, the author was offered $10,000 a year, an unprecedented figure for literary work, at least in the U.S.A., to write for *The Atlantic Monthly.* The impact of Bret Harte on American letters can be read in any history of American literature.

The public servant and substantial communal leader Emanuel B. Hart never knew that the gifted litterateur, Bret Harte, was his nephew. The reasons are rather cloudy. Evidently his father Bernard never relished the memory of his short marriage to Catherine Brett. It was therefore distasteful explaining to his large family an experience he would rather forget. Nor was there any point in talking of his son Henry, the educated *Schlimiel* who perhaps wanted no part of his Jewish kin. Bernard Hart would have been amazed to hear that his son Emanuel, ex-congressman and city father, is forgotten while his grandson Bret Harte, litterateur of America's Far West, is famous for his contributions to the national culture.

1833

LORENZO da PONTE

Librettist to Mozart

Aʙɪʟɪᴛʏ seemed native to the Conegliani family, which in the 17th century produced a physician-diplomat, who served the conflicting interests of Turkey and Venice with such deftness that both states removed from him the civil disabilities which Christendom and Islam considered good for Jews, so long as they chose to stand aloof from the Cross or the Crescent. In the 19th century another Conegliani displayed talents in political economy that would have carried him places had he lived longer than 33 years.

In 1749 Emanuel Conegliani, born not far from Venice, became an orphan when five years old. Later his father fell in love with a young Catholic girl, and she would marry only in church. Father and three sons were baptized at the same font; Emanuel received at 14 the musical name of Lorenzo da Ponte. The world now became his oyster and the bright, handsome boy could get a good education, which later on enabled him to teach literature at a seminary in Treviso.

Theological studies also fitted him for the priesthood. But in a

243

decayed and corrupt Venice he found revelries far more entertaining than celebrating the mass. In the 18th century, a Venetian
abbe could dance minuets, compose madrigals, and serenade in
gondolas by moonlight. Chummy with the famous or infamous
Casanova, he led a similar life of intrigue and dissipation. Nor
was his orthodoxy beyond suspicion. He therefore had good cause
to fear scrutiny by the City Inquisition. Not anxious to emulate
the charming Casanova in his jail break from the *Doge's pi-
ombi,* he prudently fled from Venice, from its seductive women,
from the demoralizing carousals. A decree of banishment was
filed against him.

Wandering over Europe, Da Ponte landed in Vienna. Here he
ran into a streak of fame, glamour, and well being that sometimes
fortune thrusts at a person for a brief span. He came at the opportune moment when Joseph II of Austria decided to discard
French for Italian opera. The liberal emperor appointed Da Ponte
the official poet of his theatre. His job was to write libretti for the
court musicians.

Da Ponte turned over a new leaf; at least he reduced licentious
living sufficiently to write 36 librettos during his productive years.
At the home of the Jewish banker, Baron Wetzlar, he met a house
guest, a struggling young musician named Mozart, the most spontaneous genius, perhaps, in all musical history. They came to a
quick understanding and Da Ponte wrote his sparkling comedy,
the *Marriage of Figaro,* which became Mozart's first opera. That
huge success was followed by *Cosi fan tutti.*

But their joint masterpiece was *Don Giovanni,* which will hold
the boards as long as opera is sung. According to the Danish mystic Kierkegaard, it is the greatest of all operas. Even so formidable a musician, critic, and anti-Semite as Richard Wagner had
to admit that *Don Giovanni* owes its popularity largely to the
excellence of the libretto.

The lucky streak ended with King Joseph's death. His successor
Leopold cared little for opera and less for the favorite opera poet.
Envious rivals did some knifing, for Da Ponte had a penchant

for intrigue, which made enemies wherever he went. But when things looked darkest, he received the appointment of poet for the Drury Lane Theatre in the Haymarket of London. The new post did not bring back the *gemuethlichkeit* of Vienna. The English director Taylor had neither the courtesy nor generosity of an emperor. Da Ponte even had to endorse promissory notes to hold on to his job. When the notes were protested and other debts accumulated, he skipped from England to escape the debtor's prison.

New York in 1805 was hardly the place for a 56 year old poet with a family to support. Opera had never been heard in the young republic, and the new land had little to offer an expert of Italian literature. To feed his wife and children, the poet opened a grocery store and made a living until the yellow fever epidemic caused him to sell out and to clear out.

Later the family settled in Sunbury, Penn. where he was taken for one of the powder-making DuPonts, a circumstance that helped him get credit for a fresh start. He kept store, handled groceries, measured out drams of liquor for customers, sold wheat and medical supplies. He even had an interest in a distillery. A real estate boom brought on artificial prosperity, and the former professor had leisure for giving lessons in Italian to local students. But an artistic temperament together with bad management invariably brings hard luck. Again deeply in debt, his furniture including beds was seized by the sheriff. He was glad to get back to New York.

The romantic adventurer staged a comeback at 70. He became professor of Italian at Columbia College. But the chair carried no salary and the students preferred French or Spanish to paying tuition for Italian. Undaunted, he assembled youths and maidens, set up a little theatre in his home and spread over New York a taste for Italian classics. He also operated a book store and got into a controversy with Prescott, the historian, about the merits of Italian literature. In 1823 Mozart's librettist wrote his *Memoirs,* as frank as Rousseau's and as amusing as Cellini's.

One might think an octogenarian should be content to call his lifework completed. Not so with Da Ponte. In his 84th year, he embarked on his last, if not his most difficult, venture. The inspiration came when Manuel Garcia brought his operatic troupe to New York in 1824. The cast of first-rate singers included the famous Malibran and caused a sensation. Garcia raked in the dollars and returned to Europe, leaving Da Ponte inspired with a new scheme and a new hope for profit and glory.

In partners with a French tenor, Da Ponte imported singers, gave 35 performances and folded up. This experience should have been a warning that New York in 1833 was not ready for opera. But Da Ponte was never dismayed by defeat or failure. Instead, he planned a more grandiose project and interested prominent citizens in building a special theatre. The Italian Opera House went up on Church corner Leonard Street and the opening was the social event of the year. Out of 40 scheduled performances, he produced 28. The venture then failed. The opera house was sold and later destroyed by fire. Disheartened and impoverished, Da Ponte died, close to the age of ninety.

One might question whether Da Ponte belongs in Jewish annals. Converted, he never practiced Catholicism. Given a splendid cathedral funeral, no gravestone ever marked his place of burial. Unquestionably, he rendered important services to Italian music and literature. Yet a century later, the minions of Mussolini would have handed over Lorenzo da Ponte, the Jew, for cremation in the gas ovens of Dachau or Buchenwald.

1834

COMMODORE
URIAH P. LEVY

L<small>IKE</small> <small>PEOPLE</small>, monuments often have histories. This is true, at least, of the bronze statue of Thomas Jefferson that stands in the rotunda of the national Capitol. This work of art by a French sculptor shows Jefferson on a marble pedestal holding the signed scroll of the Declaration of Independence. Of the entire group ranged about that exalted circle, it is the only statue that was never purchased by the Federal or any State government. In 1833 it was presented to the U.S.A. by Naval Officer Uriah Phillips Levy. Yet the first image to grace the Washington memorial chamber was for some reason removed. For years it stood in front of the White House. Finally in 1874 Senator Charles Sumner moved for its official acceptance. This effigy of the great Democrat stands now in the Hall of Fame.

The checkered course of the statue might symbolize the tumultuous career of its donor. Grandson of Jonas Phillips and cousin of Mordecai M. Noah, the 10 year old Uriah first sailed the seas as a cabin boy. Apprenticed at 14 to a ship master for four years,

247

he then studied seamanship at the Naval School in Philadelphia. A second mate at 18, he commanded two years later the schooner *George Washington,* of which he owned a third. Things never went smoothly for Uriah P. Levy. The crew mutinied, seized the vessel and left the captain on a remote island stranded and penniless. Picked up by a British sloop and compelled to work his way, he resisted impressment in the Royal Navy. Somehow Levy got back home. He raised money, rounded up the mutineers in foreign parts, had them tried and hanged.

The War of 1812 brought him a naval appointment as Assistant Sailing Master of the *Argus.* This brig carried U. S. Minister Crawford on a mission of high importance to France and later captured 21 enemy ships. Put in command of a prize vessel he had taken, Uriah Levy rashly attacked a warship in the English channel. The American master and crew were captured and held prisoner for 16 months. The end of the war brought about their release.

On his return, Uriah P. Levy received the rank of Lieutenant. This promotion may have satisfied his ego and fulfilled some honest aspirations; yet it is doubtful whether the rank of commissioned officer compensated for the many aggravations and vexations he endured. The Naval caste, a clique of snobbish janissaries, resented a Jewish *confrere* who dared to rise above the status of Chief Petty Officer. Uriah P. Levy was perhaps the first Jewish officer to choose a life career in the U. S. Navy, something unheard of until the early 19th century either in Europe or America. But Uriah Levy was neither meek, nor humble, nor over tactful. Sensitive at the slightest insinuation reflecting on his religion, he was quick to resent and to retaliate. He killed an adversary in a duel and had to stand six court-martials. Yet surprisingly, he rose in due course to the rank of captain.

One must not picture Uriah P. Levy a cantankerous jack tar, walking about with a chip on his shoulder. On the contrary, he was a proud sensitive Jew, with a deeply wounded soul, who bore a courageous heart that overflowed with love for his native land. At a banquet in Paris, a toast was offered to Andrew Jackson.

The name of the President, who had antagonized France, brought hisses. Levy challenged an officer and a civilian to duels. The citizen declined to fight, and the French officer sent his written apology. The vessel *Vandalia* while under Levy's command rammed accidentally a French boat. His Lieutenant tried to explain, but the irate Frenchman exploded "what else can one expect of a ship commanded by a Jew." On being informed, Levy took along his Lieutenant with a file of marines and boarded the French ship. The officer quickly apologized.

Lieutenant Levy's activities, besides the usual peacetime routine, ranged from chasing pirates out of the Caribbean to suppressing the illegal slave traffic that sprang up along Honduras Bay. Evidently naval duties during peace were not arduous; he was able to obtain frequent leaves of absence. New York in 1834 honored him with the freedom of the city. Levy wrote several important observations gleaned during travel and received appreciative replies from the Navy Department. In 1837 he was promoted Naval Commander and commissioned a Captain in 1844.

This elevation to the highest rank then given in the Navy seems more honorary than useful. For the next 11 years he lived in virtual retirement, with little else to do than writing a *Manual of Internal Rules and Regulations for Men of War*. His most important extracurricular activities centered about the abolition of flogging in the Navy. To this task he devoted strenuous efforts. Not that there was nothing else to do. When the Mexican War started, Levy pleaded in vain for active duty. He begged for a vessel to carry grain to the starving Irish. He implored for active service in protecting American commerce in the North Sea. In 1855 he applied for the vacant command of the squadron off Brazil. The answer apprised him that his name had been stricken off the Navy rolls.

At 63, Captain Levy was active, vigorous and not at all eager for the shelf. It mattered little that he was one among 200 other officers dropped by the Act of Congress "to Improve the Efficiency of the Navy." Perhaps a house cleaning was necessary. Yet it was high handed for 15 officers in secret session to terminate long, honorable careers. A storm of protest brought a Congressional Act that permitted reviewing of the dismissals.

Levy demanded and received from the Court of Inquiry a thorough investigation. The Navy introduced the six court-martials as evidence of his unfitness. He produced Naval officers and prominent civilians who testified to his patriotism, courage, seamanship, character, and general fitness. The hearings disclosed the two real reasons against him: his religion and his start in the Navy as sailing master instead of midshipman. The rampant anti-Semitism in the Navy was checkmated by the many high-minded officers with no such animus. A favorable verdict restored his rank. Given command of the squadron in the Mediterranean in 1857, he replaced Lavalette, the Commodore who testified against him with all the vindictiveness of a Judeophobe.

When the War of Secession broke out, Levy was the ranking officer in the Navy but too old for duty. He was now called Commodore, yet there is no official confirmation for that title. It is said he offered the President his entire fortune for the war efforts. Lincoln declined, and Levy subscribed liberally to the War Loan. The Commodore died the following year and devised most of his fortune, valued at $300,000, to the U. S. A. There was much discussion as to the constitutionality of such a bequest. But the Senators were spared a debate when the will was contested. The court gave the reversionary estate to Levy's heirs.

The bequest to the U. S. included Monticello, which the Commodore had purchased out of reverence for Thomas Jefferson, its designer and builder. During the Civil War, Virginia confiscated the Jefferson Shrine as the property of an enemy alien. It remained in the Levy family until acquired by the Thomas Jefferson Memorial Association.

On the tombstone of Uriah P. Levy appears: "The father of the law for the abolition of the barbarous practice of corporal punishment in the Navy of the United States." If this inscription had read "one of the fathers", it would perhaps have summed up more accurately the humanitarian contribution of the Jewish officer towards the abolition of flogging in the U. S. Navy.

ABRAHAM MOISE.

1835

PENINA MOISE

Blind Poetess

Eligible bachelors were scarce in San Domingo. So Abraham Moise, a French speaking emigrant from Alsace, found warm hospitality at the Jewish plantation near St. Eustace. He had no language difficulties in wooing and winning Sarah, the young and pretty heiress. The marriage was blessed with four boys. Their happy household increased also in possessions and in slaves; the living chattels were treated with a humanity not customary on the island.

Most of the French masters ignored the presence of their slaves while discussing the explosive events that transpired across the ocean. The Negroes thus learned about a Reign of Terror that guillotined the French nobility. The slaves, profiting from the action of the Jacobins in Paris, planned a massacre of their own white overlords. Now kindness at the Moise hacienda paid off. In the dead of one night in 1791, the aroused family was rushed to the quay and placed on board a vessel putting out to sea. The faithful black ringleader of the rescue party subsequently became General Moise and distinguished himself in the revolution that established a Negro Republic of Haiti.

The Moise family reached Charleston bringing along such valuables as they could grab in the hurried flight. Abraham Moise could never regain his former affluence. Accustomed to the leisurely pace of a West Indian gentleman planter, he found it difficult to support his growing family. When he died in 1809, his nine children had to pitch in to keep up the menage. Penina in her 12th year quit school for household duties. Her fingers could crochet lace and needle embroidery, which was sold to help pay for necessities. But never was a girl more eager for knowledge. Every spare moment found her in the attic reading voraciously whatever she could lay hands on. A legend has come down that Penina would even study by moonlight, rarely possible in Charleston, and only when the atmosphere is exceptionally clear. Self taught, Penina Moise became a marvel of extensive information.

Such hunger for learning is, of couse, intuitive. Yet environment exerts a powerful stimulus. In the early 19th century, Charleston was one of the few cultural centers of the young republic. Hugh S. Legare, a Huguenot lawyer and statesman, wrote stately prose. In novels depicting Indian customs and Southern life, William Gilmore Simms rivaled James Fenimore Cooper. The Unitarian minister Samuel Gilman contributed to the leading magazines. The College of Charleston, operating since 1790 and oldest among American municipal colleges, actively influenced scientific pursuit and literary expression.

Jewish life, always reacting to favorable environment, was influenced by Charleston's benign, tolerant, if somewhat snooty intelligentsia. The community of 1200 souls, largest in North or South America, contained, besides business men, lawyers, artists, educators, physicians and writers. Isaac Harby, educator and critic and playwright, edited *The Quiver,* a literary weekly, and later owned a newspaper. Jacob Newton Cardozo, an economist, was publisher and editor of the influential *Southern Patriot.* Jacob de la Motta, pharmacist and physician, wrote scientific articles for the *Charleston Courier.* Joshua Cantor, Theodore Moise, and Solomon Nunes Carvalho painted portraits and miniatures. Never before nor after did Charleston boast such a cultural efflorescence.

These examples no doubt affected Penina Moise, bursting with eagerness to wield her facile pen for light and even humorous composition. She became a steady contributor to the *Boston Daily Times, Charleston Courier, Washington Times, New Orleans Commercial Times,* and wrote for *Godey's Lady's Book,* a popular periodical of large circulation. Authors are often overlooked in their own locales. Recognition therefore was no doubt pleasing when her articles were in demand for the 1845 *Charleston Year Book,* a publication devoted to literary efforts of select home talent.

Penina's sensitivity, depth of feeling, frustrations, sympathies, or loyalties found a better vehicle in verse. An early collection of her poems was printed in 1835 entitled *Fancy's Sketch Book.* The steady output of her poetry appeared in the columns of the *Charleston Courier* and other journals. Her poems and articles on Jewish subjects can be found in Isaac Leeser's magazine, *The Occident.* Generally the verse flows smoothly, sometimes with a humorous touch as she comments on passing events or displays civic and sectional pride. Hardly rising above standard Southern thinking, the poetess has been blamed for never breaking a lance in behalf of the enslaved Negro. Militant suffragettes criticized her aloofness in their struggle for women's rights.

Perhaps too much was expected of the gentle spinster with plain feature and failing eyesight, neuralgia racked and steeped in poverty. Penina was hardly the fiery prophetess swayed by violent emotion. She could, however, be stirred by the wrongs inflicted upon her persecuted co-religionists. She displays passion and compassion in such poems as "The Jew of Damascus" or "The Rejection of the Jew Bill in the House of Lords."

Her most important contribution consists of 190 hymns, composed in the declining half of her lengthy life with its full measure of physical and mental pain. To this task, Penina Moise brought spiritual strivings and pious resignation, a pure heart and contrite spirit, together with a passionate love for Judaism. Unto this day no one in the English language has excelled the extent and quality of her synagogal odes. They undoubtedly lack the majestic sweep and moral grandeur of Biblical Psalmody; yet they do display humility, sincere feeling, earnest faith, thanksgiving, and saintly devotion.

These hymns were written to fill a need. In the early 1840s Beth Elohim of Charleston reformed its ritual, with a portion of the service to be conducted in the vernacular. But for the synagogue there were neither prayers nor songs in English. Penina attempted hymns with success; they were included in the service and more were printed in the Prayer Book. Newly organized Temples introduced her religious poems into the service. They are still used in Charleston, in other American cities, and even abroad where English is spoken.

The last 25 of her 83 years were spent in total darkness. Her eyes, strained in early youth from knitting and extensive study, finally went blind. To this affliction were added insomnia and neuralgia. The necessity of earning a living added to her burden. Yet nothing could dampen her ardor nor destroy that cheerful sweetness peculiar to the blind, which is a source of constant wonder to the seeing. Together with her widowed sister, the aging poetess opened a school for girls. Students showered her with love, veneration, and vied with each other for the privilege of serving their "Miss Penina". On Yom Kippur each pupil took her turn for an hour reading the prayers as the aged woman in a calico dress sat on a high-backed rocker, dark glasses shading her sightless eyes. On Friday afternoons, the humble cottage would become a literary salon, where intellectuals discussed the latest works of George Eliot, Charlotte Brontë, and Sir Walter Scott.

Resignation without bitterness is reflected in the dying request of the modest, shrinking soul that knew much suffering, of the old blind celibate never thrilled by husband or child. "Lay no flowers on my grave. They are for those who lived in the sun, and I have always lived in the shadow."

BOOK ON SEMINOLE WAR
BY M. M. COHEN.

1836

LIEUTENANT MEYER M. COHEN

In the Seminole War

On January 1, 1836 James L. Pettigru, one of America's ablest lawyers, addressed a public meeting called by the Mayor of Charleston. He was followed by Robert Y. Hayne, recently the opponent of Daniel Webster in one of the greatest debates ever heard in the U. S. Senate. These and other speakers dealt with the atrocities of the Indians against the white residents in Florida.

The sparse Florida settlements were in danger of annihilation. Chief Osceola, energetic and resourceful, was bragging he would transform St. Augustine and Jacksonville into Seminole villages. Nor did this boast seem altogether vain. Before the extensive use of telegraphs, steamships or railroads, the Federal Government needed time to assemble a force out of its 6000 regular troops scattered on both sides of the Mississippi. Meanwhile the wily Indian could burn, kill, destroy, and disappear into the Everglades, inaccessible to the U. S. infantry or cavalry. The small white colony in Florida had good cause for panic.

The widely read novels of Sir Walter Scott had conditioned the

255

public mind in the South towards chivalry and adventure. Into romance the speakers injected enthusiasm and called for knight-errants to succor their imperiled fellow Southerners. Inspired by the eloquence, many raised their hands and volunteered on the spot. Dispatches began coming from St. Augustine for men to relieve the oldsters and invalids who were guarding the city. Jacksonville begged for aid as "starvation and murder were staring them in the face."

Among those who raised their hands was Meyer M. Cohen. He even delivered a talk and immediately became one of the *Washington Volunteers*. Public speaking evidently did not faze him, since he was serving a term in the South Carolina Legislature. He had passed the bar in 1829 and presided for two years as a magistrate. Scott and the romantic movement no doubt affected him, for his writings are full of Latin quotations, classical allusions, English poetry, and literary aesthetics. His style shows the influence of teaching in the "English and Classical Seminary" which he operated in Charleston from 1824 to 1828.

Bad weather delayed until January 27th the sailing of the *Dolphin* carrying several companies of volunteers. Normally such argonauts earn a sentence in local history and are forgotten. But this Odyssey had its Homer on board. Meyer Cohen sensed from the start the historic aspect of the expedition. He made notes "sometimes on horseback, and others supine on the earth. . . . reclining against a tree, my desk being a cartridge box. . . . or scribbling under my rain beaten tent, my pine torch flaring in the wind."

The inciting force that motivated Cohen and his companions reads like a page out of a sentimental Victorian novel. "We felt that 'now's the day and now's the hour' to sacrifice something of self; to leave for a while the peaceful pursuits of commerce and the probable employ of time and capital; to give up the student's pen for the soldier's sword and his book for a shield, and to exchange the hammer of the worthy mechanic for the musket of the militiaman. . . . Animated by these impulses, we resolved to hasten to their aid in Florida; what we *could* do we would do, and do at once; not withholding our help in her hour of utmost need, and when all peril should be past, supporting her half recovered citizens with our tardy embraces."

In the same vein, Cohen describes the departure from Charleston and their reception in Savannah. The usual disillusion of rookies is playfully touched on with humor and good-natured punning. "Genteel young fellows about town . . . cooks we had never been . . . but cooks we became for lack of lackeys and minced our unspiced meat most *gingerly* and drank rye coffee without wry faces. . . . So we laughed bitterly at bitter things . . . and becoming as merry as punch, punched each other with solids for want of liquid punch. For some had a wit at their fingers' ends, who had none on their tongues."

Their arrival in St. Augustine brought a cheering sense of security. Old residents knelt in thanksgiving. For 30 days the new sentries stood guard and could catch rapid glances at Indians prowling near the city. Yet nothing would happen and time began to hang heavy. Constant guard duty, drilling several times each day, routine discipline strictly enforced became irksome. Yet their presence warded off attacks by an enemy, whose greatest glory was tomahawking and scalping.

To overcome boredom, a tiny sheet appeared with the opening notice: "We beg leave to offer (not to the public, but to the privates) a paper, which as it will be published every Tuesday and Saturday evening, may not inappropriately be called *The Sunday Morning Herald and Volunteers Gazette*." The editors A. G. Mackey and M. M. Cohen went on to say—"the ink has been stolen, the paper borrowed, and the pens purchased on a credit which will never be repaid." In each issue appeared pleasantries typical of the barracks: "Wanted in garrison coarse canvass to drink coffee thru. . . . One of the volunteers is reported to have dislocated his jaw in cracking a U. S. biscuit. . . . A Quartermaster—an officer who gives no quarter (of venison). . . . A rule of the garrison: Not more than 14 persons are hereafter to use the same tooth brush."

With the arrival of General Eustis, the volunteers are relieved by U. S. regulars. Among those who petitioned to stay on, Meyer Cohen is selected for active duty and commissioned an officer in the *Left Wing* commanded by General Winfield Scott. Thus he gets the opportunity to record incidents he witnessed in the Seminole War. He would probably have remained longer but was called home to attend the session of the State Legislature. On June 20, 1836, he leaves for Charleston, having served for five months.

His literary talents had long been recognized and friends urged writing a book of his experiences. Evidently he had undertaken the task since the expedition began. Yet it seems incredible, with his many duties, legislative or legal, as well as social, how quickly the manuscript was in the press. Before 1836 was over, publishers in Charleston and New York printed *Notices of Florida and the Campaigns,* by M. M. Cohen, an officer of the Left Wing.

Cohen's hurry about publication is regrettable. He had the source material for a more important work. Yet in spite of hasty composition, it preserved the valuable information of an eye witness. After reviewing the story of Florida's exploration, it tells of the early Indian tribes. From David Levy of St. Augustine, subsequently Senator Yulee, he obtained important transcripts of meetings between Federal agents and Indian chiefs, whose speeches cast light upon the causes of the Seminole War. His portrayal of Osceola is graphic. Nor does he fail to criticize the strategy of U. S. commanders, including General Winfield Scott, whose personal character is highly extolled. The massacre of Major Dade and his 110 soldiers moves him profoundly. It might have cheered Cohen to know that the name of the martyr soldier, preserved in Dade County, has become widely known through the marvelous growth of Greater Miami.

His next move is strange. One would think a lawyer and magistrate, a teacher and writer, a legislator with the added prestige of a war veteran might have a bright future in a city with a distinguished Jewish community. But in 1837, Meyer M. Cohen moved to New Orleans and faded into obscurity.

1837

COLONEL LEON DYER

Venturous Yet Solid

THE DYER FAMILY of Galveston acquired their name by adoption. When their ancestor Philip Heim came to America around 1812, he was befriended by a prominent New Englander, who claimed descent from Sir Edward Dyer, a commander of Queen Elizabeth's fleet which helped to destroy the Spanish Armada. According to his American descendant, the Admiral had protected homeless Jews. While Jews in the 16th century could use plenty of protection, the question is which Jews he protected, as there were very few in England and those in Spain lived in disguise. Out of gratitude to the New Englander, or his naval ancestor, Philip Heim adopted the distinguished un-Jewish name of John Maximilian Dyer.

Perhaps Philip Heim resented the name forced upon him in 1808 by the Frankfort government. In the United States he could easily reinstate the original Emanuel Gershon Feist. The name Gershon evoked pride in the family that boasted descent from Levi ben Gershon, the noted thinker Gersonides of the 14th century. It also claimed kinship with Rabenu Gershom, the Light of the Exile, who lived in Mainz in the year 1000. But the written evidence of such an exalted pedigree was destroyed when the Frankfort ghetto burned down while Gershon's father was furnishing supplies to Napoleon's army. With the *yiches brief* (letters of pedigree) annihilated, some members stretched the family antiquity to Shebuel, the son of Gershon, the son of Moses, recorded in Verse 24, Chapter 26, First Book of Chronicles in the Old Testament.

Yet the adoption of an English name did not signify any desire to escape their Jewish heritage. In fact, the Dyer attachment continued strong, and John Maximilian headed a group for incorporating the first synagogue in Baltimore. The legislature had, several years earlier, agreed reluctantly to abolish the Christian oath for office holding in Maryland. The struggle engendered bitterness, and the Assembly had its chance to display bigotry. Ordinarily an act to incorporate a congregation is merely routine. It was favorably reported and passed the first reading without comment. But spiteful forces were at work and at its second reading the bill was defeated. The committee that reported favorably then had to move for a rehearing and pilot the bill through. John Maximilian Dyer became president of the Baltimore Hebrew Congregation, the first in Maryland.

In Baltimore, he opened a butcher shop which has been incorrectly described as the first meat packing house in the land. His son Leon worked with him and in 1834 helped organize the United Hebrew Benevolent Society of Baltimore. Strong in character as well as physique, Leon was popular with the masses. With the Christian oath removed, he was able to hold several minor city appointments. But in 1834 he rendered his city an important service. Public safety was disturbed by bread riots. In the absence of the Mayor, Leon Dyer is said to have acted in his place for ten days. With pluck and leadership, besides tact and persuasion, he calmed the excitement and restored normalcy.

In 1835, Leon had occasion to go down to New Orleans on

some business. The trip must have been of a temporary nature, for the Baltimore Hebrew Congregation had just elected him trustee. Yet in Louisiana, the Governor appointed him Quartermaster General of the State Militia. About this time calls for help came from Texas. The American settlers, who had gone down with Stephen Austin and those who followed, seceded from Mexico to form the Republic of Texas. The Mexicans could not acquiesce in this rebellion. The might of Mexico was posed for attack upon the new born state organized by American colonists who came in on land grants issued by the Mexican government. But the massacre at the Alamo infuriated every one north of the Rio Grande. Leon Dyer, together with several hundred citizens, left New Orleans and came to rescue. Commissioned a Major by President Burnet, Dyer with his company reached San Jacinto just after the battle; they engaged in the clean-up campaign that secured independence.

Another minor war soon broke out in Florida. The Seminole Indians felt happier without the supervision of their hunting grounds by white overlords. Led by Osceola, the braves attacked and exterminated a company of 110 regulars under Major Dade. Again the entire country became aghast. Leon Dyer joined the U. S. Army and served as ranking Major in the staff of General Winfield Scott, while George B. McClellan, the future Civil War commander and presidential candidate, was but a lieutenant.

Returning to Baltimore, the Major increased the range and volume of his packing house. From 1840 to 1847 he held the presidency of the Baltimore Hebrew Congregation and devoted his strenuous efforts to building the granite double-tower synagogue on the corner of Lloyd and Water Street. The adventure in Texas influenced the course of other members of his family. His brother Isidore Dyer, his sister Rosanna, and her husband Joseph Osterman left Baltimore to settle in Galveston where they attained prominence. Isidore became president of the Union Marine and Fire Insurance Company of Galveston and devoted his time to religion and philanthropy. Half the residuary of his estate he left to Congregation B'nai Israel and the other half to the Protestant Orphans' Home. His widowed sister Rosanna bequeathed the Osterman Building to the poor and the bulk of her fortune to charity.

The veteran of two wars would, no doubt, have been content to attend peacefully his business and congregational duties. But his country called for enlistments in the war against Mexico. Again he found himself under the command of his former chief, General Winfield Scott. Now he was Quartermaster General with the rank of Colonel. On being mustered out of service, he returned home, no longer in good health, and unwilling to serve longer as president of the synagogue. The Congregation presented him with a medal for years of faithful service.

In 1848 Leon Dyer joined the great trek to California. He could have sailed around the Horn but preferred the more dangerous route by crossing with horse and wagon the vast plains, the high mountains, the parched deserts. He was confronted with the perils of Indian sniping, the scarcity of water, of food and the amenities of civilized living. He reached San Francisco and made up that small band of pioneers who gathered above a store to celebrate Yom Kippur in 1849. We do not know whether he went prospecting, or came for business, or in search of health or excitement. Several years later he returned east and in 1853 married a relative out of Mainz. Thirty years later he died in Louisville at 76, and his body was sent to Galveston for burial.

Lack of information makes it difficult to estimate Leon Dyer. Evidently, he displayed exceptional traits to justify important commissions and assignments. According to Rabbi Henry Cohen of Galveston, Dyer was in the guard of honor that accompanied Santa Anna to Washington after the Mexican Dictator's capture by the Texans at the battle of San Jacinto. The Dyers of Galveston could show a letter of appreciation from Santa Anna to their father. In 1852 President Millard Fillmore sent him to Berlin with confidential despatches for the Prussian government.

The career of Leon Dyer might indicate some curious contradictions. An official of the synagogue, he fought a duel in Texas, presumably on strong provocation. A sound man of business, he volunteered and fought in three wars. In San Francisco, he chanted the all-day Yom Kippur services for the assembled worshippers, yet broke the strict tenets of Orthodoxy in his restless wayfaring. A flair for action and adventure seemed imbedded in the patient organizer, the solid business man, the synagogue builder.

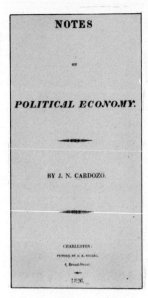

NOTES

ON

POLITICAL ECONOMY.

BY J. N. CARDOZO.

CHARLESTON:
PRINTED BY A. E. MILLER,
4, Broad-Street.
1826.

BOOK WRITTEN BY CARDOZO.

1838

JACOB NEWTON CARDOZO

Editor-Economist

THE CARDOZOS achieved distinction even before Justice Benjamin N. Cardozo was to shed lustre upon the U. S. Supreme Court. The name is too prevalent in Spain for tracing the family's origin. The first Cardozo of the American clan landed in New York about 1752. His son David Nunez found the lush climate of Charleston more agreeable than the colder city of his birth. When the Revolution started, he joined Captain Richard Lushington's company, called the *Jews' Brigade* because of its large Jewish enrollment.

In 1779 the company fought a distinguished battle at Beaufort. Encouraged, General Lincoln and Count D'Estaing conceived the plan of driving the British out of Savannah. Sergeant-Major Cardozo is reputed to have been the front non-commissioned officer to lead the storming party that assailed the Savannah fortifications. In this assault, called afterwards "The Forlorn Hope", Count Pulaski lost his life. The repulsed troops retreated to defend Charleston, which the English captured in 1780. Sergeant Cardozo was taken prisoner. He lies in Charleston's Coming Street Cemetery. His widow received the pension Congress voted to the "G. I's." of the War for Liberty.

His son Jacob Newton, born in Savannah in 1786, moved with his parents to Charleston ten years later. They seemed in poor circumstances, for at 12 he was apprenticed to learn a trade. The boy worked as a lumber clerk, all the time reading widely and acquiring the rudiments of an education. On reaching 25, he delivered before the Mothulogic Society an Oration on the Literary Character, which was promptly printed. Five years later Cardozo could hold down the editorial post of *The Southern Patriot*. This paper, one among four in Charleston, fell into financial straits. The U. S. Government held against it a lien of $20,000, which exceeded its value. Cardozo acquired *The Southern Patriot* in 1823 by replacing the lien with a mortgage. He hoped to clear it off with the proceeds received from government printing.

When John Quincy Adams became President, the Secretary of State, Henry Clay, gave the Federal printing to another. Cardozo could not meet his obligations, but help came from another source. Senator Robert Y. Hayne, later famous for his great debate with Daniel Webster, introduced a bill authorizing the Secretary of the Treasury to reduce the debt of J. N. Cardozo and extend his payments consistent with equity and justice. This bill became law with the signature of President Andrew Jackson.

Cardozo's reputation as a student of commerce and finance grew with the publication of his *Notes on Political Economy*, which appeared in 1826. The modern historian Joseph Dorfman declared in his book *The Economic Mind in American History* that Cardozo was "the only man in pre-Civil War America whose mind operated on that high level of abstraction that characterized the work of Ricardo and his school." Through *The Southern Patriot*, he was in a position of influence during the crises of Nullification that almost brought the country to war in 1832.

The issue between South Carolina and the U. S. began with the

"Tariff of Abomination" that was passed in 1828 to promote the growth of manufacture in the Northeast. But high prices for finished goods were strangling the economy of the agricultural South. Thus when Congress enacted the 1832 tariff, a South Carolina convention met in Charleston and adopted the Ordinance of Nullification, which announced the dangerous doctrine that a state might declare a Federal law null and void. Feverish excitement gripped the nation. President Jackson prepared to enforce the Tariff Law with the Army and Navy and civil strife seemed imminent.

A time of trouble calls for cool heads to calm the hot-heads. Fortunately Henry Clay was in the Senate. With a genius for negotiating settlements, America's greatest compromiser was able to reconcile at top levels the clashing sectional interests. But in the grass roots public opinion has to be moulded and nursed. In this capacity Jacob Newton Cardozo fulfilled a useful and necessary function. His reputation as a sound economist had been established by his writings. His views on free trade with foreign countries were known and respected. He advocated the South's manufacture of textiles as a liberation from the cotton mills of England. Above all he opposed the high tariffs set up in Washington. His editorials were widely read and quoted "for the solidity and extent of his views on political economy, and occasionally by the felicity of his literary criticisms," as phrased by the eminent Unitarian Minister, Samuel Gillman, in the *North American Review*.

But Cardozo refused to play the game safely by catering to the prejudices of the solid majority. He demurred to the most dangerous issue. In Charleston, the hotbed of Secessionists, he had the courage to oppose Nullification. Public excitement ran high and nerves were frayed. Duels, though outlawed, were quite fashionable. Yet he hammered away at the evils of Secession as the consequence of nullifying the Constitution. Perhaps he knew his editorials had a calming effect on the South Carolina firebrands. Possibly he played an important part in the public accept-

ance of the Henry Clay compromise, in his State's rescinding of
the Nullification Ordinance. One thing is significant: Washington
valued his influence. The succeeding administration of Martin
Van Buren selected *The Southern Patriot,* of all newspapers in
the nation, to advocate and popularize its financial policy, "the
sub-treasury scheme", before presenting it to Congress.

A better editor, apparently, than businessman, Cardozo had to
take in a partner, who in 1845 became the sole owner of *The
Southern Patriot.* He next acquired *The Evening News* but sold
it two years later, remaining however the managing editor until
1861. The 75-year-old journalist then severed his ties and moved
back to Savannah, his birthplace. During the War between the
States he worked as editor in Mobile and Atlanta. The economist
influenced the journalist. He was the first to introduce "Cotton
Statements", which has since become a regular feature in the
financial section of newspapers. When 84 years old, his *Reminiscences of Charleston* won the prize in a contest run by the Board
of Trade. He died in Savannah at the age of eighty-nine.

The self-taught economist, the self-made journalist did not
fulfill the expectations he aroused. On reaching his pinnacle during the Nullification crises, his decline was gradual yet sure.
Cardozo was what a later period would call reactionary. He belonged to the Adam Smith school of a century back and preached
laissez faire to a generation long since convinced. The utilitarian
doctrines of Jeremy Bentham and David Ricardo, to wit, that
society is best served by self-interest without interference from
authority was pretty shopworn. To advocate suffrage restricted
with property qualifications after Andrew Jackson's democratic
landslide seems absurd. His argument that the slave in the South
enjoyed a fairer share of his labor than wage earners in other
lands smacked more of the apologist than the economist.

1839

JUDAH TOURO

Philanthropist

LAFAYETTE's second visit to the U. S. A. helped to revive memories of the glorious Revolution. The twin deaths of Jefferson and Adams on July 4th 1826, the 50th anniversary that marked the signing of the Declaration of Independence, brought home the painful fact that the surviving heroes of the war were dwindling. The public was in a mood for glorifying the events of what began to seem a heroic age. Lafayette's presence in Boston during 1826 was a fit occasion for laying the cornerstone of the monument that would memorialize the battle fought on Bunker Hill half a century earlier.

The emotions evoked at the ceremony evaporated as the Frenchman left the Hub City. For 13 years, the obelisk remained a foundation stone. The committee appealed in vain for funds, and even the superlative eloquence of Daniel Webster fell on deaf ears. In 1839 Amos Laurence, of Boston's bluest blood, offered $10,000 on condition the balance be subscribed. No one responded. It appeared as if the shaft would never rise.

One day a letter came from far away New Orleans. It contained a check of $10,000 signed by one Judah Touro; a covering note requested that the donor's name remain anonymous. The committee probably suspected a hoax. Who ever heard of Judah Touro? Only a crackpot would send a check for a large sum with so strange a reservation. In those frugal days, philanthropy was practiced as rarely as witchcraft. But the check not only represented real cash; its maker Judah Touro was another "merchant of the first eminence," as Ezra Styles would have phrased it. Boston's largest enterprises, the business firms of Henry Lee and Walter E. Twing, spoke in high praise of Judah Touro, their agent and correspondent in New Orleans.

On the eve of the battle of Bunker Hill in 1775, Judah Touro was born at Newport. His father, Isaac Touro, was Hazzan during the height of the community's affluence. With the British capture of the city, import and export ceased; many of the Jewish residents scattered to other colonies. Reverend Touro had Tory leanings and left for New York. He then settled in Kingston, Jamaica, where he soon died. His widow and children sailed for Boston and found a home with her brother, the wealthy, influential, and public-spirited Moses Michael Hays, whose portrait by Gilbert Stuart reveals something of the *magnifico*.

In a patriotic atmosphere of tolerance and altruism, Judah was reared as one of the family. His future seemed bright enough. There was room in the varied and intensive enterprises of Moses Hays. But love entered and crossed his life. Love, deep and strong, gripped him and his cousin Catherine. Such a marriage would seem logical and even desirable in a small social group with religious taboos against intermarriage. But Moses Hays entertained a strong aversion against any union between cousins. Nothing could shake this deep-seated prejudice, regardless of the sorrow it brought upon his nearest and dearest. After attempts to break the attachment, he discharged Judah, ordered him out of the house, and forbade Catherine to see or communicate with her cousin.

Brokenhearted, Judah Touro sailed for New Orleans, which was under French rule. In 1802 this city had 8000 inhabitants including Negro slaves. The air buzzed with rumors about becoming part of the Federal Union. Touro landed almost penniless. Immediately he was infected with the boundless optimism of the people that prosperity would follow the annexation by the U. S. A. He opened a store and began to thrive. Old established firms in Boston made him their advisor and shipped large consignments of merchandise. The influx following the Louisiana Purchase brought prosperity to New Orleans and made Judah Touro one of the wealthy men of the nation.

The home environment of Moses Hays had a lasting influence. Touro absorbed patriotism together with veneration for Judaism. There he learned to enter into friendships with worthy Jews or Christians, to distribute charities regardless of creed. The 40 year old successful business man enlisted in the fighting forces of Andrew Jackson and was wounded in the Battle of New Orleans. His Christian friend Rezin D. Shepherd carried him to safety and saved his life.

Philanthropy was virtually forced upon Touro. Never married, he lived in rugged simplicity, nursing the memory of his Catherine. What should he do with the money that kept piling up? He thus became the earliest of American Jewish philanthropists. His benefactions were distributed with equable impartiality among Jews, Catholics, and Protestants. His famous will attracted wide attention and became an historic document bearing testimony to broad humanitarian sentiments. His bequests went to synagogues, orphanages and almshouses; to hospitals, schools, libraries, and charities; to Rabbis and Protestant Ministers; to individual Christians and Jews; to a Fireman's Association, a Seaman's Home, and benevolent societies; to the indigent of Jerusalem and the upkeep of the Synagogue and Jewish Cemetery at Newport; to the purchase of the "Old Stone Mill" allegedly build by the Vikings of Leif Ericson and the adjacent grounds, now known as Touro Park in Newport.

The gift for completion of the Bunker Hill monument received wide appreciation. The dedication took place in the presence of the President of the United States. Daniel Webster delivered the famous oration that has become an American classic. A dinner followed at Faneuil Hall in Boston, and the names of Touro and Laurence were placed on the platform under the American eagle. These verses attributed to Oliver Wendell Holmes were read:

> *"Amos and Judah—venerated names,*
> *Patriarch and Prophet press their equal claims,*
> *Like generous coursers running 'neck in neck,'*
> *Each aids the work by giving it a check*
> *Christian and Jew, they carry out one plan*
> *For though of different faith, each is in heart a man."*

Judah Touro died in his 79th year. All of frivolous, pleasure loving New Orleans virtually went into mourning. Tributes were paid by the press and the ministry to the humble man whose deeds were simple kindness, whose career could be summed up with the word philanthropy. The body was carried by ship to its birthplace. Newport decreed a public funeral and tendered the city's hospitality to all who came to honor the deceased. Jews no longer lived in the city, yet the 18th century synagogue was over crowded with public officials and prominent residents. Crowds stood reverently outside waiting to accompany the remains to the cemetery made famous by Longfellow. Fifteen feet from the grave lies Catherine Hays; she never married and died two weeks before Judah Touro.

1840

ISAAC LEESER

Orthodox Leader

Aᴅᴠᴏᴄᴀᴛᴇ, spokesman, editor, Rabbi, orator, teacher, educator, and writer, Isaac Leeser was the first to attain large scale leadership in American Jewry. Louis Marshall was the second. Neither was elected nor universally obeyed. Yet by popular consensus both stood out as top leaders in their respective eras.

After graduating from a German Gymnasium (high school) and completing several tractates of the Talmud, 18 year old Isaac Leeser crossed the ocean to accept a job in his uncle's store at Richmond, Va. Modest and humble, he found ample recreation in voracious reading at such spare time as could be snatched from "kolsche" work or assistance to the Reverend of the small synagogue. The calm of his studious life was broken by one of those slanderous attacks that come periodically upon Jews and Judaism. In 1828 a New York paper reprinted a series of articles that appeared in the *London Quarterly Review*, defaming the character and faith of Israel. The obscure young store clerk came to the defense in the Richmond *Whig*, with an answer of six essays that attracted attention. The trustees of Philadelphia's Mikveh Israel, in need of a hazan, immediately offered the post to the 22 year old newcomer, hardly yet at home in the English language.

Isaac Leeser was never ordained for the rabbinate; yet never did a formally trained rabbi acquit himself more creditably. If learning, leadership, influence, zeal, labor, understanding are necessary priestly qualifications, then he exercised the rabbinic functions with high distinction. His fame spread far beyond the Philadelphia congregation. His advice was sought and recommendations accepted by old communities on the Atlantic seaboard and the new congregations springing up as far as the Pacific coast. He traveled far and wide, enthralling audiences with his eloquence and learning. Until the Reform movement led by Wise, Einhorn and Lilienthal got under way, Isaac Leeser remained the unofficial Chief Rabbi of all American Jewry.

His prestige and authority were greatly enhanced with the appearance in 1843 of the *Occident and American Jewish Advocate*. Several such periodicals had expired shortly after birth, but this magazine was the first to succeed in American Jewish journalism. For a quarter century, it was the mirror that reflected the happenings and controversies, the events and anxieties, the gains and recessions in Jewish life at home and abroad. Year after year, Isaac Leeser hammered away in editorials and articles at vital issues that stirred the Jewish community from within and at threats posed from without. Today the researcher finds a treasure trove in the 26 bound volumes that contain the inner record, the public struggles, the social documentation of a crucial period in American and Jewish history.

After a decade, the Occident's supremacy began to be disputed by the *American Israelite*. Its publisher Isaac M. Wise, founder of Reform Judaism, also challenged the leadership of Isaac Leeser. This feud, duplicated a half century later by the rivalry between Louis Marshall and Stephen S. Wise, reflected the bitter antagonism between Orthodoxy and Reform that has not yet completely abated. Leeser became champion for Traditional Judaism. Yet his early liberalism was frowned upon by the officialdom of his synagogue. He advocated innovations that looked quite radical to early 19th century conservatism. He introduced set prayers in the vernacular and was responsible for the widespread adoption of the sermon in English. Due to his proddings, the gracious and fashionable Rebecca Gratz began in 1838 her Sunday School for Mikveh Israel. This experiment became the parent and model for the vast network of Sunday Schools, later to be copied and imitated in the Reform, Orthodox, and Conservative segments of American Judaism.

The year 1853 saw the appearance of Leeser's translation of the Hebrew Bible, his greatest literary achievement. It proved a godsend to readers who could not understand the Torah in the original and who had recourse only to the King James Authorized Version with its headnotes and overtones of Christian interpretation. Leeser's Scriptures filled an imperative need in Jewish homes of all English speaking lands until replaced in 1917 by the translation of the Jewish Publication Society of America.

The Jewish community of Leeser's day hardly numbered 100,000 souls. Yet he anticipated the needs of a century later when the population would exceed 5,000,000. Imaginative intuition prompted him to pioneer in every field of Jewish endeavor. He advocated Jewish hospitals that would prevent over pious nuns from baptizing dying patients to save them from Satan's hell fire. He called attention to flagrant abuses in dispensing charities. His ideas as to overall communal responsibility in collecting and disbursing funds by a central agency gave rise to the *United Hebrew Charities of Philadelphia.* Here we have the embryo of the Federations that would later raise gigantic sums for local, national and overseas relief. He urged agricultural settlements that would take the *luftmenschen* from peddling on highways or petty traders out of the market place.

Instinctively Leeser sensed the need of unity for American Jews. Perhaps disturbing news from abroad pointed to the necessity for organized effort. The recrudescence in 1840 of the medieval blood libel in Damascus, for the first time in a Moslem land, was followed by discrimination against American Jewish citizens traveling in Switzerland. In 1841 he made an unsuccessful attempt to organize the American Jewish community. The Board of Delegates of American Israelites, largely due to the labors of Isaac Leeser, functioned from 1859 to 1878 as a union of congregations. Forerunner of both the American Jewish Committee and the American Jewish Congress of the following century, it performed yeoman's service and remained the only authentic spokesman for Jews in the U. S. A. until absorbed by the Union of American Hebrew Congregations.

But his deepest interest lay in education. To Leeser the preservation of Judaism in its traditional form was paramount. He labored incessantly translating prayers, writing catechisms, and traveled about the land preaching, organizing congregations, installing ministers. Hoping to create a Jewish literature in English, he organized the first American Jewish Publication Society. He founded the Board of Hebrew Ministers and the Hebrew Education Society. Knowing that a laity without stimulation of a properly trained ministry could hardly stem the corrosion of creeping assimilation, he expended his last waning energies in launching Maimonides College, the first Jewish seminary for rabbis and teachers in the Western Hemisphere.

Such Herculean tasks were too onerous for the frail lonely scholar, the pock-faced bachelor whose only offspring were the institutions he created. He broke down and died in his 62nd year and left no successor behind him. In the year after his death, the *Occident* ceased publication. The Maimonides College closed after graduating four students. The Board of Delegates of American Israelites was taken over and transformed by Isaac M. Wise to become the bulwark of Reform Judaism.

1841

REFORMER
GUSTAVUS
POZNANSKI

Of Charleston

SYNAGOGUE DEDICATED
BY POZNANSKI.

Half a century was to pass before the mass exodus of East European Jewry commenced. Meanwhile the more adventurous began to straggle out of the Polish communities in a trickle. Surrounded by hate from without and stultified within by a congealing Chassidism, they had little to lose. Among these rugged individuals, Gedalia of Storchnest left Poland in 1824 and reached Germany in time to witness the reforms in the new Hamburg Temple which was spearheading a revolt against the rigidity of Orthodoxy.

He remained in Hamburg and absorbed the language and spirit of the Reform movement. The snubs experienced by a Pole from Germans probably caused him to look beyond the seas for a more inviting world. His assets consisted of a pleasing voice, a shrewd opportunism, a knowledge of the intricate Kosher cult, and a smattering of Talmud overlaid with the new *Jüdische Wissenschaft* initiated by Leopold Zunz and his coterie—surely a sufficient stock in trade for a livelihood among the naive brethren in far away provincial America. The name Gedalia became transposed to Gustavus Poznanski.

Shearith Israel in New York hired him as shohet; in the absence of the *hazan* he officiated. But this did not satisfy the ambitious Gustavus and he sought out the leader of American Jewry in Philadelphia. Isaac Leeser was evidently impressed with the native ability and capacity for leadership of the Polish newcomer, whose orthodoxy he took for granted. Nor did the neophyte disclose his leanings towards the Hamburg reforms. The doughty champion of traditional Judaism had no qualms about recommending Poznanski as spiritual leader to the old aristocratic community in Charleston, S. C.

In 1836 Kahal Kodesh Beth Elohim elected him as their "Reverend Hazan". The new leader immediately effected a revival in religious life, which had stagnated since the energies generated for Reform a decade earlier by Isaac Harby had died down. The new "rabbi" made himself indispensable while studying the parishioners. After two years he was able to wangle a life contract from the vestry. Shortly thereafter a fire swept Charleston and burned the 46 year old synagogue to ashes. The fire proved to be as beneficial as it was disastrous. The community concentrated its efforts on building a House of Prayer worthy of its fame. Poznanski sensed the prosperity that would result from feverish rebuilding in the Charleston area affected by the fire. He got into real estate and reaped what to him seemed a fortune.

The Reformers, after Harby's death, conformed outwardly without being inwardly reconciled to the synagogue majority. They increased numerically as their ideas took deeper root. Hesitant about making a public issue, they nevertheless sensed an opportune moment for asking concessions. They presented a petition for installing an organ in the magnificent synagogue about to be completed. Their request seemed destined to go the way of Harby's memorial of a generation earlier. But help came from a totally unexpected source. The Polish born hazan, a pillar of Orthodoxy, approved the daring innovation. The membership overruled the objection of the trustees by a vote of 46 to 40.

In 1841 Poznanski dedicated the new structure with a fitting ceremonial. In his discourse the Reverend Hazan not only vindicated the restoration of the organ in the synagogue as enhancing the human voice in prayer; he also advocated the use of English for parts of the service. He cut the ground from under future Zionism with the passionate declamation, as the climax of his soaring oration: "This synagogue is our *temple,* this city our *Jerusalem,* this happy land our *Palestine.*"

The hazan somehow, consciously or unwittingly, stimulated discord between the advocates for Reform and the defenders of the status quo. The organ became the central irritant. Both factions simply would not hold services together. A device was tried by way of compromise: each group to use the synagogue on alternating Saturdays. But the conservatives withdrew, resigned their rights to the building, the cemetery, the perpetual fund, and formed Shearith Israel, a new congregation for worship according to Orthodox traditional practice.

The fight over the organ, as the conservatives predicted, was simply the opening skirmish for more drastic changes. Its symbolism became clearer when the Reformers in control changed the constitution to require a three-fourths vote to suspend use of the organ. The next step disturbed even the radicals. In 1843 Poznanski in his Passover sermon declared observance of the second day unnecessary. The trustees had to pass a resolution that his preachment was "a violation of the constitution and calculated to create discord and anarchy."

The hazan countered that his opinions were known all along, and since lecturing was no part of his duties he would deliver no further sermons. A reaction appears to have set in, and the folly of withdrawal by the Orthodox now became obvious. In the face of rising opposition and resentments Poznanski resigned. No longer in need of a salary, he continued serving as a volunteer.

The opponents of further changes, to bolster their forces, invited the dissenters to rejoin Beth Elohim. But President Ottolengui refused to call a meeting which would allow the former members to be readmitted. Instead of applying to the courts for a writ of mandamus, the trustees held a meeting and voted in the 23 applicants. But when the president changed the lock of the synagogue to keep his opponents out, Abraham Tobias swore out a warrant. By this time it became clear that a peaceful settlement would never work.

A civil suit was instituted with each faction represented by eminent Christian counsel. The organ installation and reforms contrary to *Minhag Sephardim* were aired together with more technical matters. It took three years before the Supreme Court of South Carolina sidestepped the religious issues and decided that only the president had the legal right to call the meeting which voted in the seceders.

Gustavus Poznanski continued to serve Beth Elohim without compensation. With the years he grew in wealth, in experience, in prestige. Marriage into a respected old family secured his social standing. He now offered to retire; but the congregation would accept no resignation. He insisted however that a new minister would serve the best interests of the community.

In Albany a recent immigrant, one Isaac Meyer Wise, heard of the Charleston opening and sent his application. Invited to visit Charleston, he came by boat and was received by Poznanski heading a committee. A mutual antipathy arose with the hazan's stiff formality and studied address of welcome. In the carriage from the wharf, Poznanski offered to enlighten him as to the principles he was to defend. Wise answered, to the applause of the committee, that he came to set forth his own principles. The patronizing cantor advised the foreigner how to sit in society with arms folded. But when Poznanski offered to delete from his sermon any *Germanisms,* the future founder of American Reform Judaism exploded: "If there are any, you will substitute *Polisms* for them. I speak German better than you and write better English than you will ever speak."

1842

DR. ISAAC HAYS
Co-founder of A.M.A.

In Philadelphia, Samuel Hays entered the import-export business as an apprentice clerk in the brokerage office of Haym
Salomon. He worked hard to fulfill his ambitions which at the
same time gave him intellectual play. It even smacked of the
romantic when his chartered ships sailed into port carrying
the exotic wares of mysterious India. He envisioned his son broadening and extending the family business.

It therefore seemed wasteful daydreaming for Isaac to attend
the University of Pennsylvania—no doubt due to the influence
that radiated from the home of his cultured aunt, Rebecca Gratz.
Education, he argued, often impedes rather than promotes success
in business. But the father's real disappointment came when his
20 year old son, now a Bachelor of Arts, decided to study at the
medical college.

Immediately Dr. Isaac Hays displayed ability in ophthalmology,
a formidable term for the science that deals with the structure,
functions, and diseases of the eye. Within two years after gradua-

tion, he was on the staff of the Pennsylvania Infirmary of the Eye and Ear. Technically his most important contribution to American medicine remains in that field. He ranks among the very earliest to study color blindness and detect astigmatism. His invention of a special knife to operate on cataracts has recently elicited from Dr. A. A. Hubbel the authoritative statement: "Not only did this instrument admirably serve the purpose for which it was designed by Dr. Hays, but it is still an excellent knife for incision." Hays' account of the first glasses prescribed in this country for astigmatism is famous.

One might imagine that excelling in a single branch of specialized medicine would be enough for any individual. But Dr. Hays displayed unusual talent as an editor. In fact, had he devoted his energies exclusively to writing and editing he would have left a significant mark on American science. In 1820, the year Isaac Hays graduated, his teacher, Prof. Nathaniel Chapman, started *The Philadelphia Journal of the Medical and Physical Sciences.* Seven years later Dr. Chapman invited his former pupil on the editorial staff. Within a few months, Hays became sole editor. Seeing the necessity of broadening its scope, he changed the name to *American Journal of the Medical Sciences.* Thus he secured cooperation of outstanding medicos throughout the land. He remained its editor for life and was succeeded by his son Isaac Minis Hays, also a prominent physician and historian. The eminent Dr. John Billings once declared that if all the other medical literature of the period were destroyed, the real contribution of medical science would be preserved in this journal.

Nor did editorial work detract his attention from his chosen specialty. Appointed surgeon to the Wills Eye Hospital in 1834, he remained in that organization for 20 years. During that time, he edited and enlarged upon Sir William Laurence's *Treatise on Diseases of the Eye.* This work was reprinted three times and aided substantially in advancing American knowledge of the eye. Hays' American edition of Dr. T. Wharton Jones' *Principles and Practices of Ophthalmic Medicine and Surgery,* with his own original notes, was considered a valuable addition to science in that era. Hays' work on the eye received recognition when he was elected president of the Ophthalmological Society of Philadelphia.

His interests were not confined exclusively to medicine. General science and natural history also claimed his attention. His edition of Alexander Wilson's *American Ornithology* started an interesting correspondence with Charles Lucien Bonaparte. He brought out *Elements of Physics,* the revision of a work by Neil Arnott and a new edition of R. D. Hoblyn's *Dictionary of Medical Terms.* In the ante-bellum world of Andrew Jackson, not yet economically too self sufficient, nor free of youthful gaucheries, Hays conceived of an *American Cyclopedia of Practical Medicine and Surgery.* After completing and publishing two volumes, he concluded the time not yet ripe for so extensive a project.

In 1841, he became sole editor of *Hays' Journal,* which circulated for over half a century as the best of American Medical monthlies. Of *Hays' Journal* the great physician Sir William Osler said in 1929: "It is one of the few great journals in the world, and one from which it is almost possible to write the progress of American medicine during the past century."

As medical science advanced and the profession grew in numbers, in skill, in prestige, the need for a permanent national organization in the U. S. A. became evident. In 1847 a medical conference met in Philadelphia. Dr. Hays opened the convention, welcomed the delegates in behalf of the Philadelphia doctors, and took a leading part in the deliberations to form a permanent national body of physicians. His suggestions were discussed, criticized, and rejected. A generation later his ideas were incorporated in the Congress of American Physicians and Surgeons. Dr. Hays was chairman of the committee that drafted and presented a series of ethical principles for the guidance of the organization and its members. These rules of conduct in medical practice, based upon the doctrines of Thomas Purceval, were adopted at the formation of the American Medical Association. They placed the profession on the highest plane and continue as the basis of A. M. A. principles. In recognition of his work as a founder and organizer, Isaac Hays was elected the first treasurer of the American Medical Association, under the Presidency of Dr. Nathaniel Chapman, his former teacher.

The numerous activities of Dr. Hays seem bewildering. An expert oculist, he nevertheless retained a successful general practice, all the while serving on hospital staffs. Besides editing, enlarging, translating, and publishing important medical and scientific works, and the periodicals already mentioned, he established in 1843 the *Medical News* that ran until 1906. He founded the *Monthly Abstract of Medical Science,* the forerunner of the many abstracting journals that arose subsequently. An active member of important learned bodies such as the American Philosophical Society, he found time to help in organizing the Franklin Institute and served as president of ʾhe Academy of Natural Sciences of Philadelphia. Dr. Hays received formal recognition in Europe, then the world center of scientific research. Elected a member of the Royal Society for Northern Antiquities of Copenhagen, the Medical Society of Hamburg, the Universite d'Ophtalmologie of Paris, he also acted as their American correspondent.

The career of Isaac Hays appears singularly free of those tensions that often plague members of a minority as they forge ahead towards eminence. The inevitable conflicts, scientific and personal vendettas, bred by success, are even more sharply accentuated in the envious by religion or racial difference. Dr. Hays, always a member of Mikveh Israel and an active participant in Jewish communal affairs, married Sara Minis of the old Savannah family and raised his children in Judaism. A third generation American, his adjustment seems quite complete. Perhaps his good fortune stemmed from his personality. H. G. Kelly writes: "The name Isaac Hays is always associated with that which is well written and worth reading in American Medical literature. Handsome, tall, benevolent, a bland and dignified gentleman of the old school, with courteous manners and a warm heart."

1843

HENRY JONES

And the B'nai B'rith

The name of Henry Jones cannot be found in the important American Jewish histories. Both Jewish Encyclopedias simply mention him as they proceed with the progress of B'nai B'rith. Surprisingly, the Grand Lodge itself has little or no information about the origin and character, the life and personality of its founder.

Nor is this altogether surprising. Important institutions have often been initiated by unknown people. Monotheism existed before Abraham, and Hebraism had already taken form when Moses appeared. Movements that start in obscurity are dramatized with the coming of a glamorous leader. Such are the stories of many organizations that have influenced or benefited mankind.

In New York twelve obscure men met on October 13, 1843 to discuss a project they had been talking about with each other. Not quite at home in English, they conversed in German, interspersed occasionally with a stray Yiddishism; though they would have resented any insinuation that they spoke the lowly jargon of

284

Polish Jewry. Small shopkeepers and handicraftsmen, they were not members of high-toned Shearith Israel, or even of B'nai Jeshurun with a history of almost two decades. The majority present belonged to the third synagogue in New York, the Anshai Chesed, whose hazan came along to please his partisans.

The chair was occupied by Henry Jones, the efficient clerk of Anshai Chesed and considered the power behind the President. Folks said he actually ran the congregation. The discussions of these founding fathers were not recorded. What might have been said will here be imagined. The chairman called on Reuben Rodacher to repeat the conversation in the shop of Aaron Dinsheimer, while waiting for their shoes to be mended.

This worthy member of Anshai Chesed told of the bitter complaints that came to him from brethren whose applications were rejected by the Independent Order of Odd Fellows. He himself, an Odd Fellow and Mason, could only attribute such conduct to anti-Jewish prejudice. Yet nothing could be done about it, as it takes only three black balls to keep out an applicant, regardless of his worth or usefulness. The same was true in Masonry, in spite of the high position and devoted labors of individual Jews. He once heard a lecture that the Order owed a great debt to Jews; they probably brought Freemasonry to the American shores. They certainly made an important contribution before and after the Revolutionary War. Yet it was becoming increasingly difficult for Jews to pass the three degrees. In certain lodges it was useless even to try.

The jeweler at 420 Grand St., Isaac Rosenbourgh, questioned whether it would not be better to have separate Jewish lodges of Masons or Odd Fellows. He thought the Grand Masters of both Orders might issue special charters. Then all problems of rejection and blackballing on account of religion would be solved.

The barber William Reneau, who also sold "segars" in his shop at 47 Norfolk Street, passed for an intellectual. His answer to the jeweler's question sounded terse yet comprehensive. He argued that separate Jewish lodges within the framework of

I.O.O.F. or F. and A.M. would set up ghettos in fraternal organizations that preached the brotherhood of man. Nor would the Orders entertain the idea of dividing along religious lines. If anything, these Orders were set up to counteract the harm caused by religious barriers. Separation would only nullify the advantages of fraternal life. Most important was meeting the lodge brothers and showing them that Jews were normal, decent people. How could that be done if one never encounters his fraternal brother? Personally, he was convinced that Freemasonry helped to implant civil and religious rights for all in the Federal Constitution, because Masons came to know and appreciate the Jews, Deists, Quakers, and other minorities they met on the lodge room floor.

After much talk, back and forth, Henry Jones rapped for silence and said: "I do not believe our problems rest on a few black balls cast here and there in clubs or lodges. After all, numerous Israelites are members in both fraternities. Good men are often rejected, yet all of us know some, not so worthy, who are Masons and Odd Fellows. I therefore agree with Mr. Reneau that separate Jewish lodges in the great Orders are undesirable.

"But we have far more serious problems. The eight New York synagogues eye each other with hostility. Unified action seems impossible. We are in urgent need of a hospital, an orphan house, an old folks home. Jewish education is sadly neglected. We have no library, and not one ordained rabbi. And look at the social snobbery. To the Portuguese, no one exists outside their own charmed circle. The English and native born regard us foreigners or intruders. We in turn look down upon our brethren from Poland. Now a new segregation is taking form in the growing antagonism between Orthodoxy and the new reformers. Free thinkers are increasing, and they say 'a plague on both your houses.' Every boat brings in immigrants. Yet no organized effort helps these newcomers to learn the language and strange ways of a new land. They depend on the goodness of relatives and *landsleute* to start earning a living. These *greenhorns* are subject to mocks and scorns that might be avoided. Our lack of unity can only lead to confusion, or even anarchy.

"What we need is a Jewish lodge, a *Bundesbrüder* that would assume the mission of uniting Israelites in the work of promoting their highest interests and those of humanity; of developing and elevating the mental and moral character of the people of our faith; of inculcating the purest principles of philanthropy, honor, and patriotism; alleviating the wants of the poor and needy; visiting and attending the sick; coming to the rescue of victims of persecution; providing for widow and orphan; in short to act as befitting the *b'nai b'rith* of Abraham."

Then and there began the Independent Order of Bnai Brith. The success of the first secular Jewish fraternity was immediate. Sister lodges sprang up in New York and in the larger American cities. Branches were opened in such foreign lands as permitted fraternal organizations to function. The necessity for a B'nai B'rith was best attested by the emergence of rival lodges patterned after the original archetype. The influence of B'nai B'rith upon the rising American Jewish community is incalculable.

The anonymity of Henry Jones is baffling. His impact must have been significant if attention is paid the pronouncement of I.O.B.B.'s official historian. President of the order for 32 years, Julius Bien writes, "The speeches and addresses of Henry Jones were all marked by a rugged, sturdy common sense, studiously devoid of all ornamentation so as to strike home to the plainest intellect, and accomplish the best practical result. It will be seen that he was the man at the helm, guiding the frail bark at the outset of the voyage with a mind, created as it were for the purpose of finding the safe channel, and laying out a route upon which the voyage could proceed with unerring direction. His was also the strong hand that kept the wheel straight in the course which he had determined upon, and only a man endowed as he was with strength of intellect and character, could succeed in the accomplishment of his great purpose."

1844

HENRY CASTRO

Texas Colonizer

IT HAS been observed that only a small part of human experience is recorded. The general gets credit for the victory that is painfully won by numerous subordinates together with the common soldiers. The story teller is primarily concerned with the dramatic or the bizarre. Events cluster around big names. Consequently the major portion of what actually transpired is forgotten.

This is particularly true of Jewish history. The 4000 year saga, condensed by Heinrich Graetz into 11 volumes, could easily number 100 books had Jews taken the trouble to preserve records of the momentous odysseys they experienced. The long chronicle is punctured with many lacunae that black out events of great magnitude. The Jesus of Nazareth story should never have been left to enemies for generating eternal hate against Jewry. The connection of Jews with the formation of Islam has come down only through hostile Mohammedan sources.

We should therefore be grateful to any one who saves historiography from oblivion, as Rabbi Henry Cohen preserved stories of Texan Jewish pioneers. The noted Galveston clergyman was

288

born after the death of Henry Castro. People were rapidly forgetting the achievements of the Jewish colonizer who brought to Texas thousands of hardy settlers, badly needed in the continental wilderness of a new state that had just seceded from Mexico. There were no authentic records. Rabbi Cohen evidently decided to write down all he heard, factual or apocryphal, and leave it to future researchers to separate the wheat from the chaff. Unfortunately, the pulpiteer transformed the chronicle into an obituary.

Rabbi Cohen strikes a romantic note by giving Henry Castro a noble ancestor in Joao de Castro, the fourth Viceroy to the Indies for the King of Portugal. This relationship is farfetched, since the Inquisition kept careful records and saw to it that no Marrano would get a post of such high importance. Incidentally, the De Castro clan must have been very numerous, for there are few Sephardim who do not claim descent from this distinguished family that hailed originally from Spain.

In 1786 Henry Castro was born in France. According to the Rabbi's account, the Prefect of Landes appointed the 19 year old boy to welcome Napoleon on his visit to the Department in 1805. The following year the French Emperor invaded Spain, and Henry "was one of the guard of honor" to accompany the conqueror. The selection of a youth to greet the august visitor at the height of his glory seems rather remarkable. The "guard of honor" is probably a euphemism for *interpreter,* needed by the invading army.

An officer of the French National Guard in 1818, Castro fought with Marshal Moncey at Clichy, then emigrated to the U.S.A. and became a citizen. While living in Providence, Rhode Island, in 1827, he was appointed Consul for the Kingdom of Naples. Eleven years later he returned to France and formed a partnership in the banking business with an M. Lafitte.

In 1836 Texas seceded from Mexico and set up an independent republic. The new government needed money, and President Sam Houston established contact with Castro's bank. But the banker soon perceived far greater business opportunities than negotiating loans for the new state. Texas had millions of acres awaiting the plow, the ax, the labor and industry of new settlers. Mexico had been granting large tracts to enterprising pioneers. So in 1842 Pres. Houston entered into a five year agreement with Henry Castro conveying a land empire west of San Antonio for colonization. At the same time Castro received the appointment of Consul-General to France. But during that year hostilities broke out between Texas and Mexico and thus retarded the progress of colonization. With peace established in 1844, the Texas Government recognized the handicaps confronting Castro and extended his contract for three years longer.

Castro hurried to France to assume his official duties. He rendered valuable service in assisting General James Hamilton to advertise and popularize Texas. For a time, his colonization scheme was stymied. The timing proved bad. France had taken over Algiers and was utilizing every pressure to encourage the emigration of settlers to North Africa. Risking official displeasure, he published maps of Texas, distributed pamphlets in French and German, and circulated advertising material in Alsace and the Rhenish provinces. Despite opposition, he succeeded by the end of 1842 in shipping 113 emigrants from Havre to Texas.

In his Preface to the *History of Mexico,* Lorenzo Castro writes that his father rendered great services to the Texas Republic and received grants of land that comprise the county of Medina and parts of Frio, McMullen, Zavalla, Uvalde, Baxar, and Bandara. Between 1842 and 1847 he brought over 5000 emigrants in 27 ships. These farmers, fruit and vine-growers became industrious, law-abiding colonists, who built homes, laid out gardens and tilled the soil. He founded the towns of Quihi, Vandenberg, Dhanis, and the settlers named in his honor Castroville, the county seat of Medina.

Colonizing has always been a difficult affair, and Henry Castro expended much energy and labor in launching his project. During the first year he fed the settlers and furnished them with live stock, seeds, medicines, farming implements and other necessities. Altogether he invested over $150,000, and it is doubtful whether he saw the returns in his lifetime. He had plenty of land in a vast state where several decades later the ex-Confederate statesman Robert Toombs could on his return from France purchase a large tract of good soil at 50 cents an acre.

Henry Castro was not destined to spend a peaceful old age in the midst of his colonies. When the American Civil War broke out, he was evidently in difficult straits. He found it necessary to leave for France, but the Texan ports were blockaded. Tireless in his energy, he attempted to journey through Mexico. He died in his 76th year at Monterey and lies buried at the foot of the Sierra Madre.

The success of Castro's colonies elicited admiration. Great dangers beset his task. The settlements between San Antonio and the Rio Grande were exposed on the west to attack by Mexican bandits and on the east from Indian tribes full of understandable hostility. Castro's achievements earned him the friendship of three Texas Presidents—Houston, Lamar, and Jones. His efforts received the blessings of the first Catholic Bishop of Texas who visited Castroville to welcome newcomers from France and the Rhineland. Fifteen years after the Founder's death, the State of Texas named a stretch of land in the Panhandle region *Castro County*.

The Jewish origin of Henry Castro is not mentioned in histories of Texas. Lorenzo ignores, if not suppresses, his father's religion. But in his brief sketch, Rabbi Henry Cohen states: "The instinct of the Marrano must have been strong within him, as it is related, upon the authority of a contemporary, that during his surveying tours he would leave his companions in order to retire to the forest for the purpose of binding his phylacteries (tephillim). He did not often speak of his family, although he was proud of his uncle, Dr. Barota, an eminent physician of Jamaica." Such legendary testimony may not be authentic history, yet sufficient to include Henry Castro among the Jewish builders of America.

1845

ABRAHAM HART

Publisher

Hᴏᴡ ᴅɪᴅ ɪᴛ ʜᴀᴘᴘᴇɴ? A Jewish lad, without money or connections, was given a partnership in one of America's oldest and best publishing houses. In 1829, eighteen year old Abraham Hart had been an orphan for six years. His father, a small shopkeeper, came from Hanover and died in 1823.

The boy went to work to earn enough money for maintaining his mother in the little shop that stood opposite the thriving bank operated by Philadelphia's affluent and eccentric Stephen Gerard. Her stock being meager, Abraham approached an established bookdealer for some credit. The books which he received sold quite well. The incident attracted the attention of Moses Thomas, who sold, published and auctioned off books as was then customary in the book trade. Thomas saw and utilized the ability of the young fellow who became his protegé. In Boston an important sale was scheduled and Thomas could not attend. He gave 16 year old Abraham a letter of credit for $5000 with full *carte blanche* to use his best judgment in the transaction. Later, Moses Thomas recommended Abraham Hart to the Careys.

Mathew Carey, the noted Catholic liberal and reformer, had been printing books and periodicals since 1785; he became a leading publisher in the America of his time. His itinerant bookseller, Parson Weems, wrote the fabulous story of George Washington and made the cherry tree legend world famous. Carey took in as partners his son Henry Charles, who became a leading economist, and his son-in-law Isaac Lea, whose son, the learned Henry C. Lea, attained high distinction as author of Histories on the Papal and Spanish Inquisitions—still the standard works on those subjects. When Mathew Carey's youngest son, Edward L., became 21, he was also taken into the business. Scholarly and ethical, they nevertheless could not work in harmony after their father's death. It became necessary to divide the business. Henry C. Carey and Isaac Lea continued their partnership. The 24 year old Edward L. needed a partner and selected Abraham Hart, who was six years his junior.

Success greeted Carey and Hart almost immediately. Not handicapped by conservative traditions, they accepted "The Yellowplush Correspondence" of an obscure young writer, one William Makepeace Thackeray, whose work was rejected by the publishers in England. The partners thus launched Thackeray's literary career. They printed some of the best literature of the time and within 10 years became leading publishers in America.

A single anecdote might reveal Hart's alert efficiency. The novel, *Rienzi,* by Bulwer Lytton, created a sensation in Europe; an American edition was eagerly awaited. The boat which carried a copy of the historic romance for Harpers in New York brought one also to the Philadelphia firm. In the era before international copyrights the strongest rivalry prevailed to get out a book first. Hart quickly distributed sections of *Rienzi* among 12 printers. By nine the next morning the sheets were ready for binding. That afternoon 500 copies were finished. Hart bought all the space in the mail coach and rushed the shipment to New York, where it was placed on sale a day before the Harper edition was published.

The firm showed enterprise and foresight in being the first to assemble the essays of Macaulay that were scattered and buried in English periodicals, chiefly the *Edinburgh Review*. This miscellaneous collection they brought out in five volumes. Carey and Hart were also the first to publish an illustrated edition of Longfellow's poems. Among their many popular publications were anthologies of New England poetry, as well as of Pennsylvania, the Life of David Crockett, Captain Marryat's Tales, an anthology of European poets assembled by Longfellow, novels by Cooper, writings of Poe and Emerson. Philadelphia itself attained a preeminent reputation as a book center by virtue of the excellent printing, illustrations and high standard of the Carey and Hart publications. As a publisher of Jewish books in the English language, Hart made equal contributions. Leeser's translation of Jacob Schwartz's *Descriptive Geography and Brief Historical Sketches of Palestine* was the most important Jewish book printed in the United States up to that time. The works of Grace Aguilar and the poems of Rebecca Hyneman were non-profit ventures that added to the culture of America.

Abraham Hart made a tidy fortune, and after publishing for 25 years decided to retire. The Philadelphia book trade took the opportunity to show esteem for a competitor. At a farewell dinner the top publishers of the nation paid Hart high encomiums. He must have displayed character and ability to win the respect of such founders of the great American publishing houses as Fletcher Harper, Charles Scribner, J. B. Lippincott, William H. Appleton, George A. Putnam, and George W. Childs. The impact of these pioneers upon the national culture has been considerable. Harper actually suggested Hart for Mayor of Philadelphia, or even for Governor of Pennsylvania.

Noteworthy were his intimacies with eminent men in high places. After all, Abraham Hart did not have the advantages of a formal education. Yet he retained the lifelong friendship of Thackeray and two distinguishd Jews, Isaac Leeser and Morris Raphall. His home on Arch Street attracted such celebrities as Ulysses S. Grant, Anthony L. Drexel, and George G. Meade, the

hero of Gettysburg. But most remarkable was the friendly attitude of Thomas Carlyle, who was no lover of Jews. In a letter
that dyspeptic precursor of Fascism pays Hart the highest com-
pliment he ever gave to any business man.

Far too young at 44 to withdraw from all activity, Hart became
interested in mining and industry, in the new sewing machine,
as well as in real estate. As he grew older, his participation increased in civic and communal affairs, in religion and charities.
For a number of years he served as Parnass of Mikveh Israel. He
held office in Philadelphia's Hebrew Education Society, in Maimonides College for the training of ministers, in the first and
short-lived Jewish Publication Society, in the Hebrew Charity Association, in the Jewish Foster Home and Orphan Asylum. His
benefactions were liberal, his gifts to the poor generous. He presided at the meetings that organized Philadelphia's Jewish Hospital and the Young Men's Hebrew Association. Recognition outside of his home town came when he was elected President of the
Board of Delegates of American Israelites, the first organization
to attempt the unity of all American Jewry.

Absorption with local organizations did not obscure Hart's
grasp of the larger issues that affected Jewry as a whole. He
caught the perilous significance of the Damascus blood libel,
which the leadership of Shearith Israel in New York completely
ignored. The resurgence in Syria of the medieval slander that
Jews require Christian blood for the Passover ritual posed a threat
not only to the community in Damascus but to that of Philadelphia as well. He utilized his influence to bring about the intervention of the United States Government. On August 27, 1840
Christian and Jewish speakers expressed their abhorrence at a
mass meeting at which Abraham Hart presented a resolution stat-
ing: "That we invite our brethren of Damascus to leave the land
of persecution and torture and to seek asylum in this free and
happy land, where all religions are alike tolerated."

About 18 years later, Hart as President of Mikveh Israel again
addressed the State Department. World wide attention was fo-

cused upon the Mortara case when the Roman Church refused to return a child to its parents because several years earlier a nursemaid had secretly baptised it during infancy. Hart's correspondence with Lewis Cass, Secretary of State, reflects the indignation of enlightened public opinion.

During the Civil War his whole hearted loyalty to the United States found expression in active support of the newly organized Union League. He evidently sensed the need of assurance by President Lincoln in that dark period of suspicion, defeat and treachery. As *Parnass* of Mikveh Israel he sent in the address and invocation delivered by Rabbi Sabato Morais in response to the Presidential proclamation for consolation and prayer. Abraham Lincoln thanked Abraham Hart by letter for his "expression of kindness and confidence."

1846

DAVID CAMDEN DE LEON

The Fighting Doctor

Aʀᴏᴜɴᴅ the middle of the 19th century the best Jewish minds thought in terms of integration into the life, culture, and religion of the Christian environment. Voltairean enlightenment had all but demolished the foundations of belief among the intellectuals. If religion was merely a mish-mash of superstition, priestcraft and politics, then why cling to the most unpopular among the sects that persisted in standing apart as if in defiance of the civilized majority's progress.

Yet it was not quite the thing to plunge into the baptismal font and glow with the fervor of a rustic convert. It took the genius of a Disraeli to perceive that since "half of the civilized world worshipped a Jew and the other half a Jewess" it was absurd to shy away from such august relationship. Boldly avowing pride in his Jewish lineage, Disraeli created the profoundest impress upon his generation and achieved immortality. The DeLeons of South Carolina, though capable, patriotic, and even idealistic, sought to conceal their origin and were forgotten.

In 1791 Mordecai Hendricks DeLeon was born in Camden,

South Carolina. He became a physician and married the charming, brilliant Rebecca Lopez of Charleston. Of their six children, Edwin made his mark in diplomacy and literature, Thomas Cooper as journalist and playwright, and Agnes as translator and writer. But David Camden chose his father's calling and studied medicine. After graduating at the University of Pennsylvania in 1836 with the degree of M.D., he enlisted in the army and was sent to the Florida tropics to treat the sick and wounded soldiers of the Seminole War.

By the time the Mexican War began, David Camden DeLeon had developed into a competent surgeon. He served in the army of Gen. Zachary Taylor. In a furious battle with Mexico's Santa Anna, all the American officers were killed or wounded. The U. S. troops stood in danger of being routed for lack of leadership. In a critical moment the Jewish surgeon jumped into the breach at Chapultepec. Without military training, David Camden De-Leon took command and snatched victory from the jaws of defeat. This bold act earned him the sobriquet of "Fighting Doctor" and a double *thank you* from Congress.

In 1860 DeLeon obtained a military leave of absence because of sickness and visited his brother Edwin, who was Consul General in Egypt. Uneasily did the brothers scan the political horizon and watch the clouds hovering over their native land. Both were proud and happy in the service of their country. Both faced the same dilemma that confronted Robert E. Lee, the Southern Senators and many eminent Americans. In the event of secession, which Dr. DeLeon did not at all approve, what was his patriotic duty? Remain in the army that would fight the South? Or resign his commission and follow his state?

A letter to his brother Edwin reveals the bitter state of his divided loyalties. "Treason and patriotism are next door neighbors and only accident makes you strike the right knocker. Revolution is treason even if right, if unsuccessful. . . . A Southern Confederacy seems as near a fact as human foresight can dive in the future. The wire pullers have fixed their line so that the electricity has been infused into the masses. Interest has been superseded by pseudo patriotism and they do not count the pecuniary loss. The loss of country, or the status we will occupy as separate confederacies; love of country is merged into unnatural hate of section . . . I have loved my country. I have fought under its flag, and every star and stripe is dear to me. . . . But I am still convinced that no man can be a patriot who is afraid of being thought a traitor."

But when war came his troubled conscience decided for the Confederacy. Getting out of the army was not too easy. DeLeon's letter came to General Winfield Scott, his old friend and commander during the Mexican days. The General refused to accept the resignation of his surgeon, who as major now ranked pretty high in the army medical staff. Scott begged him to remain and offered a post in the Northwestern frontier, too far away for any fighting he might have had to do against his Southern comrades. The commander threatened arrest, and DeLeon virtually had to flee across the new frontier.

In Richmond President Davis assigned to DeLeon the important and difficult task of organizing the medical department of the Confederate Army. He served as Surgeon General until superseded by Dr. Samuel Preston Moore, also of South Carolina, who had outranked him in the U. S. Army. DeLeon also served in the field, in hospitals, in various capacities until the war's end.

The war that almost wrecked the Union also complexed the minds of Americans on both sides of the conflict. Puffed up with victory, the radical wing of the Federals now thirsted for vengeance. The Confederates also lost a sense of proportion in their premonitions and resentments. Men of large intellectual calibre such as Judah P. Benjamin, Robert Y. Toombs, together with a host of lesser celebrities, refused to live on in their home country by the grace of the conqueror. They left and some never returned.

David Camden DeLeon was among the loyal Dixians who quitted their homeland. He tried Mexico, but could find little happiness there. He suffered, and it is difficult to determine which affected him most, the defeat and prostration of his beloved South or the collapse of his fervent faith in that symbolic entity summed up by the *Stars and Stripes*. He returned to the U. S. A. upon the invitation of his former colleague in the Mexican War, General Ulysses S. Grant, now the most eminent personality in all America. The Fighting Doctor settled in the state of New Mexico, where he had property. He practiced medicine and displayed the family penchant for literary expression. His terse and vigorous writings in medical journals were widely read and admired. Never married, he died in Santa Fé 59 years old.

In Dr. DeLeon one senses a deeper tragedy than mere disillusionment. A more profound intellect would perhaps have perceived in the defeat of the Confederacy and in the Reconstruction that followed the birth pangs of a greater and purer Federal Union. The blood shed by a million Americans cemented more firmly the foundation of a United States that one day would lead the world in progressive self government. The South itself, cleansed of the moral taint of slavery, subsequently emerged richer and spiritually purified.

The DeLeon malady stemmed from escapism. In their desire to forsake their origins they cut the cables linking them with a rich spiritual tradition. They attempted to substitute patriotism for religion, only to learn that the state can also disappoint and disillusion. It would seem that after the loneliness of self-imposed exile in Mexico, David Camden would seek a more stimulating environment than the frontier town of Santa Fé, a veritable sahara of anything intellectual in the 1870s.

A prominent personality and physician of stature would certainly be recognized in the rapidly expanding communities of New York, Philadelphia, New Orleans, or San Francisco. Charleston or Savannah would recall youthful or ancestral memories. The military doctor admitted loneliness on disclosing that he would marry in a minute if he found so charming a girl as his brother Edwin's Irish wife. The question remains how closely did he seek? Presumably not among his co-religionists, or even among the elite Sephardim, who like himself, were rapidly dying out without leaving offspring to preserve the memory of a once glorious past.

1847

JACOB de CORDOVA

Publiciser of Texas

THE DE CORDOVAS displayed abilities in several fields. Nevertheless their chief pride stemmed from the claim of descent from Gonsalvo de Cordova, a truly noble figure of Spanish chivalry. *El Gran Capitan,* beloved of Isabella and conqueror of Naples, presented an exceptional contrast to the fierce fanaticism rampant in 15th century Spain. Yet a connection with such *Old Christian* prestige offered slight protection when the Inquisition sank its fangs into a victim of sufficient means to make extensive investigation profitable. The family chose the staff of exile. Several centuries later some of the de Cordovas found refuge in Jamaica.

Sickness plagued Jacob de Cordova all his life. In search of health at 22, he left Kingston for Philadelphia, a medical center in the 1820s and 30s for both Americas. For a time, he engaged in the West Indies trade in partnership with his father. But he was soon confined to his room for a year. The energetic patient whiled away the dragging days in learning the printing trade from his cousin's husband, who set up a press in the sick chamber. The doctors advised his return to the island, prescribing the accustomed climate as more conducive to recovery.

Returning to Kingston, Jacob found it queer that no morning paper appeared on Mondays. Spanish lethargy or Puritan observance of the English Sabbath banned Sunday printing. To fill the gap, he started in 1834 a daily with a novel feature. At 5 A.M. an advance advertising sheet could be obtained free. An hour later the regular issue was distributed. *The Daily Gleaner* subsequently became the leading paper on the island, and after a century is still published by the de Cordova family.

The Caribbean air did not contain the healing benefits predicted by the medicos. Jacob had to keep moving and tried New Orleans. This port city began a thriving trade with the newly increasing settlements in Texas. The printer-publisher went into business and shipped cargoes of merchandise which he disposed of by auction. The new frontier beckoned, and as soon as Texas declared her independence of Mexico he decided to settle there. Jacob de Cordova moved to Galveston in early 1837 and became a citizen of the infant republic.

Still restless and in quest of health, Jacob tried Houston in its early years. He remained until 1842 and sickness again compelled a change of place. Doctors now thought that his only chances lay in colder climates. But attachment to the new republic became strong. Furthermore, it began to dawn upon him that the potentialities of Texan real estate were unlimited. He gave up merchandising and turned to land. But buying and selling were complicated by the land laws inherited from Spain and Mexico. For the next ten years he traveled from county seat to county seat examining records and attempting to unravel the complications in land titles. A benefit far more important than money making accrued unexpectedly. He spent most of his waking hours in the saddle. Open air and exercise operated to improve his health beyond the expectations of learned physicians.

He threw all energies into finding and acquiring land. *De Cordova's Land Agency* did a proverbial "land office business" and became widely known, not only throughout Texas but in the larger centers of American wealth. Admission into the Union increased public confidence in the Lone Star State. Residents of New York, Philadelphia, and Baltimore purchased large tracts. No one located as much desirable land as de Cordova, and the largest proportion of patents issued by the State were on certificates held or controlled by him. His reputation grew. The people of Harris County in 1847 elected him to the House of Representatives to fill out an unexpired term.

His abundance of land called for development. De Cordova selected a tract for a townsite. He invited the two neighboring landowners into a joint venture. He plotted land parcels and laid out the City of Waco. The lots were then put up for sale at auction. Nothing was overlooked that would insure the success of the undertaking. He presented each religious denomination with a lot upon which to build a church. The Presbyterians delayed construction, and when ready found that the city had disposed of their lot for another purpose. Another plot of ground was promptly substituted. These liberal offerings made a deep impression on the community. Several years later the Independent Order of Odd Fellows honored their Deputy Grand Sire, Jacob de Cordova, by ordering his portrait painted in full regalia. At its presentation to the Grand Lodge, the Grand Master paid his tribute to the Jew who presented lots for Christian churches of all denominations. It was inevitable for an optimist with boundless confidence in the future of Texas to over extend himself. Jacob de Cordova accumulated far in excess of a million acres. The boom was over and land became a drug on the market. He now faced the difficulties affecting a "land poor" operator. Meeting the ad valorem taxes on such vast holdings became a yearly hurdle. A real challenge had to be met and overcome.

The knowledge of printing and newspaper publishing now served him to good advantage. He sent for his brother Phineas, who had literary ability coupled with considerable experience gained in the office of the influential *National Gazette of Philadelphia*. The brothers started *The Texas Herald* and distributed copies over the state and other settled parts of the West. Boosting and advertising the sparsely inhabited state became their personal affair. Their articles concerning Texas, their description of her untapped resources, their information about the vast empire of potential riches were reprinted in other newspapers of the West and of the South. Many immigrants were attracted by these glowing, yet unexaggerated, accounts.

The Texas Herald evidently made its influence felt. Governor Bell urged the removal of its printing plant to the state capital. The brothers then published out of Austin the weekly *South Western American,* which became a force in state politics. It stressed Texan rights over New Mexico and pressed for the passage of the Compromise Measure of 1850, which brought about the payment of $10,000,000 to Texas for her claims.

A more important victory was scored in connection with the paper's program for building railroads throughout the state. The *South Western American* advocated the donation of excess public lands and even lending the school fund. A prominent politician of Travis County ridiculed the proposal. He was astonished when the voters defeated him for the legislature on that very issue. Both de Cordovas always felt proud of their contribution to the bringing of railroads into Texas.

Efforts for the public welfare did not stiffen the real estate market. Jacob de Cordova tried lecturing. He attempted "to sell Texas" to audiences in New York, Philadelphia, and Brooklyn. He read a paper before the New York Geographical Society. He crossed the ocean and tried in vain to convince the Cotton Supply Association of Manchester that Texas could supply the entire world with cotton if she had the population. This organization was interested in locating lands where more cotton could be raised so that English mills might reduce unemployment. Yet the Britons would not believe his assertion that Texas had 10,000,000 acres that could grow a bale to the acre.

The crisis of the Civil War was followed by hard times. Jacob de Cordova did not live long enough to realize his golden expectations. When three score, he died in 1868 feeling quite poor in spite of possessing land that in a generation could be sold for untold millions. Constant sickness notwithstanding, his life was eventful. A practical man with vision, he was not indifferent to things of the mind. Well versed in Judaism, he could write fluent Hebrew. In his Austin plant he printed in 1856 *The Texas Immigrant and Travellers Guide Book*. Two years later he published in Philadelphia, *Texas; Her Resources and Her Public Men,* which a prominent bibliographer describes as a "fine Texas cyclopedia at the time."

1848

WARDER CRESSON

Convert

S ELDOM DO WE SEE Jews converted to Christianity. But far more rarely do we hear of Christians embracing Judaism. If we rule out those cases of marriage for financial advancement, the scarcity of proselytes to the faith of Moses is not too easily explained.

This paucity of converts does not stem from the burdensome rites demanded by Orthodoxy. There is something in the psychology of a genuine proselyte that grasps quite eagerly at the onerous practices of a new faith. The unpopularity of Jews may possibly deter the more worldly. Yet the history of many a *ger tzedek* simply proves that a seeker of religious truth is never frightened by persecutions from without or by the resentments within the new congregation he enters.

A plausible explanation lies in the unwillingness of Jews to welcome an apostate from another religion. Everything is done to discourage the stranger who comes knocking at the synagogue door. He is assured that his soul can be saved in his ancestral faith if he leads a blameless life. The *ger* is accepted only after he demonstrates the sincerity of his conversion beyond all doubt. Such, at least, was the experience of a Quaker from Philadelphia.

Warder Cresson was given to Bible study and religious speculation. At the age of thirty, he wrote *Babylon the Great Is Falling,* a diatribe against Catholicism. In the same book he deplores the evil of the times and exhorts his own Quakers to a better life. But the religion of the Friends was not quite satisfying. Spiritual unrest drove him to try several other sects which appealed for the moment. In 1840 he met Rabbi Isaac Leeser, and this leader of American Orthodoxy created an impression that ultimately changed the life and faith of Warder Cresson.

Early in the 19th century pious Jews, particularly older men, were seized with a desire to forsake the *galut* and die in the Holy Land. But before dying they would marry and bring forth children. This led to an increase in the population of *luftmenchen,* without support of any kind from agriculture, commerce, or industry. Their wretched poverty inspired some English missionaries to form the "London Society for Conversion of Jews". At Jerusalem, the pickings in the vineyard of the Lord seemed too good to be overlooked.

The American missionaries looked hungrily at the harvest of souls that stood ready for gleaning in the Holy Land. They sensed the benefit to their own prestige if the growing power of the U. S. A. would be represented by a consulate in Palestine. They were also aware of the religious yearnings in Warder Cresson and saw in him excellent material for a missionary. It seemed therefore an inspiration from heaven that induced Washington to appoint Warder Cresson the first American Consul at Jerusalem.

Cresson had a wife and six children and operated a successful farm near Philadelphia. Only strong religious cravings could prompt him to leave home and forego the prospects of material success. He felt the sacrifice and wrote, "I left all these in pursuit of the Truth and for the sake of Truth alone." In the city, holy to three faiths, he was most impressed by the tenacity of its impoverished Jews who resisted the blandishments of the missionaries. The soul snatchers promised not only salvation but offered a yearly stipend that meant affluence to the hungry dwellers in filth and squalor. In Leeser's *Occident,* Cresson wrote some scathing denunciations, castigating the well-fed self-sufficiency of the missionaries in the midst of starvation.

Instead of fraternizing with the missionaries, the American Consul sought out Jerusalem's noted rabbis. He studied Hebrew and was soon able to delve into the 24 massive folios of the Talmud. Fondness for the mystical led him into the portals of the Cabala. His entire person became immersed in the Jewish spirit. He identified himself with the Sephardic group and formally applied for admission into the community of Israel. The Chief Rabbi cast a side glance at the missionaries and Moslems and became apprehensive. It was less than a decade since the notorious Damascus affair demonstrated that Christians and Mohammedans can merge their hates into a joint persecution of Jews. The Beth Din (Rabbinical Court) interposed their learned objections. The 50 year old consul overcame all opposition and entered the Covenant of Abraham. In 1848 Warder Cresson became Michael C. Boaz Israel.

The convert returned to Philadelphia. He intended making a fair disposal of his property for the benefit of his family and return to live in Jerusalem. Instead he found himself in an asylum. A commission of lunacy had been filed by his wife and family. Only one son stood by him. A *cause célèbre* followed; over 100 witnesses were heard; physicians, psychiatrists and missionaries testified. The press over the land argued his sanity. People stared at him in the streets. Finally the Circuit Court concluded that conversion to Judaism was not *prima facie* evidence of insanity. The former Quaker was ordered released.

In Jerusalem, the American proselyte married a Sephardi and became a leader in the community. Serious thought about relieving the appalling poverty led him to evaluate the "Chalukah", the charity system, which supported almost the entire Jewish population. He saw the degrading effects of the inadequate doles that came in from "pushkes", the Meir bal Haness charity collection boxes nailed up the homes of pious Jews in all lands. He also detected the inevitable corruption that accompanies the unequal and often unfair distribution of the charity funds.

Quite naturally the Philadelphia farmer came to the conclusion that the soil was the proper support intended by God for his creatures. He rejected the general opinion that Jerusalem Jews were lazy, shiftless, unable and unwilling to work. The practical American put his convictions to the test. He purchased land in the Emek Rephaim near Jerusalem and was able to prove that the Jewish poor made excellent, efficient farm workers. He preached and wrote constantly about the wholesome, uplifting effects of agriculture. His words evidently produced results. About the same time Judah Touro of New Orleans and Sir Moses Montefiore of England became interested in similar projects. Warder Cresson has a place among the forerunners of Zionism for being the first to advocate agricultural colonies for the Jews in Palestine.

When the American *ger tzedek* died in 1860, the entire community followed his coffin for burial on the Mount of Olives. Regarded a saint, his grave became a shrine to which the devout offered prayers.

1849

ABRAHAM WATTERS

Itinerant

U NREST has never been the compelling spur that caused Jewish migration. Hoboes or tramps as a class never existed among Jews. On the contrary, the Jew is a classic *pater familias,* the sober, industrious home builder who provides for the education of his children.

And yet no people have done more wandering. Not that Jews travelled about for the sheer joy of roving. Religious persecution, legal oppression, economic restriction, or forced migration were the factors that produced the *Wandering Jew.* In the course of centuries migrating became a habit, less burdensome perhaps than to more stationary folk, yet not without leaving its mark on the national character. The career of Abraham Watters might reflect the tendency to go places, not always compelled by necessity.

In Prussia Wolf Wasser acted as broker for a wealthy landowner and often had occasion to dispose of the wool, hides and other produce raised on the estate. He would sometimes take along to London his oldest son Abraham, who thus acquired English when quite young. After his father's death Abraham settled in England, translated Wasser to Watters and appears to have married a sister-in-law of Samuel M. Isaacs, the Amsterdam rabbi who became prominent in New York and father of a gifted family. After the death of his young wife Abraham Watters, still in his twenties, immigrated to the United States.

In 1837 he is registered a Mason in Charleston. Five years later, a lodge in Griffon, Georgia, presents him with a golden keystone. Spending about 10 years in the South, he proceeded by easy stages to the Mississippi Valley. In 1847 he is admitted to citizenship in St. Louis. Always a devotee of fraternal organizations, he joined the Order of Odd Fellows at Independence, the "jumping off place" in Missouri for travellers about to penetrate the great Wild West. His presence at that outpost might indicate the intention of crossing the continent in a covered wagon.

While in Missouri, Abraham Watters no doubt witnessed a strange cavalcade. Before him proceeded a multitude that sprang up in the grass roots of America, a sect calling themselves Latter Day Saints. They aggravated the rustics by their practice of ancient polygamy after the manner of Hebrew patriarchs. Against these hated Mormons raged a persecution that must have struck a tremulous note in the consciousness of the Jewish émigré out of Prussia. Before him they trekked in Biblical fashion with their wives and children, their kine and sheep, on another Exodus, ready to cross fearsome deserts in search of a promised land to build their Zion.

Two years later gold was found in the Sacramento valley, and a mighty rush started for California. In 1849 Abraham Watters is found attending a Yom Kippur service in San Francisco. A series of meetings in his home result in the formation of the first *Chevra* on the West Coast. Under his chairmanship, a committee raised $4400 for building a synagogue and Watters became the first Vice-President of the Congregation Emanu-El.

We do not know how Watters reached California. He might

have returned to New York and boarded a schooner, more or less seaworthy, that for six to nine months would sail down the Hemisphere, round Cape Horn, then up the West Coast. Or he could venture on a ship to Panama; then cross the isthmus, if not robbed and murdered by bandits, and finally pick up the second boat on the Pacific bank—that is, if the captain did not squeeze more money from another prospector and leave the lawful passenger stranded. Abraham might have joined a safari and risked the hazards of thirst, Indians, heat, hunger, disease, cold or mountain passes in crossing the vast stretch between the Missouri and the Pacific.

Business evidently did not fare too well after the gold rush subsided. Watters formed a partnership with Moses H. Lichtenstein and together they braved new dangers in the wilds of Mexico. With a good stock of jewelry and silverware they boarded a British ship and landed on the Sonora coast. Prospects were not too bright for "gringos" in a defeated enemy country, and so the partners returned to the port city ready to sail for San Francisco. But getting out of the country was no simple matter. They deposited their merchandise with the U. S. Consul and signed up as "assistant hands" on the American transport that could not take passengers. The Mexican Prefect then took away their passports and blocked their departure.

Nor were the suspicions of the Mexicans altogether groundless. It was an era when the South sought expansion by increasing the number of slave states. The Mexican officials had information about William Walker's filibuster that was fitted out in San Francisco to take over Sonora. The Americans might well be spies. Actually Lichtenstein had contacts with Walker and had even served under him in the expedition to conquer Nicaragua. The partners were in peril, yet the Consul could do nothing without their passports. In fact he was not even sure of their American citizenship.

Their situation looked desperate when they applied to an English sea captain for help. The all powerful British commanded great influence. Captain Provost induced the Prefect to return the passports and took the partners on board. In San Francisco they published in the newspapers their gratitude to the "Virago's" captain and filed a claim for redress against the Mexican Government. Watters sailed to Honolulu for an affidavit from the engineer of the British ship. Former Governor Bigler of California and his brother, the ex-Governor of Pennsylvania, pressed the case in Washington. After many hearings nothing came of their claims.

Abraham went into partnership with his younger brother, Ichel Watters. In Sacramento they purchased and fitted up "Sutter Hall" as a recreation casino, engaging at the same time in the jewelry business. Abraham traveled several times to Mexico and Cuba. Business interests carried him to Venezuela and the Virgin Islands, then to England, France, and Germany. The brothers were passengers on the British ship "Trent" when the famous incident of Nov. 8, 1861 took place. Mason and Slidell, the Confederate commissioners on board, were forcibly removed by Captain Wilkes of the U. S. Navy. This was contrary to international law and especially galling to England. It took all the tact and common sense of President Lincoln to avert war between the U. S. and Britain.

After the war, the brothers settled in Salt Lake City. The rise of the mining industry made money in the Mormon agricultural economy more plentiful. Their business prospered and branched out to other towns in the Far West. The Watters brothers were the first in Utah to manufacture jewelry of gold and silver. Ichel took a leading part in the growing Jewish community and conducted services in the synagogue prior to the arrival, or in the absence, of any rabbi. To the end of his days Ichel was active in communal and civic affairs.

In his "Pioneer Jews of Utah" Dr. Leon L. Watters tells of Mormon esteem towards the early Jewish settlers. Joseph Smith the Moses, and Brigham Young the Joshua, of Mormonism had Jewish mentors and friends. The Latter Day Saints regarded themselves as descended from the ancient Israelites and looked upon all non-Mormons as Gentile enemies. One still hears the famous quip, "Utah is the only place in the world where Jews are Gentiles." It is true that during a bitter civil and religious feud Ichel Watters was severely beaten and almost lost an arm. But, ironically, he suffered because he was classed a "Gentile". It is significant that the only "Gentile" governor ever elected in Utah was Simon Bamberger, a Jewish business man.

Abraham Watters married again in his 53rd year. For 11 years he lived in Birmingham, England, probably to please his wife. He returned alone, and when 82 years old died in Salt Lake City.

1850

ERNESTINE L. ROSE

Suffragette

Iɴ Nᴇᴡ Yᴏʀᴋ a crowd had gathered in the Broadway Tabernacle to hear about improving the crude public school system. A member of the British Parliament spoke and was followed by the Rev. Robert Breckenridge of Kentucky. The distinguished clergyman used the occasion for lambasting infidels and to rally the audience for religion. As the assembly was rapidly turning into a prayer meeting, a voice from the gallery interrupted the evangelical harangue. "Throw her out! She's an infidel!" screamed a part of the audience. Disrespect to the cloth was unheard of during the 1830s, the golden era for American preachers.

But the female refused to be hushed. Her foreign accent, not without its piquant charm, enhanced the magnetic timbre in her voice. She continued in protest against deflecting the purpose of the meeting. The catcalls subsided. Before sitting down she managed to score roundly the opponents of free education as the very forces who fought the emancipation of women and the rights of labor and the growing abolitionist movement. She stole the show. Those who booed now gave her an ovation.

The incident brought wide publicity to Ernestine Louise Rose and perhaps marks the opening of her strenuous career in America. The next half century saw her preoccupied with petitions to State Legislatures, with lecturing before audiences, large or small, with the inner direction of conventions, with traveling by wagon, on foot, and later on trains, across the length and breadth of the land, speaking and organizing for causes affecting the public in general and women in particular.

Who was this capable, vibrant woman? Little is known of her origin, and that little has been sentimentalized into a romantic haze by the Victorians of the suffrage movement. They tell us Sismondi Potowski was born in 1810 in Piotrkow, a small town in Poland. Her father, a "prominent" rabbi with all the seven virtues, taught her the Bible in Hebrew. But the precocious child would ask questions the learned Talmudist could not answer, except with the well-worn formula "a little girl shouldn't ask questions."

At 16 her mother died, leaving her a small legacy. The paragon of a father, whom the child adored, married again and would not let her have the money without a lawsuit, which she conducted Portia-like without help from any one. She won and, with a Spinoza-like gesture, she nobly relinquished the inheritance and departed. How a 17 year old girl without means could travel about in Poland, Russia, Germany, Holland, Belgium, and France is a detail too petty for her female admirers to notice.

The young girl appears to have met little difficulty in associating with leaders, thinkers, Socialists, and even celebrities. In Berlin Sismondi, a very unusual Italian name for a girl in the Polish ghetto, confers with the Prussian King and castigates him for the restrictions against Jews. Frederick III is impressed and she is permitted to stay as long as she likes, without the red-tape demanded of other Jews native or foreign. In Paris, she witnessed the revolution of 1830. In the Hague the case of a sailor's wife unjustly accused moves her girlish compassion. Again she is admitted to the royal presence. The petition she had drawn up herself secures justice for the unfortunate woman. It is not easy to separate the factual wheat from the fanciful chaff in the early years of the future "Queen of the Platform," a female knight-errant who went about the country tilting against human slavery, religious absolutism, and restrictions of the rights of women.

Hitherto a rebel merely against social inequalities or religious tyranny, she acquired a more positive philosophy of government and society on coming under the influence of Robert Owen, the founder of Utopian Socialism in England. It must have appeared a gesture of defiance to a generation that still denied full civil rights to Jews in England for a young girl liberated from the stifling obscurantism of Russian Poland to preside over an organization with the all embracing title: *The Association of All Classes of All Nations, Without Distinction of Sect, Sex, Party, Condition or Color*. About this time Sismondi Potowski met William H. Rose, an Abolitionist. They married and left England for the more promising field of the United States, which was a broad arena for social reform.

In the young republic, Ernestine L. Rose found ample scope for her talents and inexhaustible energy. The New World, except in political freedom, had advanced but little beyond the social injustice that obtained in Europe. Negro slavery flourished until the frightful carnage of a bloody war established the aims of the Abolitionists. Workers had neither the power to strike nor the right to organize labor unions. Married women, in subjection to their husbands, ranked as incompetents at common law on a par with infants and lunatics.

Besides agitating on many platforms against the existing evils, Ernestine presented to the New York Legislature a petition that would give married women a legal right to their separate property and a share with their husbands in the guardianship of children. Her petition, which carried only five signatures, was rejected. But she persisted year after year in pressing these reforms until the law was finally adopted.

But thinking women were not satisfied with sporadic reforms, wrested here and there from unwilling law makers. They correctly attributed the cause of their inferior status to political disfranchisement. A group of intelligent idealistic women dedicated their lives to secure equal rights with men at the ballot box. In the top echelon of leadership in the newly launched women's suffrage movement stood Ernestine L. Rose.

For 30 years—until her health failed—she worked at full speed in the National Women's Suffrage Association. Her recorded speeches show intellect, passion, logic and fearlessness. At conventions she took a leading part as organizer, politician, orator and parliamentarian. She must have displayed extraordinary capacity and character to win the respect and admiration of Susan B. Anthony, Lucy Stone, Wendel Phillips, Julia Ward Howe, William Lloyd Garrison and Elizabeth Cady Stanton. At a time when women were not yet conditioned for parliamentary procedure, or to catcalls and hectoring at public meetings, she was an indispensable spokesman. If Susan B. Anthony was the soul, then Ernestine L. Rose was the brain of the suffrage movement.

Her contributions towards the emancipation of women, though now forgotten, were appreciated during her lifetime. In 1869 she was chosen the American delegate to the Women's Industrial Congress in Berlin. She scored her greatest personal triumph when the Territory of Wyoming adopted equal suffrage. This was the first American legislative body to give the ballot to women, an exploit due to her almost unaided efforts.

Her daguerreotype shows a vital, energetic woman of regular attractive features and firm character. In the *History of Women Suffrage,* L. E. Barnard says of Ernestine L. Rose: "She had a rich musical voice, with just enough foreign accent and idiom to add to the charm of her oratory. As a speaker she was pointed, logical and impassioned. She not only dealt in abstract principles clearly, but in their application touched the deepest emotions of the human soul."

1851

MAX LILIENTHAL

Educator and Spokesman

I N THE horse-and-wagon era of 1840, Russia seemed shrouded
in preternatural darkness to the young German Rabbi who received an offer to superintend the new school at Riga. He was
intrigued when informed of the light that began to penetrate the
opaque mist enveloping Russian Jewry. He might even spear-
head the revolution engineered by the *Maskillim* to bring modern
culture to a people, extraordinarily astute and receptive, yet
steeped in obscurantism.

Max Lilienthal forsook Munich to introduce up-to-date methods of the German Jewish school, designed to displace the *cheder*
and *yeshiva,* in operation since the 16th century when the Talmud
was a beacon light in a world of Christian hate and bigotry. He
succeeded and his name spread. Government officials presented
Lilienthal with a diamond ring as a mark of the Czar's approval;
he was invited to St. Petersburg for a conference.

Russian autocracy, full of fears over its ability to preserve the
feudal status quo in a world charged with revolutionary ideas,

leaned heavily on organized religion. It could only regard Judaism as the hereditary foe of Greek orthodoxy. The German race myth had not yet been invented by the French Count Gobineau. Czardom saw a simple way towards monolithic conformity in the conversion of Jews to the state religion. Stiff-necked obstinacy lay grounded in Rabbinic ideology. The bearded Chassidim, with corkscrew curls dangling from temples under furred turbanlike headgear, wearing long caftans that scarcely concealed their white stockings, appeared to officialdom as the spirit incarnate of the Talmud. If the modern teacher, schooled in secular learning, could displace the melamed, then conversion and assimilation would follow apace.

At least so thought the Minister of Education, Sergius Uvarov, who passed for a liberal in the milieu of black reaction. To Lilienthal he represented the Czar's government as abandoning persecution or compulsion and genuinely concerned with Jewish enlightenment as a remover of hatreds and humiliations. Cultural reforms through state supervised schools would transform the Rabbinate as well as the masses. But he needed a qualified intermediary, a spokesman for the Government and trusted by the Jews. Lilienthal accepted the assignment.

For a time Max Lilienthal stood out as one of the famous men in Europe. The eyes of civilized people everywhere focused upon the person who might bring amelioration to Jews in Russia. Forward looking Maskillim considered him "as wise as Solomon and as enterprising as Moses." Crowds extended a royal welcome to the harbinger of emancipation, to the enlightener of their persecuted brethren, sunk in a quagmire of fanaticism.

But the leadership in both wings of Orthodoxy were suspicious of Greeks bearing gifts. In Vilna the acute Lithuanian mind questioned the good faith of a government that declassed an entire people and made them into pariahs, confined and overcrowded in a vast ghetto called the Pale of Settlement. Could confidence be placed in a tyrant who *ukased* that little children be kidnaped and inducted to military service for 25 years? What was the value of modern culture without human rights? What could *aufklae-rung* without emancipation accomplish, except to lead the discontented intellectual to baptism? Lilienthal replied that if he thought such were the aims of the Government, he would resign his post immediately.

It was a tough assignment for the 27 year old school teacher. Any move could offend some group. Intimacy with ultra-Orthodox elements might alienate liberal Maskillim, and vice versa. Aloofness brought the accusation of German arrogance. Yet Lilienthal's recommendations were adopted by the Government. A rabbinical commission, evoked to supervise the proposed new schools under the Ministry, served as security against reforms that might sabotage Judaism. Montefiore in England, Cremieaux of France and Phillipson of Germany were invited to attend the deliberations. Yet nothing could persuade the plain people of the Government's benevolent intentions.

Shortly after the prominent community in Odessa offered him the post of rabbi, Dr. Lilienthal applied for leave to visit his family in Germany. Once out of Russia, he never returned. Instead he turned to the free society of America. It is possible that he finally saw through official duplicity that had intended to use him as a stooge for converting and Russifying his coreligionists.

The fame of Lilienthal preceded him in the New World. The second ordained rabbi to settle in New York, he served three German Orthodox Synagogues jointly in 1846 at the then generous salary of $1000 a year. He instituted some mild reforms in abolishing archaic prayers and improving decorum. He introduced the confirmation ceremony, subsequently adopted in all three forms of American Judaism. Although the ablest speaker among American rabbis, yet somehow he did not quite realize the glowing expectations raised on his arrival. Recognizing the pressing need for Jewish education, he withdrew from the ministry to conduct a private school that earned approval from all factions. It anticipated the modern Hebrew day school. He preferred to act as honorary rabbi for several German congregations, preaching and performing services without compensation.

His lack of impact on New York stemmed probably from a gradual change affecting his ideology. A growing interest in the Reform movement led him to join forces with Isaac M. Wise. Called to the rabbinate of Bene Israel in Cincinnati, he also became editor of and contributor to the *American Israelite*. He wrote for the German and Hebrew publications as well as for Isaac Leeser's *Occident*. In the citadel of Reform he spent his last 27 years and there made his chief contribution to American Judaism, publishing several volumes that included sermons, speeches, and poems. He even left three dramas in manuscript.

Dr. Lilienthal brought scholarship, impassioned eloquence and literary expression to Reform Judaism. A crusader by instinct, he nevertheless was unwilling to go all the way with the radicalism of David Einhorn. He preferred the more moderate course of Isaac M. Wise and assisted in founding the Hebrew Union College, in which he taught history and literature. The conservatism of Max Lilienthal exerted a wholesome influence in shielding Reform from the centrifugal dangers that threaten all revolutions.

1852

JUSTICE
SOLOMON
HEYDENFELDT

Charleston resembles a venerable matriarch. Her sons might glory in the kinship, yet were never loathe about cutting loose from her apron strings. Since early 19th century it became a habit, almost a fashion, for them to seek fame or fortune in climes less mauve, but more promising. Among these émigrés Solomon Heydenfeldt attained distinction at the far end of the world, as California appeared in 1850.

An orphan at eight, Solomon managed to study Latin, Greek, and mathematics at Pennsylvania. Unable to graduate, he returned to read law at the office of Charleston's celebrated jurist, Chancellor de Saussure's son. Settling in Alabama, he impressed the new environment sufficiently to make him at 24 a county judge. Two years later, he sought one of the best paying jobs in the state, County Judge of Mobile. Though not elected by the Legislature, he made a good race, which was encouraging for a newcomer 26 years old.

Married, a promising lawyer politically ambitious and well

323

thought of, he damaged his future by meddling with slavery, a hot potato for any opponent in the South. Not that all Southerners were rabid proponents of the system. Many recognized its evils and, like the Grimke sisters of Charleston, hoped to see slavery eradicated. Heydenfeldt addressed to the Governor a pamphlet advocating an amendment to the State Constitution that would prohibit further importation of slaves into Alabama.

We do not know what effect his brochure produced. He was no fire eating radical intent on abolishing slavery even at the cost of disrupting the Union. A believer in States Rights, he felt that the South should on its own accord eliminate human bondage. He advocated the solution of the slave problem by the states themselves, without interference from the national government.

Middle of the road measures are seldom popular in times of stress and excitement. Sane people might appreciate Heydenfeldt's appeal to justice and sound policy. Yet it is doubtful whether the slave trading interests read the pamphlet with calm detachment. Early in 1850 Judge Heydenfeldt left Montgomery for San Francisco. This departure can hardly be construed as a flight, for two years later he came back for an extended visit to his family. In the histories and records of Alabama, he left a reputation of "very fair ability and excellent character," which brought him universal esteem.

The real cause for leaving lay in the feverish excitement that swept the country with the discovery of gold in California. Recovering gradually from the disastrous depression that followed hectic speculation brought on by extensive railroad building, the nation became intoxicated when a farm hand found gold on Sutter's farm in the Sacramento Valley. The grand exodus of the "49ers" started. Fortune hunters sailed around the South American Horn, or by boats to Panama, crossing the isthmus on foot to proceed by ship to the Golden Gate. The boldest hazarded the perils of nature and Indian hostility by traversing the plains, mountains and deserts of the Great Wild West in covered wagons.

In San Francisco Heydenfeldt found himself among prospectors and criminals, honest pioneers and shady adventurers, professionals discredited at home and capable men stirred by honest ambition, mountebanks and gamblers, restless wanderers and home builders anxious for domestic comfort. He opened a law office and is praised in *Shuck's Bench and Bar in California* for "excellent habits, business assiduity, generous disposition, broad legal knowledge, and dignified presence, which made him a man of mark in that era of restlessness and won for him a fine civil practice."

Despite all the confusion and turbulence of gold prospecting, a lawful government was set up. The new Legislature met in 1851 for its second session, pretty equally divided on the issues that were agitating the nation. The Democrats, having a slight majority, selected Heydenfeldt to succeed the daring explorer John C. Fremont in the U. S. Senate. But the Northerners distrusted the Southern sympathies of the Democratic candidate. After 142 ballots his name was withdrawn, and the session closed without electing a Senator.

Such deadlocks are usually compromised. At the next session John B. Weller was elected, with Heydenfeldt managing his campaign. The State Democratic convention nominated Solomon Heydenfeldt on the first ballot to succeed the retiring Chief Justice of the California Supreme Court. At the general election he received 24,420 votes as against 20,670 for his opponent. A Jewish colleague, Henry A. Lyons of Philadelphia, already sat on the bench, but Heydenfeldt was the first Jew elected by popular vote. The office carried the high salary of $10,000 a year.

On the bench Heydenfeldt made a good record, writing more opinions than the two other judges combined. His decisions on Mexican grants, on disputed land titles arising out of the gold rush, on the conduct of Vigilantes during the hectic period of lawlessness, remained with few exceptions the law of California. His work in drafting a system of equity and jurisprudence received strong commendation. Yet the associates on the court were not congenial. His trip to Europe was ruined on hearing of Justice Terry's imprisonment for stabbing a man. His other colleague, Judge Murray, was corrupt, immoral, venal and claimed the title of Chief Justice which rightfully belonged to Heydenfeldt by virtue of a prior election. The Legislature then cut salaries down to $6000, which he felt inadequate for the support of a rising family. After five years service, he resigned and went into private practice.

When the War of Secession broke out, Heydenfeldt became a victim of ambivalence. He believed in preserving the Union, yet opposed the use of force. An opponent of slavery, he nevertheless favored recognizing the Confederacy. Engaged in a lucrative practice, he would not subscribe to the "ironclad" oath of loyalty demanded of lawyers before the argument of every case. Claiming his oath to the Alabama Bar sufficient for any American, he evidently failed to grasp that Alabama had seceded from the Union. Conscientious in his scruples that a principle was at stake, he refused a retainer of $35,000 to appear in court.

In religion Solomon Heydenfeldt remained a faithful observer of Judaism. Defending a fellow Jew for violating the Sunday Law, a rather trifling offense in the period of lawless violence, he had the highest state court reverse the conviction on constitutional grounds. In 1859 he presided at a mass meeting which joined the mass protest against the abduction of the child Edgar Mortara from the arms of his parents to be forcibly retained in the Catholic faith.

1853

MORRIS JACOB
RAPHALL

Fundamentalist

DURING THE Administration of James Buchanan, Judaism received official recognition. The Orthodox Rabbi of B'nai Jeshurun in New York was invited to open a morning session of the House of Representatives. Rabbi Morris Jacob Raphall, wrapped in a *talith* and wearing a skull cap, prayed before the national lawmakers in Washington.

Today the morning prayer in Congress is routine. The papers scarcely name the Protestant, Catholic or Jewish minister who happens to officiate. A century ago the situation was quite different. The Catholic minority regarded the Know Nothing Party a threat to its civil rights or religious freedom. Jews were distressed at the constant efforts to insert the word Christian into the Federal Constitution. Rabbi Raphall's invocation took on meaning during the War of Secession when the controversy about appointing Jewish chaplains for the Armed Forces became a disturbing issue.

The selection itself would indicate that Raphall occupied the highest place in the American rabbinate. To us this is surprising, for the names of Leeser, Wise, Einhorn or Lilienthal are much more familiar. It should be remembered, however, that Raphall was but 14 when he came to England. A mastery of English and a purer diction gave him the advantage over his German reared colleagues. Besides he carried himself with the born-to-wealth assurance of one whose spirit 'was never blighted by crushing poverty or humiliating persecutions.

When a child, Morris Jacob became seriously ill. His father, a banker to the King of Sweden, vowed he would dedicate his son to the rabbinate, should he recover. The boy was sent to Copenhagen for his Jewish studies. On receiving his doctorate at the German University of Erlangen, he traveled in Europe, then returned to England. Soon his lectures on post-Biblical history and Hebrew poetry attracted attentive listeners among Jews and intelligent Christians. He published in 1834 the "Hebrew Review and Magazine of Rabbinical Literature", the first Anglo-Jewish periodical to appear in the British Empire. His reputation as scholar, rabbi and orator spread throughout the United Kingdom. Rabbi of the Birmingham Hebrew Congregation for eight years, he translated parts of the Mosaic Pentateuch, of the Mishna, of Maimonides and of other Hebrew classics. As Secretary to Chief Rabbi Solomon Hershell, he participated in the influential synod over British Jewry.

On arrival, Rabbi Raphall toured the larger American cities and repeated his famed lectures. In a letter to her brother, the gracious Rebecca Gratz testifies to their stimulating effect upon her relatives and upon Christian clergymen. His coming would be greeted as an intellectual event in many communities. B'nai Jeshurun Congregation elected him rabbi and, under his direction, became the largest synagogue in New York. Believing that a knowledge of the Jewish past would remove Gentile ingrained prejudices, he wrote a *Post-Biblical History of the Jews* that continued the story from the close of the Old Testament to the destruction of the Second Commonwealth. Everything tended to enhance his prestige. The Congressional invitation merely indicated and confirmed his preeminent place in American Jewry. Suddeny a single incident brought about his decline.

Lincoln had been elected but not yet inaugurated. President Buchanan proclaimed a National Fast Day as a final, desperate act to avert the impending crack-up of the Union. People of all denominations gathered in their houses of worship for prayer. Rabbi Raphall, seizing this occasion to preach a sermon on "The Bible View of Slavery," declared with a display of learning that the Bible, which is the highest authority and superior to all laws, sanctioned human bondage. It was therefore idle for Protestant ministers to pervert the text and argue that Biblical Law intended to abolish slavery. He stressed the inherent humanity in the Jewish Law that regarded the slave, not as a *chattel* as in the South, but as a person; that the Mosaic dispensation protected his body, his rights and even his dignity. Consequently, the Rabbi placed Judaism in diametric opposition to the aim and ideology of the Abolitionists.

The sermon created a sensation. Copied by newspapers, it was reprinted in pamphlets and widely distributed. The Southern slave-owners were elated. Testimony out of the Bible, supported by scholarly interpretations of Jewish lore, received acclamations from Fundamentalists and slavery sympathizers in the North. But liberals were shocked, angered and ready to accept the anti-Jewish canards circulated among the masses for centuries. Bitterness came from the infuriated Abolitionists, among whom could be found Judeophobes of the classic type, who referred to "the race that stoned the Prophets and crucified the Redeemer of the World."

In the main, rabbis and laymen tended to consider Raphall's sermon just another partisan pamphlet in the bitter political controversy. But the more acute minded among them saw Judaism besmirched. Attacks from enemies were too familiar to cause surprise. Yet for a prominent rabbi to condone slavery as divinely ordained (though he did not actually say so) seemed blind and callous. The liberals contended that even if laws drafted 3000 years ago did not forbid human bondage, yet enlightened religion must progress beyond the penumbra of a semi-barbarous age. Jews, of all people, should feel particular compassion for the unfortunate and downtrodden.

The Rabbi of Har Sinai in Baltimore entered the lists against Raphall. With fiery sermons and vitriolic articles in German, David Einhorn exhausted logic, theology and invective against his reactionary colleague. As a consequence he had to flee for refuge in Philadelphia to save his family from mob violence. Even more effective were the intellectual dissertations of the encyclopedist Michael Heilprin, who did not hesitate to label Raphall a fool or a knave. These articles, written for the influential *New York Tribune* by the most learned Jew in America, helped to mollify even those fanatical Abolitionists who were in a mood for some anti-Semitic sniping.

Raphall's influence waned. Today he is forgotten except for the unfortunate sermon. Was the Fundamentalist trying to be honestly objective? Or were his views in keeping with an arrogant, bigoted, unkind disposition? He was cordially disliked by his colleagues in the Reform and Orthodox wings. A single anecdote might shed light upon his character. When he arrived in New York, Dr. Max Lilienthal, of Russian fame, called to pay his respects and expressed surprise that Raphall should forsake Britain for the immature community in the New World. The over-bearing Pharisee replied with the Talmudic dictum: "Where there are no men, strive thou to be a man." Lilienthal immediately took his leave.

1854

MAJOR
ALFRED MORDECAI

Conscientious Objector

In the early years of the struggling American Republic, many Jewish volunteers enlisted in the Armed Forces. Some rose from the ranks and attained the grade of Colonel. But after the wars each soldier, as he was mustered out, went back readily to his business or occupation. With the possible exception of Samuel Noah, the first Jew to choose the army as a life profession was Major Alfred Mordecai; and he might have reached the rank of Major General if conscience had not interfered.

Born 1804 in North Carolina, Alfred grew up care free and well adjusted in Warrenton, near the Virginia border and remained there until 1819. His father, Jacob Mordecai, owned and operated the famous Warrenton Female Seminary. Disqualified from attending a girls' school, Alfred nevertheless managed to pick up from the teaching staff, chiefly his own family, sufficient education to read ancient classics in the original Latin and Greek. Grounded in history, geography, French, mathematics, and literature, he was perhaps the best prepared cadet when admitted to West Point in his 15th year.

Graduating first in his class, he was detailed as assistant professor at the U. S. Military Academy until relieved several years later to become assistant engineer in the construction of Fortress Monroe in Virginia and Fort Calhoun at Norfolk. On completion of the fort he was appointed assistant to the Chief Engineer of the U. S. Army and detailed to construct ballistic pendulums. Made assistant inspector of arsenals, he had three under his direct charge. In command of the Washington arsenal, he was raised to the rank of Major for meritorious service in the line of duty during the Mexican War.

The War Department considered Major Mordecai more than a hard-working, efficient officer. He was sent on a mission that required penetration, boldness and honesty in the investigation of a delicate issue that involved good relations between Governments. As part of the peace treaty, Mexico agreed to pay American citizens in her territories such of their losses as grew out of the war. The Mexican Government had paid out under protest an exorbitant claim which it was now seeking to recover. Alfred Mordecai received the assignment to adjust this claim. He went into the wilds of Mexico and made a report which recommended the repayment of $500,000. The U. S. Government approved Mordecai's recommendation and paid this amount to Mexico.

When the Crimean War broke out, Major Mordecai was sent over as an observer together with Capt. George B. McClellan, later to become the top ranking commander of the Union forces in the Civil War and the opponent of President Lincoln in the 1864 campaign. The capable but reactionary Nicholas I, Czar of all the Russias, is said to have received the American-Jewish officer at a private conference. Mordecai's observations in Europe during the war in Crimea were published by order of Congress in the Senate Executive Document No. 60.

The fates had been singularly kind to Alfred Mordecai. Handsome in person, with the social graces and easy manner derived of a refined and cultured family well integrated in its milieu, he never knew any discriminations in the society of the military caste. As a student in West Point all references to religion, except in philosophic discourse, were studiously avoided by his classmates. Moreover he was happily married and father of a family. His peace time services packed with achievement were recorded and reflected in the numerous tracts, digests, manuals, and reports he wrote on military and scientific techniques. Secure in the estimate of his superiors as an officer of high merit and uncommon ability, his future seemed bright with honors and promotions.

But his sky became darkened by the same clouds that overcast the United States and soon broke into a furious storm. Like many another soldier or civilian, Major Mordecai found himself in the quandary of conflicting loyalties between his State and the Federal Union. No believer in secession, he nevertheless could not force himself to shower death and destruction upon his native state, the home of his happy childhood and adolescence. He could find no other alternative than to resign his commission and remain in Philadelphia. Thus ended suddenly the labors of a lifetime, filled with valuable military experience.

After a career of 42 years in the army, the Major found himself out of a job. Raising a family on officer's pay hardly left much reserve in the savings bank. He needed work, but at 57 good jobs are not easily obtained. His daughters were teachers. So the father also managed to get work teaching mathematics. Their combined salaries enabled the family to maintain their accustomed living standard.

But Alfred Mordecai had too much ability and personality to remain in eclipse. He was offered by the Mexico and Pacific Railroad a position as engineer in the construction of trunk lines from Vera Cruz to Mexico City and thence to the Pacific. In Mexico he lived without his family, moving chiefly in the society of Confederate expatriates. With several former army officers, he was presented at Court to Maximilian and Carlotta, the ill-starred Emperor and Empress of Mexico. He returned to Philadelphia in 1867 and for the next 20 years held down the important position of treasurer and secretary of canal and coal companies controlled by the Pennsylvania Railroad.

One cannot escape the conclusion that Major Alfred Mordecai's honest scruples cost him a place in American history. Few professional soldiers were better equipped for high service when the Civil War started. Of the vintage of Lee and Grant and as well trained, he could have made his mark on either side of the conflict. His less sensitive son and namesake joined the Union forces in 1861 and died a general. Alfred Mordecai is forgotten. And yet he might have been mentioned in the same breath with Philip Sheridan and Stonewall Jackson, with William Sherman and Joseph Johnston. Like all conscientious objectors, he was a victim of principle. To him applies the German maxim: *idealism destroys*.

SOLOMON NUNES CARVALHO

Artist-Explorer

Jᴏʜɴ C. Fʀᴇᴍᴏɴᴛ ranks among the most colorful figures in American history. Teacher, civil engineer, surveyor for railroads and army officer, he eloped with Jessie Benton, the talented literary daughter of Missouri's Senator, then a top leader in national politics. Thereafter Fremont became an explorer on a par in daring with Daniel Boone, Kit Carson and those adventurers who penetrated trackless country never before trodden by a white man.

There was also in his make-up an element of the irrational that sometimes got him into trouble, but also won him everlasting fame. But for Fremont, California might not have been a part of the U. S. A. His unorthodox conduct clashed with the army authorities. He was court-martialed and found guilty. By this time his popularity was such that President Polk found it necessary to pardon him. He had purchased a tract of land on which gold was subsequently found. Instead of earning millions, this land was lost after protracted litigation. In 1850 he was sent to represent California in the U. S. Senate.

One day in August, 1853, this Byronesque leader with plenty of personal magnetism met and invited Solomon Nunes Carvalho to join his new expedition for exploring the Far West into California. Carvalho succumbed to Col. Fremont's charm and immediately consented. This was surprising in a 38 year old aesthete who had led a sheltered life and who had written a treatise on the Biblical origin of the universe, entitled *The Two Creations*. Born in Charleston, he had in his 20th year set up as a portrait painter and had received a silver medal from the South Carolina Institute for his *Moses Receiving the Tablets of the Law on Sinai,* which was destroyed in 1838 when the Beth Elohim Synagogue burned down. Fortunately Carvalho had drawn a sketch of its interior so that today we can still see the "spacious and elegant" Synagogue described by LaFayette and dedicated in 1794 before Gov. Moultrie and his large entourage of military and civilians. But his best known paintings are the portraits of Rabbi Isaac Leeser, the leader of American Orthodox Jewry, and of Thomas Hunter, the founder of Hunter College in New York.

It also seems strange that Fremont should have selected a sensitive artist to join his party of ten Indians, two Mexicans and five Americans for an expedition that called for the toughest kind of physical and moral fibre. But Fremont was born in Savannah and studied at the College of Charleston. Evidently he recognized the loyal, impulsive, hardy, adventurous nature of Carvalho and put on his persuasive charm to win over a fellow Southerner, whom he understood and appreciated. Besides being a painter, Carvalho was expert in handling the recently invented daguerreotype photography, never before utilized in explorations.

Autumn was well advanced by the time the expedition got under way. Winter is obviously not the season for climbing the Rocky Mountains. The planning and timing reveals the queer streak in Fremont's make-up, the impractical knight-errantry that fails to provide sufficient food against starvation.

Month after month the heroic band blazed its vanishing trail through dense forests in ice and snow. Winding alongside the majestic mountains, a slip on the narrow ice-frozen path might plunge man or beast into the deep valley or river beds far below. Food supplies dwindled; the explorers had to kill their pack horses and fry the meat in melted tallow candles. When a beaver was shot or a porcupine killed, the starved men celebrated a holiday feast. Finally all beasts of burden were consumed, and there was danger of cannibalism among the desperate hunger-crazed crew.

Carvalho was second in command and a favorite with the tough-minded group. No hardship could weaken his confidence in or loyalty to his chief. He writes, "While suffering from frozen feet and hands, without food for 24 hours, traveling on foot over mountains of snow, I have stopped on the trail, made pictures of the country, repacked my materials, and found myself frequently with my friend Egloffstein, who generally remained with me to make barometrical observations, and a muleteer, some five or six miles behind camp, which was reached only with great expense of bodily as well as mental suffering. The great secret, however, of my untiring perseverance and continued success was that my honor was pledged to Col. Fremont to perform certain duties, and I would rather have died than not have redeemed it. I made pictures up to the very day Col. Fremont found it necessary to bury the whole baggage of the camp, including the daguerreotype apparatus."

The vice-commander on one occasion saved the entire party from massacre. A stray horse had been shot for food and some Indians collected its value. About 30 miles further a different band of Indians claimed the horse. The Utes had good horses, were armed with bows and arrows, rifles, and greatly outnumbered the explorers. Fremont saw the peril and resorted to strategy. He knew his lieutenant to be a crack shot and gave him an order in secret.

Carvalho started gun practice with a Colt six shooter and hit the bull's-eye six times. Cleverly shifting revolvers, he invited the chief to try his skill with a pistol which the Indians thought had already fired six times. The only guns the red men knew needed reloading after each shot. Amazed that the whites had a weapon that could shoot indefinitely, the Indians withdrew and went their way.

Conditions became desperate. Malnutrition brought on scurvy and diarrhea. Their emaciated bodies wrapped in tattered shreds scarcely had sufficient strength to drag over the snow that might cover a hollow deep ravine. One of the band died of starvation and exposure. When all hope began to abandon even their indomitable leader, help came unexpectedly from a Mormon outpost. Carvalho was taken to Salt Lake City. With rest, food and care, he gradually regained health. He remained for a time with the Mormons and did a painting of Brigham Young, their governor.

As the story of the hazardous adventure spread, Fremont's reputation as a daring romantic explorer captured the public imagination. Carvalho enhanced his Colonel's fame by writing a book: *Incidents of Travel and Adventure in the Far West; With Col. Fremont's Last Expedition Across the Rocky Mountains; Including three Months' Residence in Utah and a Perilous Trip Across the Great American Desert to the Pacific.*

In 1856, the newly formed Republican Party nominated Fremont for President. But for his anti-slavery views he might have defeated the pedestrian James Buchanan, and the name Abraham Lincoln would have remained unknown outside of Springfield, Ill. Carvalho would probably have been a member of Fremont's cabinet.

At all times Solomon Nunes Carvalho remained faithful to traditional Judaism. His articles in Leeser's *Occident* reveal concern over the assimilationist tendencies in the older strata and the leaning toward extreme Reform in the more recent arrivals. In the early days of Los Angeles he helped to form a Hebrew Benevolent Society for mutual aid and for burying the dead. In Baltimore and Philadelphia he took a leading part in Jewish communal and religious life. While not a great artist, his paintings are nevertheless sought after by collectors. They would deem it a fortunate stroke to find anything from the brush of the dashing artist who achieved fame as a pathfinder in a great American adventure.

CARVALHO'S SKETCH OF CHARLESTON SYNAGOGUE
DESTROYED BY FIRE IN 1838.

1856

ISIDOR BUSH

Abolitionist

GLANCING BACK at the Jewish exodus from Europe, one might conclude that it was the spontaneous act of a people weary of persecution and straining at the leash to reach the American haven of freedom and opportunity. Yet this obvious conclusion is not quite correct. Far-sighted leaders had to employ their talents to bring into being the migration trickle that ultimately became a mighty stream.

Among such leaders appeared the 26 year old Isidor Bush, whose maternal grandfather was the first Jew raised to the nobility in Austria. His father had moved from Prague to enter an established publishing house in Vienna. Father and son printed many important works, including the Talmud. Isidor also edited his own *Jahrbucher fur Israeliten,* which carried contributions by the outstanding scholars of the *Wissenshaft des Judentums.*

The Revolution of 1848 had its effect on Isidor Bush as well as other liberals dreaming of a free world. He began publishing a weekly which was the only organ in Austro-Hungary open to free discussion of Jewish affairs. For this paper the novelist Leopold Komport, famous for his ghetto stories, wrote "On to America", a clarion call for Jews to disregard everything and migrate to the U.S.A. Not every one agreed. Some thought it incumbent to remain and fight for freedom on the soil they had inhabited for centuries. Others feared that the ancient faith, for which rivers of blood had been shed, would disappear in the free new world. Isidor Bush, inspirer of Komport's appeal, had little faith in the triumph of liberalism under Austrian rule. He planned to leave even before the revolution failed. On January 8, 1849 he landed in New York.

Immediately, Bush started publishing *Israel's Herold,* the first Jewish weekly in America. He attempted to transplant another *Allgemeine Zeitung des Judentums* on American soil for German speaking residents and immigrants coming in by the droves. The paper displayed the solid learning and literary standards of Europe and, in a milieu of Orthodoxy, it carried only the writings of radical reformers. Neither the time, the place, nor the few readers were ripe for such a publication. *Israel's Herold* ceased after 12 issues. Bush left New York to join his relatives in the Missouri hinterland.

On reaching St. Louis, Bush together with his brother-in-law opened a general store that operated with moderate success for six years. Acquiring 100 acres, which he named Bushberg, he planted grapes and became an authority on viticulture. His catalog, translated in several languages, had a circulation in foreign lands. Engaging in real estate and banking, he became president of Peoples Savings Institution. General freight and passenger agent for a railroad, he succeeded in life insurance as an actuary figuring risks, rates and premiums. Interested in a wine and liquor business, he also served as president of the Mechanics Savings Institution. Such a variety of occupations and enterprises for a man of Bush's abilities reflect the troubled conditions in a sparsely settled state torn with Civil War strife.

On the other hand, Isidor Bush's deeper interests lay primarily in books, journalism and public events. An earlier revolutionary striving for greater freedom often leads in later life to fuller participation in civic and political affairs. To Bush, public service had the force of a religious obligation. Elected to the City Council, he also served on the Board of Education. Possessing a knowledge of finance, he worked out a scheme for the Federal Government to raise a popular war loan of $100,000,000 and submitted the plan to the Secretary of the Treasury. Salmon P. Chase thought well of the idea but did not believe that Congress would adopt it. As a mark of approval, Chase offered Bush a position in the Treasury Department. After the War of Secession, a Board of Immigration of the State of Missouri was formed to "repair as readily as possible the losses of population sustained through the desolation of war." Bush served as its secretary free of compensation for 12 years. He advocated a liberal policy to attract immigrants, who would create wealth and increase the population. Evidently the plan succeeded, for in 12 years the voters increased more than 340 per cent. When Bush resigned the Board ceased functioning.

But his most significant impact was felt in the abolition of slavery. Missouri had been a slave state since Henry Clay effected the famous 1820 compromise. The slave owners, eager to join the Confederacy, persuaded the Legislature to call a convention to consider secession. The opposition organized a Union Party to counteract the secessionists and selected a slate of 15 candidates, known for their loyalty to the Federal government. Isidor Bush was elected on this ticket. The Union Party gained control of the convention. Widely known as an Abolitionist and a firm believer in preserving the Union, he stood high in the confidence of his party. Somewhat sensitive about his German accent, he did not push himself forward, although his speeches were second to none in that capable assembly which took charge of state affairs, deposed the Governor, the Secretary of State and discharged the Legislature.

After Lincoln's Proclamation, the convention met again to consider emancipating the slaves. A special committee of nine, one from each congressional district, was selected to study the question and bring in recommendations. Bush, one of the nine, found himself in sharp disagreement with the majority who wished to put off emancipation for the future. Alone, he filed the minority report, urging immediate freedom and an end to the barter of slaves. In a stirring speech to the plenary session, he cried: "Slavery demoralizes, slavery fanaticism blinds you. It has arrayed brother against brother, son against father. It has destroyed God's noblest work—a free people." The convention passed a resolution postponing emancipation until July 4, 1870.

But events moved rapidly. Lee surrendered and Lincoln was martyred. The radicals now in control called a constitutional convention to bring Missouri up to date. Bush, elected a delegate, received special recognition when appointed on the committee of three to take charge of arrangements for the convention. The assembly quickly adopted the Emancipation Ordinance, thus justifying completely the stand Bush took two years earlier. Yet he was again in the opposition minority. Out of sympathy with the narrow, vengeful spirit of the victors drunk with power, he opposed restricting the citizenship rights of former Southern sympathizers, or disfranchising those who fought for the Confederacy. He was one of the 13 who refused to sign the Constitution. A decade later a new Constitution repudiated the instrument of 1865 and vindicated Bush's intransigence.

An accident in childhood from a fire rendered Bush unfit for military service. But during the war he served as a civilian secretary to Gen. John C. Fremont. In his *Reminiscences,* Isaac M. Wise complains of Bush's aloofness from Jewish affairs. The Rabbi expected a closer participation from the Abolitionist and humanitarian who had absorbed Jewish tradition in its European setting. To Wise, the secular outlook represented no great rift with a Reform Judaism that had broken the hard shell of excessive religiosity. Isidor Bush did assist in forming the first synagogue in St. Louis, yet stressed philanthropy rather than faith. He labored tirelessly to establish the Cleveland Jewish Orphan Asylum. To the end of his days he was prominently identified with the Independent Order of B'nai B'rith.

1857

AUGUST BONDI

*In Bleeding Kansas
with John Brown*

Fifteen-year-old Anshel Bondi joined a student corps in Vienna to assist Louis Kossuth in freeing Hungary. The failure of democracy to attain a foothold in the Europe of 1848 caused many liberals to emigrate. The Bondi family settled in St. Louis and "Anshel" was Anglicized to "August".

Hearing of an expedition to free Cuba from Spanish oppression, August enlisted, but the attempt died stillborn. After several years in Texas he returned to St. Louis and got a job in the store of Theodore Weiner, an emigrant from Poland. At this time the Indian Territory in Kansas was opened to white settlers. Weiner and Jacob Benjamin, lately from Bohemia, decided to pool resources and join the pioneers trekking to Kansas; it was a good opportunity to establish business on the ground floor of that wild and woolly country. With a stock valued at $7000, Weiner set out in covered wagons and took August Bondi along as chief clerk with an interest in the business.

The new territory became a pawn in national politics, caught between the anti- and pro-slavery forces. The newly arrived settlers were to decide whether they wanted a free or slave state. Northern home-seekers came in greater numbrs, but the Southerners were far better organized. The minority rammed through a Constitution that permitted slavery. This led to civil war in "Bleeding Kansas". Pro-slavery sympathizers, who came in from Missouri to vote, remained to harass and persecute the Free Soilers. They laid waste to the town of Lawrence. Arson, robbery, and murder became daily occurrences. The settlements were drifting towards anarchy, with the pro-slavery forces as aggressors and victors.

The three Jewish pioneers might have pulled through this conflict had they minded their own business. But they spoke their anti-slavery sentiments openly and aroused the ire of the "Border Ruffians", as the Northern settlers called the violent proponents of slavery. When the news spread that Theodore Weiner had given material assistance to the Free Soilers, he became a marked man. Dutch Bill Sherman, bully and gang leader, notified him to leave Kansas in three days, "or else". The three Jewish newcomers applied to the Brown brothers for assistance. About this time their father, John Brown, arrived from the East.

John Brown was like a figure out of the Old Testament. A fanatical enemy of slavery, filled with righteous wrath, he substituted action for the words of Garrison's Abolitionists. A quixotic adventure several years later in Virginia brought him martyrdom and hastened the Civil War. With eighteen white and black crusaders he attempted to free the slaves in the South. Breaking open the armory at Harpers Ferry, an act of sheer lunacy, was tantamount to declaring war on the U.S.A. Besides, Virginia law prescribed hanging for treason resulting in murder. Legally there was no question as to Brown's guilt. Yet Emerson declared: "The new saint awaiting his martyrdom will make the gallows glorious like the Cross." Armies marching to battlefields sang:

> *"John Brown's body lies a-moldering in the grave,*
> *But his soul goes marching on."*

In Kansas John Brown took command and called for volunteers. Among the first seven to respond were August Bondi and Theodore Weiner. (Benjamin seemed to have joined another band or formed a company of his own.) Now the anti-slavery group took the offensive and used the tactics of their enemies. Led by John Brown, the settlement on Pottawatomie Creek was attacked and five "Border Ruffians", including Dutch Bill Sherman, were lynched.

The Weiner store with its merchandise was soon reduced to ashes. The three Jewish comrades were in the midst of the fighting, shooting and looting. Throughout the two years' warfare in Kansas, they were as guilty or innocent as the rest of John Brown's company. Bondi had some education and wrote an eye witness account of the stirring events in his autobiography, which is valuable source material for historians and biographers. The following excerpt should be of interest to readers understanding Yiddish:

"We followed Captain Brown up the hill towards the 'Border Ruffians' camp, I, next to Brown and in advance of Weiner. We walked with bent backs, nearly crawled, that the tall dead grass of the year before might somewhat hide us from the 'Border Ruffian' marksmen. Yet the bullets kept on whistling. Weiner was 37 and weighed 250 lbs. I, 22 and lithe. Weiner puffed like a steamboat, hurrying behind me. I called out to him. 'Nu, was meinen sie yetzt?' (Well, what do you think of it now?) His answer, 'Was soll ich meinen? (What should I think?) 'Sof odom muves.' (The end of man is death.) In spite of the whistling bullets, I laughed when he said 'Machen wir dem alten mann sonst broges.' (Look out, or we'll make the old man angry.)"

Bondi remained in the state and joined the Fifth Kansas Cavalry at the outbreak of the War of Secession. Promoted to First Sergeant, he fought in every engagement of his company and survived. Returning to Salina, Kansas, he found his home burned to the ground, yet was enormously pleased to discover unscathed the flintlock which John Brown had given him. Bondi presented the musket to the Kansas State Historical Society, of which he had become a director. The former immigrant and ex-soldier evolved into a well integrated citizen. He farmed, was a real estate broker, became a lawyer, got into politics, held the office of Township Trustee and served as Clerk of the District Court.

During the time of trouble in "Bleeding Kansas" the three comrades were little people. Yet they are not without significance. The 100,000 Jews in ante-bellum America were largely refugees from European oppression and hardly yet sufficiently acclimatized in their newly adopted land to interfere in explosive issues that were leading the nation to the brink of an abyss. It comes, therefore, as a refreshing surprise to find three Jewish lads in the small, devoted band of John Brown, fighting to prevent slavery from taking root in Kansas.

1858

ABRAHAM JONAS

Friend of Lincoln

ONE OF 22 children, Abraham Jonas was born in Exeter, England. Either the family multiplied too numerously or conditions in England were not too favorable. In 1817 his brother Joseph Jonas left Exeter to become the first Jewish settler of Cincinnati. Two years later Abraham followed and began his new life in the auction business. Things looked rather encouraging, for he soon married the daughter of Gershom Mendes Seixas, the Rabbi-Hazan who with Christian clergymen stood near the platform at the first inauguration of President Washington.

His first wife died shortly after they were married. Jonas, restless in his twenty-fourth year, began to take an active part in the affairs of the budding community. An incorporator of the first synagogue, he is also recorded as a purchaser of the plot for a Jewish cemetery from Nicholas Longworth, the great-grandfather of the Nicholas Longworth who married Alice, daughter of Theodore Roosevelt and became Speaker of the House of Representatives in the Administrations of Coolidge and Hoover. Abraham Jonas left Cincinnati and settled in Kentucky. There he went into business and entered politics.

Freemasonry was a powerful magnet in the early days of the republic. Important personages in the circles of Washington, of Franklin, of Marshall, or of LaFayette joined this secret fraternity, said to have been the nest in which the American and French Revolutions were hatched. Jews were especially attracted to a lodge which professed a progressive liberalism based on the enlightened concept that all men are brothers under God the Father. A powerful attraction lay in the unequivocal monotheism that enabled men of every religion to enter its mysteries, a toleration seldom conceived or practiced prior to the 18th century.

But as the 19th century advanced the Masonic skies clouded. When a Freemason of unscrupulous character, one Henry Morgan, disappeared from Batavia, a reaction set in against an order which teaches the best of principles. Out of an atmosphere of hate and suspicion arose a new political party of anti-Masons. They poured slander and vitriol upon the heads of Freemasons, yet were encouraged by John Quincy Adams. They were led by the club-footed Thaddeus Stevens, whose liberal views did not apply to Masonry. This sinister bigot, in his old age, almost succeeded in impeaching President Andrew Johnson. His political gang in the 1830s caused Masonry to shrink in New York from 20,000 to 3,000 members, from 500 to 30 lodges.

Clearly it was hardly the time for any one with political aspirations to join the Ancient and Accepted Order of Freemasonry. Politicians are noted for their eagerness to affiliate with any organization that might promote their interests; conversely they shy away from associations which may retard their advancement. But Abraham Jonas entered politics and Masonry at the same time. He served a term in the Kentucky General Assembly and was reelected in 1833. The same year he became the Grand Master of Masons for Kentucky. His portrait hangs on the wall of the Grand Lodge in Louisville. Moving later to Quincy, he became the first Grand Master for the State of Illinois. Immediately following his death the Masons honored his memory with a plaque in the hall of the Grand Lodge. On celebrating 50 years of Masonry in Illinois the Grand Lodge struck a bronze medal commemorating its first Grand Master.

Holding the highest position in Masonry and serving four years in the General Assembly might have enabled Jonas to become a power in Kentucky. But he followed the pioneering trend of the times and with many other Kentuckians moved to Illinois. Like Lincoln, he opened a store and used his spare time studying law. For two years he led a movement to transfer the county seat from Quincy to Columbus and edited the *Columbus Advocate,* the newspaper favoring his group. The venture failed, but he made many friends. In 1842 he ran for the Legislature and was elected; although a comparative stranger in Illinois, he received the third largest vote among 21 candidates.

Jonas had a genuine flair for politics. According to a contemporary, the German immigrant Gustave Kerner who subsequently became a Justice of the Illinois Supreme Court, Jonas was highly successful as a public speaker and "the best debater and best politician" of all the Whig members in the Legislature. With such promising talents, he felt justified in turning over the business to his two brothers. When 43 years old, he was admitted to the Bar and practiced successfully for the next 20 years. Active and influential, Jonas became an important factor in state politics. Appointed Postmaster of Quincy by President John Tyler, he was reappointed by Millard Fillmore.

In his first session he met a tall, raw-boned, lanky representative from Springfield named Abe Lincoln who attracted but slight attention. Something about the homey features and rustic humor of this legislator appealed to Jonas; they became fast friends. Both attended the national conference which founded the Whig party. When Lincoln had business in Quincy, he did his work at the office of Jonas and Asbury. In 1856, Jonas and Lincoln were chosen Presidential Electors by the Illinois State Convention.

After the formation of the Republican Party, Jonas joined Lincoln at the first national convention in 1856 and attempted to have his friend nominated for the Presidency. But he followed Lincoln in supporting John C. Fremont. In the great debate on slavery between Lincoln and Stephen A. Douglas held at Quincy, Jonas served as chairman of the Republican Committee on Arrangements. He inserted a notice in the newspapers requesting the presence of Lincoln's friends. In the midst of the bitter national campaign of 1860 Lincoln, the candidate for the Presidency, was accused of membership in the anti-Catholic, anti-alien Know Nothing Party. In a long letter the future President denied ever being a member, but cautiously intimated that his friend Abraham Jonas might make the denial for him.

One of Lincoln's first Presidential acts was the appointment of Jonas as postmaster of Quincy. Nothing could shake Lincoln's esteem, not even the information that three sons of Jonas were fighting in the Confederate Army. His son Edward Jonas, however, served the Union with distinction and rose to the rank of Major. Divided family loyalties were by no means rare in those troubled times. Another son, Benjamin F. Jonas, later to become U. S. Senator from Louisiana, stated that President Lincoln would inquire after the Jonas boys of anyone coming from New Orleans, after the city was taken over in 1862 by the Union forces. Lincoln's confidence in Jonas may be inferred from the incident following the arrest of Thomas Thorough at Quincy for treason. Acting on the suspect's appeal and a flock of petitions for his release, the President directed his Secretary of War Stanton "to dispose of the case at the discretion of Abraham Jonas and Henry Asbury, both of Quincy, both of whom I know to be loyal and sensible men."

Jonas was dying. He wished to see his son, who was a Confederate soldier imprisoned at Lake Erie. Jonas refused to bother the President. His wife and daughter had Orville Browning telegraph the Great Emancipator. Lincoln divulged his feelings for his old friend by an order to the War Department: "Allow Charles H. Jonas, now a prisoner of war at Johnson's Island, a parole of three weeks to visit his dying father, Abraham Jonas, at Quincy, Illinois. A. Lincoln." After the death of Jonas, the President immediately appointed his widow postmistress of Quincy.

1859

DAVID EINHORN

Radical Reformer

Wʜᴇɴ ᴀ ᴛʜɪʀᴅ ᴀᴛᴛᴇᴍᴘᴛ at unifying American Jews was made, it had possibilities of success. Growing immigration had increased the population to about 100,000 souls, and the lack of organization among Jews presented vital problems. Orthodoxy resented the new reforms as threatening schism in Judaism which was striving against odds to establish a foothold in the new land. The Reformers themselves were divided between moderates and radicals. A conference of synagogue representatives was called by Isaac M. Wise, initiator of American Reform. Orthodox leader Isaac Leeser came and eyed the Reformers suspiciously. Both spokesmen agreed as to the value of a national religious federation.

The conference felt elated when a compromise formula was agreed to by Wise and Leeser. Union in Israel appeared certain when the Cleveland Conference of 1855 adopted the resolution: "The Bible is of immediate Divine origin; the Talmud contains the traditional, legal and logical exposition of the Biblical Laws which must be expounded and practiced according to the comments of the Talmud." The victory seemed permanent. Even the extreme traditionalists, who opposed participation with infidels, conceded a victory to Isaac Leeser.

But prospects for harmony were quickly blasted. A newcomer that very year from Germany was able to shatter the unity in American Judaism. David Einhorn, the new Rabbi of Har Sinai in Baltimore, protested: "Who authorized you (American Sanhedrin) to make alliances with the Orthodox and their Talmudic ideas?" Other Reformers lined up behind the radical firebrand. American Judaism was not destined to see unity. Each denomination ultimately organized its own rabbinical councils.

In Germany Einhorn had become entangled in the *kultur kampf,* raging within and without the *Judengasse.* During the first half of the 19th century conflict was inevitable as soon as Emancipation opened the ghetto and let in a flood of modern thought. The sudden light of the *Aufklaerung* almost blinded the dwellers in a medieval world. The more progressive sought a new formula that would enable the liberated Jew to live in the Fatherland as a good patriot and useful citizen, differing only in religion from the dominant Teuton. But the difference was more than creed or confession. Centuries of living within the circumscribed ghetto, obedient to a closely meshed code of traditional law, produced a bearded and caftaned sectarian who appeared incongruous to the hostile surrounding society.

Extremists and conservatives recognized the necessity for reform. Samson Raphael Hirsch and Zacharias Frankel sought gradual evolution consistent with a Torah revealed by Divinity. Abraham Geiger and Samuel Holdheim advocated drastic changes, which the pious believed would subvert Judaism completely. The radicals proposed a violent operation that would cut away Rabbinic legalism and revert to the universalism of the Prophets. They stressed the ethical and spiritual as transcending the burdensome adherence to 613 *mitzvos.* They deleted from the prayer book all reference to the restoration of a national homeland in Zion. Close observance of the Sabbath was relaxed. The cult of ritual slaughter and the kosher preparation or separation of foods were abolished. The synagogue now became a temple with a shortened service that initiated the sermon and organ, minimized Hebrew in favor of German and admitted women on a parity with men. The personal Messiah was rejected and transformed into a messianic era. The immortality of the soul was retained as a substitute for the resurrection of the body.

Such fundamental changes in practice and doctrine proved far too revolutionary to go unchallenged. A violent controversy ensued, with David Einhorn taking a significant part. But radicalism in politics or religion was frowned upon by the reactionary governments of Central Europe. Instigated by Orthodox zealots, officialdom refused to confirm his appointment to the rabbinical post of Wellhausen in Bavaria. The young rabbi tried Budapest. This time his temple was closed by the Austrian monarchy. The invitation to become Rabbi of Har Sinai in Baltimore was especially pleasing to the fighting reformer weary of secular power meddling in religion.

In America, Einhorn found an open field for reforms which would never, as in Europe, run counter to a deeply rooted tradition. He quickly sensed that the seeds sowed by the Jacobsons and Friedlanders, the Geigers and Holdheims would sprout forth to their fullest efflorescence in the virgin soil of the New World. In fact, the furrows lay fallow awaiting the planter. A year after his arrival, Einhorn began publishing monthly his periodical *Sinai,* which together with Wise's *Deborah* reached the German speaking immigrants now constituting the majority in American Jewry. Einhorn's impassioned eloquence, his wide scholarship and written word battered incessantly at the moderation of the Western rabbis. His German sidur *Olath Tamid* brushed aside Wise's *Minhag America* and subsequently became, with slight modifications in translation, the official Union Prayer Book. Isaac M. Wise, with his gifts for leadership and organizing, found it necessary to acquiesce in the extremist reforms of David Einhorn.

For Einhorn's courageous stand on the slavery issue, American Jewry must ever be grateful. The combative oppositionist could not contain his feelings on human bondage in a free land. His bitter invectives, though voiced in German, became known to the Southern sympathizers in pro-slavery Baltimore, which had jailed the Abolitionist William Lloyd Garrison and mobbed a German editor for expressing anti-slavery views. Public feeling boiled over in a riot on April 19, 1861. The military and the police warned Einhorn that his name appeared on the mob's list. Friends pleaded that he display the Dixie flag. He refused. He finally consented to remove his family from the danger spot. He abandoned home and belongings and secretly brought his wife and children to Philadelphia. Martial law forbade his return. When the situation calmed down, he prepared to take up where he had left off. But the trustees denied him the freedom to discuss dangerous questions. He resigned and accepted a pulpit in Philadelphia.

The benefits of Einhorn's victory over the progressive conservatism of Wise and Lilienthal might be questioned. For besides sabotaging unity in American Jewry, he diluted Reform Judaism to a pallid monotheism. His gaudy concept of Israel's mission to the world hardly deterred the assimilation that brought thousands to Christian Science and Unitarian churches. Today, a century after Einhorn's arrival, finds the descendants of the German mid-century immigrants almost as rare as the Portuguese scions of Colonial days. His fantastic proposal to turn Tisha B'av, the *Yahrzeit* mourning tragedies and extermination, into a feast day for rejoicing over the scattering of Jews among the nations reveals a lack of psychologic insight as well as historic blindness. His attempt to substitute German for Hebrew as the language of prayer in America spells downright folly. But history is the best commentator. As the 20th century advances, American Jews are rejecting the disintegrating radicalism of David Einhorn. Even the term *Reform* seems to be losing its former appeal. *Liberal Judaism* is coming into favor as the more fitting name for the growing tendencies. The increasing urge to amalgamate the Reform and Conservative wings may yet bring new force and vitality to non-Orthodox Judaism.

1860

MICHAEL HEILPRIN

Encyclopedist

THE RUSSIAN-POLISH TOWN of Piotrkow was the birthplace of several persons who made their mark after leaving the Czarist Pale. Ernestine L. Rose and Fabius Mieses hailed from Piotrkow. Here in 1823 Michael Heilprin was born. A few years later, 1830, Poland attempted to throw off the Russian yoke. Memories of this ill fated revolt sank deep in the consciousness of the seven year old child and conditioned his future attitude toward all oppressed peoples.

The Heilprins were intellectual and intelligent. The record of their scholarly achievements over three centuries can be found in the major libraries of the world. Yet this gifted family had faith in Central and Eastern Europe. They even believed idealism would develop in a free Poland. But as the repressive measures of Russia became intolerable, Michael Heilprin, 20 years old and married, moved to Hungary, then seething with revolt against the oppression of the Austrian Hapsburgs. He opened a bookstore and quickly acquired an amazing proficiency in the Magyar lan-

357

guage. The Hungarian gentry soon recognized his worth. Still garbed in his kaftan, the Polish Jew was received in the local club of the nobles.

Swept into the revolutionary vortex, he wrote patriotic articles and poems that attracted some attention. He was welcomed in the circle of Louis Kossuth, the Hungarian National leader. When the Nationalist Liberals attained temporary power, Michael Heilprin accepted the post of secretary to the Literary Bureau, an agency attached to the Government. But the revolution soon collapsed. He became a marked man and barely avoided capture by the Austrians. For several months he remained in hiding until he managed to escape. He tried France, England, and even attempted a comeback in Hungary. Convinced that the New World offered the best prospects for free living and inner expression, Heilprin joined the other Hungarian exiles, including the Kossuth family, already living in the U. S. A.

While attempting to earn a precarious living by teaching, he met Ripley and Dana, editors of Appleton's *New American Cyclopedia*. Impressed by the extent and accuracy of his erudition, they engaged Heilprin to revise all historical, geographical and biographical articles in the first major American attempt at compiling a cyclopedia. He also contributed many of the important articles. The excellence of his work, its unification and verification, received commendation, as "no other similar work of collaboration published in the English language had ever this merit in so high a degree in which, for example, there was a spelling of proper names, a uniformed system of transcribing words (especially proper names) from foreign languages not using the Roman alphabet."

Meantime, the contradictions of slavery in a democracy were breeding a state of disunion and war. While absorbed in his arduous labors, Heilprin was startled on reading in the newspapers a sermon by Rabbi Morris A. Raphall of New York, bristling with citations from the Torah to prove that the Mosaic Law sanctioned slavery. Southerners and their sympathizers welcomed the discourse and reprinted it in pamphlet form, as proof that Holy Writ sustained their cause. In 1861 the country was in an ugly mood. The learned sermon angered liberals and exasperated Abolitionists. Nor were there wanting editorials casting aspersions on Judaism.

The *New York Tribune,* edited by Horace Greeley, denounced Raphall and cast strictures upon Judaism. This leading anti-slavery daily published Heilprin's lengthy reply, a scathing refutation of the rabbi's thesis and an exoneration of Judaism on theological and historical grounds. The *Tribune,* by accepting Heilprin's forcible, scholarly arguments in lieu of Raphall's exposition, exerted considerable influence on American public opinion. Judaism escaped further sniping from anti-slavery elements.

Rabbis and informed laymen also denounced Raphall's sermon, but they could not reach a wide public for their vehement anti-slavery views. Besides, Heilprin's reputation as a scholar of wide attainments grew daily. With a memory almost as phenomenal as Macaulay's he could read eighteen languages and speak eight. After completing his task on Appleton's Cyclopedia, he joined the *Nation* at its inception and remained with that important publication for the last 20 years of his life.

·The extent, depth and variety of Heilprin's encyclopedic knowledge are best reflected in his continuous output of criticisms, editorials, reviews and articles in the *Nation.* They ranged from modern criticism of the Old Testament to daily events in European revolutions, from theology to politics, from the time and place of 600 battles, large and small, of the American Civil War to a comprehensive view of universal history, from archeology to Hebrew poetry. His reviews of the Encyclopedia Britannica as volume after volume appeared showed a catholicity of knowledge hardly equaled by any American scholar of the post-Civil War period.

Out of Michael Heilprin's multitudinous writings, it is some-

what disappointing to find but a single two volume work published in his life time. The *Historical Poetry of the Ancient Hebrews,* which embodies his lifelong studies in Biblical literature,
is a critical analysis of poetic passages in the Old Testament in
harmony with the modern views of 19th century research. He did
not live to complete the third volume. But his monumental labors
are largely anonymous, buried in periodical and encyclopedic
editing. A search in the files of the *Nation* would reveal a 20 year
literary output of criticism rarely surpassed in the English
language for content, variety, exact scholarship and broad yet
sound estimates. The editors of the *Nation,* in their obituary
tribute, declared:

"How great is the loss sustained by American scholarship
through the death of Mr. Michael Heilprin, the general public,
owing to the man's invincible modesty, cannot know. To this
journal and its readers it may fairly be pronounced irreparable,
so largely has he contributed during the past twenty years to
whatever reputation the *Nation* may have acquired for literary
accuracy or breadth of information."

Michael Heilprin neither observed formal Judaism nor participated in purely Jewish affairs. His contacts and friendships were
largely in scholarly Gentile circles. Satisfied with the Austro-Hun-
garian compromise that was reached on Magyar aspirations and
happy over the abolition of slavery, he looked forward to the
peaceful pursuit of study and writing. His calm was broken when
the Russian pogroms broke out. Shiploads of refugees came
streaming into New York harbor. Could a fighter for human
rights ignore the plight of his own flesh and blood?

The historian in Heilprin grasped the significance of the Czar's
persecutions. Proudly conscious of Jewish achievements and contributions to universal history, he resented the wrongs and humiliations heaped upon his people. Pained at their degradation,
he nevertheless knew the vast potentialities beneath the uncouth
exterior of the new arrivals. He also sensed the complications
that would follow any influx of large numbers, ill-fitted and un-

prepared for a quick adjustment in a strange environment. Throwing his fast ebbing energy into the task, he rendered a service to the Jewish cause.

Going beyond mere philanthropy, he advocated agriculture as a substitute for the petty trading associated with Jews. He labored to establish Jewish farm settlements in New Jersey, Dakota, Oregon and Kansas. Virtually on his deathbed, he wrote a memorandum at the request of Oscar S. Straus, then Ambassador to Turkey. This plea influenced Baron de Hirsch to invest $4,000,000 which established Russian Jews as successful farmers in many American states.

1861

DAVID LEVY YULEE

Florida's First Senator

Dᴀᴠɪᴅ Lᴇᴠʏ was born in 1810 on the Island of St. Thomas in the Caribbean. Shortly thereafter, his father acquired extensive lands in Florida for a Jewish colonization project. David spent his boyhood in a private school at Norfolk, Va. Between father and son began a coolness which continued throughout life. We do not know the cause. Possibly the young blade spent money too freely, vying with the sons of Virginia slave owning planters. Could it be that the boy showed a leaning for the dominant religion? In his 17th year David Levy had his allowance cut off and thereafter shifted for himself.

After staying a while on one of his father's plantations, David found his way to St. Augustine and studied law in a private office. His father's precipitate action might have been conducive in developing a self-made man out of a potential spendthrift. The young fellow entered politics and became clerk of the Territorial Legislature, a coveted post. He took an active part in the State Constitutional Convention and then made a successful race for

Congressional Representative-at-large for the Territory of Florida.

In Washington he attracted attention through an incident which proved fortunate. His seat was contested on the ground of non-citizenship. His opponent had the backing of former President John Quincy Adams, the future President Millard Fillmore, and such eminent personalities as Everett, Giddings, Roosevelt, and Cushing. But his maiden speech in defense of his title made a marked impression. It gave him standing as well as notoriety. He was able to do an effective job in hastening the admission of Florida as the 27th state in the Federal Union.

David Levy's work was evidently recognized. For in the very first campaign in the new state he was elected to the U. S. Senate. A strong advocate of slavery, he lined up behind the leadership of John C. Calhoun and at the age of 36 was an important member of that body. He then met the daughter of ex-Gov. Wickliffe of Kentucky, a former member of President Tyler's Cabinet. He must have put forth some effort to win the beautiful girl, known in Washington as "the Wickliffe Madonna". We find the Florida Legislature changing his name, or to be more exact, adding a patronymic. On the roster of the U. S. Senate, he appears thereafter as David Levy Yulee.

Here we must pause a moment, and inquire into the necessity for this move. If David Levy actually intended to obscure his origin, he might have selected an Anglo-Saxon name. Wilson, Lowell or Williams would have served his purpose far better. Yulee sounds quite Seminole and serves to emphasize rather than hide his foreign origin. Besides, he moved in Washington society and every one knew his Jewish antecedents. A clue is furnished by George R. Fairbanks, a prominent attorney of St. Augustine, who represented Moses E. Levy, yet remained on friendly terms with his son. On account of their strained relations, the father was never able to reveal his family history. Mr. Fairbanks told the Senator the fantastic story of his grandfather's position as Grand Vizier to the Morocco Sultan; of a plot by the heir apparent to dethrone the ruler; of the Crown Prince's succession to the throne following the sudden death of the old Sultan; of the Vizier's sudden flight. The love-struck Senator must have used the story with telling effect upon the romantic young girl. Instead of a Jew, his grandfather was a Portuguese who became the Mohammedan Prince Yulee, married to an English Jewess. But since his father had to go into trade, he didn't want to sully the princely name; he merely adopted his mother's surname Levy as more suitable for a business career. The Wickliffe Madonna must have clapped her hands excitedly and demanded the reinstatement of the princely Yulee.

On the next election, Yulee was defeated; but in 1856 he was elected for a second term. In 1861 he was the first Senator to announce the secession of a Southern state and took a sorrowful but courteous leave of his colleagues. This marks the high point in his career. He served in the Southern Congress, but without distinction. After the defeat of the Confederacy, the Governor of Florida appointed Yulee on a commission to proceed to Washington and have his state peacefully reconstructed into the Federal Union. But the ex-Senator was arrested, and on orders from Washington was confined at Fort Pulaski near Savannah. After a year's imprisonment he was released upon the intercession of General Ulysses S. Grant.

Ex-Senator Yulee now retired from public life and devoted all his energies to rehabilitating the Florida railway system, of which he was president. It is a tribute to Yulee's persuasive talents that on the eve of the Civil War he was able to induce northern capital to invest $5,000,000, a large sum for those days, in a prospective Florida railroad. During the war he exposed himself to the animosity of Jefferson Davis in his efforts to prevent the rails from being torn up and converted into cannon. Cars, locomotives and tracks were all rusting together. For 20 years he fought unremittingly to restore the decrepit railway. His efforts were finally rewarded when English capitalists bought out the stockholders.

Senator Yulee was, without doubt, an eminent American and a loyal Southerner. His services to Florida earned him a permanent and important niche in the State's history. Today the frenzy for secession and slavery may seem queer, even in the South. Yet the chivalrous Confederates can only be judged by the state of mind that obtained during such a highly emotional era.

Yulee and Benjamin merely reflected the hysteria prevalent in a highly controversial period. From the point of view of their state or section, both were patriots stirred by the loftiest sentiments of loyalty. They should, therefore, be judged together with Calhoun and Rhett, Lee and Jackson, Jefferson Davis and Alexander Stephens.

But Yulee and Benjamin were not attacked as misguided fanatics in a cause that crushed all feelings of humanity and justice. They were assailed as Jews, even though both had severed all ties with Judaism. Yulee's enmity towards his father, his obscuring the family name, his eagerness to marry outside the faith and his membership in the Presbyterian church would indicate a coldness, perhaps resentment, towards his ancient folk and faith. Yet according to the diary of Charles Francis Adams, the Senator from Tennessee, Andrew Johnson, later President of the United States, declared to him: "There is that Yulee, miserable little cuss! I remember him in the House—the contemptible little Jew —standing there and begging us—Yes! begging us to let Florida in as a state. Well! we let her in, and took good care of her, and fought her Indians; and now that despicable little beggar stands up in the Senate and talks about *her* rights."

1862

CESAR J. KASKEL

Shtadlan for a Day

THROUGHOUT the American Civil War, Kentucky, though a Southern State, remained loyal to the Union. In Paducah the small Jewish group lived on good terms with their fellow townsmen, and Cesar J. Kaskel, a good-looking merchant with a flair for public affairs, helped to organize the local Union League.

On a December morning the friendly sheriff walked into his store, "Good morning, Mr. Kaskel, I'm afraid I have bad news for you. Look at this." He handed the merchant a certified copy of General Order No. 11 issued on December 17th, 1862, at Holly Springs, Miss. by General U. S. Grant: *The Jews, as a class violating every regulation of trade established by Treasury Department and also department orders, are hereby expelled from the department (Tennessee, Mississippi and Kentucky) within 24 hours from the receipt of this order.*

Kaskel was thunderstruck. The sympathetic expression of the sheriff helped him recover his composure.

"Can anything be done? Does the order require immediate action?"

"That's why I'm here," answered the sheriff. "The army officer handed me the paper this morning. He looked relieved when I told him I would handle the matter, since I know all the Jewish people here."

"What about appealing to General Grant?" ventured Kaskel hopefully.

"The Lieutenant said it has been tried, but Headquarters would not accept any such petition." A sudden light illumined Kaskel's features as he exclaimed, "I know, I shall telegraph President Lincoln. Honest Abe will not permit this outrage." "Say that's a good idea," declared the sheriff. "I didn't think of that. Go ahead, and I will hold up execution for three days."

Trading with the enemy goes on in every war. During the War of Secession a situation arose that was too tempting to pass up. Cotton was sorely needed in the textile mills of New England. The spindle looms in Birmingham and Manchester were idle and thousands of English workers went hungry. In the Confederacy millions of bales of cotton were stocked in warehouses, in depots, in the fields. The Southerners were in dire need of medical supplies, munitions, foods and manufactured goods, A barrel of salt brought $100.

After Ulysses S. Grant captured Fort Donaldson, he penetrated into Mississippi. Now came the opportunity for each side to obtain the articles so badly needed. Brisk trading behind the lines sprang up. Washington would not interfere, since the demand for cotton was too urgent. Speculation became rife and army officers were involved in secret partnerships. It was known that Jesse Grant, father of the General, received a cut from cotton buyers who, through his recommendations, obtained permits from the son. After making a tidy fortune, a relative of Mrs. Grant was ordered to leave the camp. President Lincoln remarked to a friend: "The army is diverted from fighting the rebels to speculating in cotton." Treasury agents sent to investigate became themselves implicated in the traffic. Some army officers captured $2,000,000 worth of cotton and pocketed the proceeds.

At the time the Jewish population in the United States numbered approximately 150,000. Many were native born and Americanized. But in the decade preceding the Civil War large numbers had migrated from Germany. Conspicuous for their foreign ways and thick Teutonic accents, they were as easily identified as the poor and uncouth refugees that would come flocking in from Russia a generation later. Mainly peddlers carrying their packs of merchandise to the farms and villages of rural America, they descended with the Gentile traders into the conquered area and exchanged the articles badly needed for Confederate cotton.

No answer came from the White House. The telegram may not have been delivered in the clamor and rush of war messages. Order No. 11 applied to all Jews in the Tennessee Military Department, to citizen and foreigner, to soldier and civilian, to office holder, professional or business man. Thirty men and their families left Paducah; two dying old women were permitted to remain.

Cesar J. Kaskel displayed true leadership. He decided to go and appeal directly to the President. He brought along a Bill of Particulars: a copy of the infamous order; affidavits of leading citizens testifying that Jews in Paducah were never engaged in trading with the enemy, that two of them had served enlistments in the Union Army. On the boat to Cincinnati he spent all the time writing letters and telegrams to daily papers, to Jewish publishers and community leaders.

An Ohio congressman, friend of Rabbi Isaac M. Wise, obtained an immediate conference at the White House. Pres. Lincoln looked searchingly at the expelled citizens, listened to the affidavits, and humorously queried: "And so the Children of Israel were driven from the happy land of Canaan?" To which Kaskel replied: "Yes, and that is why we have come unto Father Abraham's bosom, asking protection." Said Lincoln: "And this protection they shall have at once." Lincoln sat down at his big table and wrote a note to General-in-Chief Henry W. Halleck directing a telegraphic cancellation of General Grant's order. He shook hands with the committee, told them they were free to return to their homes and wished them well.

Since Washington unofficially encouraged trading behind the lines, we can only wonder why the notorious order was issued. Unquestionably, Grant and Sherman opposed bitterly the buying of cotton for gold, which enabled the Confederates to obtain munitions and prolong the war. But surely the generals knew that Jews were only the small fry. Big business sent down agents who stopped at the best hotels and wined and dined army officers, with whom they were often in cahoots. Did the order come from Washington at the behest of interests desirous of removing Jewish competition? As to the scandalous corruption of trading with the enemy, there is no record of court martials or Senate investigations.

Grant never defended the issuance of this order, nor did he ever make any apologies for it. Yet the General was no anti-Semite. When President, he made more Jewish appointments than any of his predecessors. His subsequent concern for the Jews in Russia and Roumania and his desire to relieve their distress might reflect his inner urge to make amends for an act that can only be regarded as unjust and cruel.

1863

JUDAH P. BENJAMIN

Statesman and Jurist

THE FAMOUS QUIP about "an Israelite with the principles of an Egyptian" was hurled at a U. S. Senator, who ranks high among America's great lawyers and orators. A statesman, leader and politician, the jurist who wrote a legal classic, a successful sugar planter and refiner, the lawyer who declined an appointment on the U. S. Supreme Court, a man of affairs and imagination, Judah P. Benjamin has come down in American Jewish history as its most brilliant, colorful, and all-around ablest personality. Yet he retains no place in the affection or esteem of Jewry.

Together with Empress Josephine, Alexander Hamilton, Senator David Yulee and the painter Camille Pissarro, Judah Phillip Benjamin was born on a Caribbean island. His impoverished parents brought their eight year old boy to Wilmington, N. C., then to Charleston. With assistance from a Jewish philanthropist he was educated in Fayetteville Academy and Yale College. Settling in up and coming New Orleans, young Judah studied law, tutored a beautiful Catholic Creole and married her. His success at the bar was rapid; his name became associated in celebrated cases that attracted international attention. President Fillmore offered to nominate him Associate Justice of the Supreme Court. There is hardly another instance of a 41 year old attorney refusing such a post.

Trouble with eyesight caused Benjamin for a time to retire from law practice. Purchasing a plantation in the Louisiana bayous, he applied his superb energies to sugar planting. Researching, he made a signal contribution to the new industry in extricating and refining sugar from the cane; he popularized his methods by example and by publication in journals. But he had to resume law practice when. called upon to pay a $60,000 note endorsed for a friend. Entering politics, he was elected to both houses of the State Assembly and took part in the Louisiana Constitutional Convention.

While in the U. S. Senate, Benjamin attracted attention at home and abroad. His eloquent speeches on the legal basis for slavery and the constitutional grounds of States Rights were the most brilliant and logical of all Southern leaders. In 1855 he warned that secession was inevitable unless a reasonable compromise could be effected between the conflicting interests of the North and South. But sectional passions on both sides rushed the nation into a catastrophic civil war. On February 4, 1861 Benjamin delivered to the Senate his farewell, a deeply moving masterpiece in American oratory, taking leave of his colleagues and defending with brilliant argument secession of the States from the Federal Union.

Upon the formation of the Confederacy Benjamin received the appointment of Attorney General. His abilities were soon demanded for Secretary of War, a post difficult enough for any civilian who had to impose views and orders upon such paladins as Lee, Jackson, Beauregard and Johnston. With mounting stringencies, hardships, short rations and military reverses, complaints ripened into criticisms against "the Jew whom the President had retained at his council table, despite the protests of the Southern people." With the surrender of Roanoke Island, a Congressional Committee investigated the failure to send powder. He took the censure stoically and refused to reveal, for the enemy's comfort, that he had no munitions to send. A universal howl went up to remove "Judas Iscariot Benjamin". The President had to acquiesce.

Jefferson Davis found Benjamin indispensable. In the face of hostile opinion, he promoted his War Minister to Secretary of State, a position virtually identical with that of a Prime Minister in Europe. Here Benjamin shone at his best. The corner-stone of his policy, recognition of the Confederacy as a belligerent by Britain and France, would break the Union blockade and enable the South to sell its cotton in Europe and obtain armaments and supplies essential for winning the war. Benjamin's objectives seemed attainable until Gettysburg shattered his dream. Thereafter the defeat of the South was a matter of time.

Following Lee's surrender at Appomattox, Benjamin fled the country, as did other Confederate leaders. After hair-breadth adventures, including a Robinson Crusoe shipwreck at sea, he landed in Europe. His wife and daughter lived in Paris, yet he refused excellent connections with French banking concerns. Instead, he chose to start anew at law practice in England. Applying to the Benchers of Lincoln's Inn, he sat among 150 youngsters, students from Oxford and Cambridge, gravely listening to law lectures. Even English conservatism saw the absurdity of a 55 year old famous statesman and renowned lawyer pretending to learn what he already knew so well. After six months, the authorities dispensed with the three year course of study, and the ex-Secretary of State was called to the English Bar.

During leisure periods while getting started in London, he wrote and published a *Treatise on the Law of Sale of Personal Property.* Popularly known as *Benjamin on Sales,* it became a standard textbook, an authoritative work purchased by practitioners in all English speaking lands. Gradually bench and bar began to take note of the foreign Jewish lawyer, starting at an age when many contemplate retirement and staging a comeback unequalled, perhaps, in legal annals. Appearing before the Privy Council of Chancery Court of the House of Lords, he argued cases of the highest import, generally referred to him by brother barristers.

Phenomenal success brought him in some years as much as $100,000 in fees, unprecedented legal earnings for the 1870s. From all sides came recognition, including the appointment of Queen's Counsel, an honor conferred only upon the most distinguished lawyers. At 71, when ready to retire, a farewell banquet was tendered him. Graced by the Lord Chancellor, the Lord Chief Justice, high officials of the Empire and the most eminent members of the profession, Benjamin was toasted and eulogized as the only man "of whom it can be said that he held conspicuous leadership at the Bars of two countries."

Yet Judah P. Benjamin holds no place of honor in Jewish tradition. With all the scintillating of his nimble intellect, he reflects little glory upon his people. Senator Wade's dig about "Egyptian principles" might be unfair, since Benjamin merely enunciated with forensic eloquence the moral and intellectual convictions of the South. Yet there is a germ of truth in the scathing gibe. Memories of degrading oppressions from the Pharaohs to the Czars should have held back any Jew from advocating human slavery. But Benjamin had no contact with Judaism. Never a conscious convert to any other religion, he nevertheless lies in a Catholic cemetery. There is significance and symbolism in that burial.

LA BELLE MENKEN

Enchanting Rebel

LIKE Alexander the Great, Adah Isaacs Menken began her career at 20, had the world at her feet and died in her 33rd year completely exhausted. The Macedonian hero inherited a compact kingdom, an army splendidly trained and equipped, together with a blue print for world conquest. But the American Jewess single-handed had to fight and conquer her world.

Seldom was a woman blessed with more provocative gifts of body and soul, of mind and spirit. A slender curvacious form supported a Byronic head, a pale face of classic feature with dark flashing eyes and curling hair, raven black but cut short. Adah Menken had the intellect to write trenchant essays, a heart over-flowing with emotion, a soul attuned to the mystical and the poetic. Her beauty and charm attracted the wordly and the capable as well as the literary giants of her day. Though possessing a slight stage talent, she became the most famous actress of her turbulent, eventful decade.

Adah Menken was among the very first to bob her hair, thus

anticipating by three generations the flapper who emerged during the Coolidge era. At the height of Victorian prudery, when women wore the ultra-modest hoop skirt and crinoline, she had the daring to bare her body in public and become the forerunner of the modern strip tease. But she was no mere burlesque diva. Adah wrote poetry of a quality that gives her rank among American minor poets. Her understanding of publicity would in our own day place her among experts in public relations. Thus in Adah Menken we have a Gypsy Rose Lee, a Rita Hayworth, an Emma Lazarus and Helena Rubinstein all rolled into one.

But who was Adah Menken? Mystery beclouds her origin and birthplace. The best book about her is Allen Lesser's *Enchanting Rebel*, a masterful job uncovering the secret of Adah Menken. Opinions differ as to her real name. Some doubt her Jewish birth and ascribe her devotion to Judaism to the zeal of a convert. Interest and curiosity continue to cling about her fascinating memory; a movie of her life story is now being projected in Hollywood.

It appears that Adah was born not far from New Orleans. At 20 she married Alexander Menken of a Cincinnati German Jewish family, a black sheep who had drifted into the theatre of the Mississippi valley. Through her husband she became leading lady in the stock companies that brightened the monotony of provincial life before the advent of moving pictures. Never a great actress, her beauty, her vivacity, her fascinating personality somehow got across the footlights. After the financial crash of 1857, she actually supported her discouraged husband. They moved to Cincinnati, where she had already made a reputation with her poems and articles published in the *American Israelite,* the famous weekly edited by Rabbi Isaac M. Wise, the founder of American Reform Judaism.

Inevitably, Adah the Bohemian would clash with the stuffy ante-bellum respectability of her in-laws. She left her husband after seeing that he obtained a divorce according to Jewish law. In New York she managed to act in the lesser theaters and chanced to meet John C. Heenen, the prize fighter who became heavyweight champion by default. Swept off her feet by violent passion, she married him secretly. But the news somehow got out; there being too much romantic appeal in the marriage of the extremely handsome Irish boxer with the beautiful, bewitching actress. But Alexander Menken was peeved. He wrote to a New York newspaper denouncing her as an adventuress who was using his name. Heenen had gone to England to accept a challenge. Alone and pregnant, Adah was all but crushed by the storm that broke over her head. She was subject to the bitterest villification in the press which dragged her name in the mire. Heenen repudiated her by denying the marriage. Ordered out of her hotel, she hid her face in a squalid room across the New Jersey line. In the midst of everything, her baby died. Her mother followed. Penniless and broken there seemed to be nothing left but suicide. She wrote her farewell letter, then changed her mind.

But from the depths Adah rose and soared to the stars. A producer decided to revive the melodrama *Mazeppa* and offered her the leading role. She must impersonate the male hero, even if it took heroic grit to act the part. In the play, Mazeppa's clothes are ripped off and the Tartar is tied to a wild horse. The stallion rushes off headlong, plunging over mountain and valley. A dummy was always substituted for this dangerous part. But the dare-devil Menken dispensed with the dummy and risked her life in each performance. Adah inflamed her audience with the strip scene and electrified them with her perilous ride over the scenic mountain gorges. Overnight she became a national sensation and packed the theatres of New York, Washington and Baltimore. The prospectors of California's Gold Rush, no mean judges of spirit and courage, paid hysterical tribute to her glamour and mettle.

Her greatest triumphs were scored across the Atlantic. In London and Paris she became a world celebrity. Her performances were witnessed by royalty and commoners; her receptions were attended by nobility, by the talented and the celebrated. Her personal friends were Charles Dickens, the poet Swinburne, Charles Reade, Alexander Dumas, George Sand, and a host of the lesser literati. Invitations to her sumptuous dinners were eagerly accepted by the famous and the select. But human endurance could not hold up under the strain of her strenuous drive. Her remarkable vitality cracked. She attained her 33rd year and died of tuberculosis. She lies in the Jewish section of Montparnasse Cemetery in Paris.

In the Menken dual personality lay deeply imbedded a sensitive soul that knew suffering. As a publicity seeker she might have invented tall tales to further her stage career, but never was there any evasion as to her genuine attachment to Judaism. No convert could have resented so fiercely the humiliations heaped upon her persecuted people. Neither the prospect of glory nor profit could tempt her to perform on Yom Kippur, her day of prayer and fasting. Half a century before Herzl issued his clarion call to the first Zionist assembly, she advocated a Jewish state in Palestine. In the Hall of Fame for early American precursors of Zionism, the niche between Mordecai Manuel Noah and Emma Lazarus is occupied by Adah Isaacs Menken.

EDWIN DE LEON

Confederate Agent

THE SOUTH CAROLINA DeLeons were an exceptional family. Edwin's older brother, David Camden, had distinguished himself in the Seminole and Mexican Wars and served the Confederacy as a physician. His younger brother Thomas Cooper and his sister Agnes were noted writers in their day. The famous Lafayette had presented a gift jewel to his uncle Abraham DeLeon, whose wife, Isabel Nones, was a daughter of the Revolutionary soldier and devoted Jew, Benjamin Nones. Edwin's mother, a Lopez of Charleston, was highly intelligent, cultured, and charming. Here was a stock to be proud of; yet Edwin DeLeon forsook his people and his religion.

Edwin DeLeon began to practice law in 1840 at Columbia, but soon drifted into journalism. His grandfather had settled in Camden, and Edwin quite naturally imbibed the Southern attitude towards slavery. His articulate editorials advocating that strange anachronism for 19th century America attracted attention. He was invited to Washington to edit a newspaper that would present the Southern side. The paper was not successful, though financed by slavery sympathizers. Editorials and speeches advocating Franklin Pierce for President brought DeLeon the diplomatic post of Consul General for Egypt.

The American Consul exhibited a special penchant for handling difficult assignments. Unconsciously he revealed his submerged Jewish sympathies for a helpless religious minority in danger of attack. During the Crimean War, Turkish anti-Russian feelings found an outlet in projecting a persecution of Christians unprotected by any strong state. Ordering the Greek Consul out of Egypt would be the prelude for looting and attacking Greek nationals by Moslem hooligans. The Christians were without protection, as neither the English nor the French consulates could afford to embarrass their own governments in alliance with Constantinople.

Without authority from his superiors, DeLeon took the initiative and declared all Greek Christians in Cairo under American protection. This was possible under the peculiar extra-territorial practice recognized at the time in the treaties of Turkey and China with the Christian powers. Such unauthorized procedure might have created a difficult situation for the U. S. It succeeded because the Khedive, secretly pleased at the discomfiture of his Turkish overlords, interposed no obstacles. The Greek colony expressed gratitude by presenting DeLeon with a silver tea service appropriately inscribed. The King of Greece invited the American Consul to Athens and offered him a cross and decoration of a Greek order, which DeLeon felt bound to decline respectfully. While the issue created hung in doubt, the State Department maintained a discreet silence. But with its success, Secretary of State Lewis Cass sent the Consul his warm approval.

Another crisis was averted by DeLeon's capable handling of the incident created by the murder of American missionaries in Palestine. He demanded immediate transportation to Jaffa by the U. S. Frigate stationed in Alexandria harbor. The unimaginative commander refused without specific naval instructions. The matter seemed urgent and DeLeon rushed to the spot by private conveyance. The U. S. Consulates in Jerusalem and Jaffa could do nothing with the rascally Governor who blandly offered to entertain them socially.

DeLeon brushed aside both Oriental courtesy and knavery and demanded punishment for the guilty. The Turk produced five vagabonds, who obviously were not involved. DeLeon threatened reprisals that would lead to war. The Governor, thoroughly alarmed, went to considerable trouble in capturing the five murderers. They were tried and condemned to death. Now the distressed Consul expected a serious reprimand for taking a desperate chance without authorization. Instead, he received thanks from the President and Secretary of State for his courageous action.

The prestige of the U. S. thus enhanced in the Near East, the State Department registered its approval by extending DeLeon's term for an additional four years. Still comparatively young, his prospects in diplomacy appeared particularly bright when South Carolina seceded from the Union. Resigning immediately, he encountered the dangers and adventures of blockade running and offered his services to the President of the Confederacy. DeLeon had been friends with Jefferson Davis during his Washington residence while editing the *Southern Press*. The President appointed DeLeon his personal representative in Europe and special advisor, a post far more important than a commission in the army.

The mission of DeLeon consisted in public relations and propaganda with the overall objective of getting France and Britain to recognize the Confederacy as a belligerent. It was a tough assignment. Mason and Slidell, the accredited envoys of the South, could not get the British Premier nor the French Emperor to receive them officially, although these statesmen secretly hoped for the division of the Federal Union. But the plain people simply would not support a state that fought to preserve human slavery. DeLeon succeeded in conferring personally with

Palmerston and Napoleon III, but got nowhere. Discouraged, he wrote a confidential letter revealing apprehension and small faith in the statesmanship of Secretary of State Judah P. Benjamin or his diplomats in Europe. These dispatches were intercepted and published in the New York Press. The President was unable to save the scalp of his confidential agent.

The diplomatic assignment cost DeLeon his life savings. After the war he wrote for leading magazines. Experiences in Egypt were recorded in several well written novels, of which *Askarso Kassis* is the best. His memoirs, *Thirty Years of My Life on Three Continents,* give intimate pictures of an eventful career that brought him in close personal contact with the novelist Thackeray; DeLesseps, the Suez Canal builder; Morse, inventor of the telegraph, and leading figures in American politics. *The Khedive's Egypt* was adopted by the British Parliament as essential reading for all officers serving in the Near East.

DeLeon married a charming Irish girl. Her influence brought him into the Catholic Church. She died six days after him. Both lay buried side by side in New York's Calvary Cemetery. Yet no memorial stone has ever been erected to mark their graves.

GLOSSARY

Adjunta	governing council of a synagogue among Sephardim.
Allgemeine Zeitung des Judentums	title of a German newspaper.
Anusim	Hebrew for Marranos, Jews professing Catholicism outwardly, and practising Judaism in secret.
Ark	cabinet in the synagogue in which the Torah scrolls are kept.
Ashkenazim (singular Ashkenazi)	Jews of Central or East Europe, or their descendants, as distinct from the Sephardim of the Mediterranean perimeter.
Aufklaerung	era of enlightenment in Europe in later 18th and early 19th centuries.
Auto-da-fé	act of faith, burning at the stake of a heretic, witch, or Christian convicted by the Inquisition of backsliding to Judaism.
Beth Din	Rabbinical Court competent to decide questions of Jewish law.
Beth Elohim	House of God, name of a synagogue.
Beth Hamidrash Hagodol	great house of study, name of a synagogue.
Beth Shalome	House of Peace, name of synagogue in Richmond.
B'nai B'rith	Sons of the Covenant.
B'nai Jeshurun	children of Jeshurun, a poetic term for Israel. Name of the second oldest synagogue of New York.
Bodek	inspector and examiner of meat ritually slaughtered.
Bundesbrueder	fraternal brothers.
Cabala	a study of Hebrew mysticism.
Chalukah	relief fund for the poor in the Holy Land prior to the State of Israel.
Chassidim	literally saints, a sect in 18th century Poland started by Israel Baal Shem Tov.

Cheder	Hebrew elementary school.
Chevra	group, society, association.
Cohen	priest, descendant of Aaron.
Conversos	Jewish converts to Christianity in Spain or Portugal.
El Gran Capitan	the great Captain.
Galut	Dispersion of Jews throughout the world.
Gemuetlichkeit	pleasant, intimate, and comfortable atmosphere.
Ger	proselyte to Judaism.
Ger Tzedek	saintly proselyte.
Gringos	Mexican nickname for Americans.
Haham	Sage, Rabbi among Sephardim.
Haskalah	secular learning as distinguished from Talmudic or Rabbinical lore.
Hidalgo	Spanish nobleman of the second class, not quite a grandee.
Hof-Jude	a Jew influential in the Royal Palace and spokesman for his people.
Judengasse	street inhabited by Jews.
Juedische Wissenschaft	Jewish learning.
Junker	a Prussian of the privileged, agricultural and military caste.
Junta	governing body of the synagogue among Sephardim.
Kaddish	prayer for the dead recited by mourners.
Kahal	community, congregation.
Kahal Kodesh	holy congregation.
Kashruth	the kosher cult.
Kolshe	communal, congregational.
Kosher	meat ritually slaughtered, food prepared ritually and permissible for usage to pious Jews.
Kulturkampf	an ideological struggle.
Lamdan	a scholar versed in Hebrew lore.
Landsleute	group of fellow countrymen.
Landsmann	fellow countryman.
Lettre de cachet	letter under the seal of the King of France confining someone to prison without trial.
Luftmenschen	people without occupation, living by their wits.

Maggid	preacher, pulpiteer.
Marranos	professing Christians practising Judaism secretly in Spain and Portugal.
Maskilim	zealous advocates of secular culture in lieu of exclusive Rabbinical learning.
Matzos	Unleavened bread eaten during passover.
Medinat Israel	Land of Israel.
Melamed	a slovenly Hebrew teacher, generally without proper training.
Meschianza	a revel in the grand style, with entertainments, pageants, regattas, tableaux, closing with a gala ball.
Meshulach	solicitor for charitable institutions or religious academies.
Meshumed	convert and renegade to Judaism.
Mikveh Israel	Hope of Israel, congregation in Philadelphia.
Minhag	custom, established tradition.
Minhag America	customary usage in America. Name of the prayerbook composed by Isaac M. Wise.
Minhag Sephardim	ritual followed by the Sephardim.
Minyan	quorum of ten Jewish males qualified to conduct services as a congregation.
Mishna	digest of Jewish law, to which the Gamara is a commentary.
Mitzvos	acts of merit performed as a religious duty.
Nusach	method and manner of prayer.
Olath Tamid	An Everlasting Offering. Name of prayerbook by David Einhorn for American Reformed Judaism.
Parnass	President or Warden of the congregation.
Pater familias	father of the family.
Pentateuch	five books of Moses.
Prima facie	at the first view before investigation.
Pushkes	Tin boxes for collecting money in Orthodox homes for the poor in the Holy Land.
Rav	a Rabbi.
Rimonim	pomegranates.
Rosh Hashanah	Jewish New Year.

Sanhedrin	members of the Council in ancient Jerusalem.
Sanhedrion	the Council in ancient Jerusalem that functioned as a religious Synod, Legislature, and Supreme Court.
Schlemiel	a failure, an inefficient ne'er-do-well.
Semicha	ordination of rabbis.
Sephardim (singular, Sephardi)	Jews originally of the Spanish peninsula, or long settled in the Mediterranean perimeter.
Sepher Torah	scroll of the Torah.
Shames	sexton, beadle.
Shearith Israel	Remnant of Israel. Name of the oldest synagogue in America.
Shema Yisroel Adonoi Elohanu Adonoi Echad	Hear, O Israel, the Eternal our God, the Eternal is One.
Shofar	ram's horn, used in the New Year's service.
Shohet	slaughterer of cattle or fowl in accordance with Jewish law.
Shtadlan	unofficial representative, spokesman, intercessor, for the Jewish community in ruling circles.
Shtadlanuth	the Shtadlan's profession.
Shul	synagogue, house of prayer.
Sidur	prayerbook.
Talith	shawl used by Jews during prayer.
Talmud	24 tractates of commentaries of Jewish law.
Tanach	entire Hebrew Bible.
Tedesco	Sephardic term for a German Jew, or Ashkinaz.
Tephilim	Phylacteries.
Tisha B'av	the 9th day of Ab, a fast-day in memory of the destruction of Jerusalem.
Torah	The Old Testament, also five books of Moses.
Trefa	non-kosher or unclean food.
Ukase	decree of the Czars.
Weltanschauung	a philosophical attitude towards the world.
Wissenschaft des Judentums	Jewish Science, a learned movement originated by Leopold Zunz.

386

Yahrbücher für	Jewish Yearbook.
Israeliten	
Yahrzeit	anniversary in memory of dead relatives.
Yiches	pedigree, pride of descent.
Yichesbrief	letters of descent, family genealogy.
Yom Kippur	Day of Atonement.

BIBLIOGRAPHY

ALTFELD, E. MILTON, *The Jews' Struggle for Religious Liberty in Maryland*. Curlander. 1924.

AMERICAN JEWISH ARCHIVES. Cincinnati. Hebrew Union College Jewish Institute of Religion.

AMERICAN JEWISH HISTORICAL SOCIETY PUBLICATIONS, 1893–1954, 44 Vols.

AMERICAN JEWISH YEAR BOOK, 1899–1955. Philadelphia. Jewish Publication Society of America.

BARCLAY, GEORGE L., *The Life and Remarkable Career of Adah Isaacs Menken*. Philadelphia. 1868.

BAROWAY, AARON, *The Cohens of Maryland*. Maryland Historical Magazine, Vol. 15. 1920.

——, *Solomon Etting*, Maryland Historical Magazine, Vol. 15, 1920.

BARRETT, WALTER, *The Old Merchants of New York City*. New York, 1863.

BIEN, JULIUS, *A History of the Independent Order Bne Brith*. Minorah I, II, III.

BLUM, ISIDOR, *The Jews of Baltimore*. Historical Review Publishing Co. Baltimore. 1910.

BONDI, AUGUST, *Autobiography of August Bondi*. Galesburg, Ill. 1910.

BRADFORD, GAMALIEL, *Confederate Portraits* (Judah P. Benjamin), Houghton Mifflin Co. 1912.

BUTLER, PIERCE, *Life of Judah P. Benjamin*. G. W. Jacobs and Co. Philadelphia. 1907.

BYARS, WILLIAM VINCENT, *B & M Gratz*, Merchants in Philadelphia. Hugh Stephens Printing Co. Jefferson City, Mo. 1916.

CARVALHO, SOLOMON NUNES, *Incidents of Travel and Adventure in the Far West*. Derby and Jackson, New York. 1857.

COHEN, GEORGE, *The Jews in the Making of America*. Boston, Stratford. 1924.

COHEN, MYER M., *Notices of Florida and the Campaigns*. Charleston. Burges and Honour. 1836.

CRESSON, WARDER, *The Key of David*, and other articles, including Rea-

sons for Becoming a Jew, with a *Revision of the Late Lawsuit for Lunacy on that Account.* Philadelphia.

DALY, CHARLES P., *The Settlement of the Jews in North America.* New York. Cowen. 1893.

DECKEY, MALCOLM, *Benedict Arnold.* Tarrytown, William Abbott, 1932.

DeLEON, EDWIN, *Thirty Years of My Life on Three Continents.* London, 1890.

DE LEON, THOMAS COOPER, *Four Years in Rebel Capitals.* Mobile, 1892.

DICTIONARY OF AMERICAN BIOGRAPHY, 22 Vols., Scribners, New York. 1928–1946.

DORR, RHETA CHILDE, *Susan B. Anthony,* (Ernestine Rose). New York, Frederick A. Stokes Company. 1928.

DRAYTON, JOHN, *Memoirs of the American Revolution.* Charleston, A. E. Miller. 1821.

ELZAS, BARNETT A., *The Jews of South Carolina.* Lippincott Company, Philadelphia, 1903.

———, *The Reformed Society of Israelites,* New York. 1916.

EZEKIEL, HERBERT T. AND LICHENSTEIN, GASTON, *History of the Jews of Richmond from 1769 to 1917.* Richmond, 1917.

FISH, SIDNEY M., *Aaron Levy; Founder of Aaronsburg.* American Jewish Historical Society. New York. 1951.

———, *Barnard and Michael Gratz. Their Lives and Times.* Philadelphia, In Manuscript.

FONER, PHILIP S., *The Jews in American History, 1654–1865.* International Publishers, New York. 1946.

FREUND, MIRIAM K., *Jewish Merchants in Colonial America; Their Achievements and Their Contribution to the American Development.* Behrman's, New York. 1939.

FRIEDMAN, LEE M., *Early American Jews.* Harvard University Press. Cambridge. 1934.

———, *Jewish Pioneers and Patriots.* Jewish Publication Society of America. Philadelphia. 1942.

———, *Pilgrims in a New Land.* Jewish Publication Society of America, Philadelphia. 1948.

GOLDBERG, ISAAC, *Major Noah; American Jewish Pioneer.* Jewish Publication Society of America. Philadelphia. 1936.

GOLDSTEIN, ISRAEL, *A Century of Judaism in New York.* New York. 1930.

GOODMAN, ABRAM VOSSEN, *American Overture.* Philadelphia. The Jewish Publication Society of America. 1947.

GRINSTEIN, HYMAN B., *The Rise of the Jewish Community in New York.* Jewish Publication Society of America. Philadelphia. 1945.

GUTSTEIN, MORRIS A., *The Story of the Jews of Newport; Two and a Half Centuries of Judaism.* Bloch Publishing Co. New York. 1936.

HANDLIN, OSCAR, *Adventure in Freedom; 300 Years of Jewish Life in America*. McGraw-Hill. New York. 1954.

HANNA, A. J., *Flight into Oblivion* (Judah P. Benjamin). Richmond. Johnson Publishing Co. 1938.

HECTMAN, FRANCIS B., *Register and Dictionary of the U.S. Army*. Washington, 1903.

HENRY, F. P., *Standard History of the Medical Profession of Philadelphia*.

HENNIG, HELEN KOHN, *Edwin DeLeon*, in manuscript, a thesis for Masters Degree, University of S. C., Columbia, S.C. 1928.

HUHNER, LEON, *The Life of Judah Touro*. Jewish Publication Society of America, Philadelphia. 1946.

———, *Moses Elias Levy, an Early Florida Pioneer*. The Florida Historical Quarterly, Vol. XIX, No. 4. 1941.

ISRAELS HEROLD, the First Jewish Weekly in New York.

JAMES, EDWIN, *Biography of Adah Isaacs Menken*. New York. 188?.

JEWISH ENCYCLOPEDIA, 12 Volumes, Funk and Wagnalls Company. 1901–6.

JOURNAL OF MT. SINAI HOSPITAL, *Story of Mt. Sinai Hospital*. Vol. VIII 6.

JUDAH, S. B. H., *Gotham and the Gothamites*. New York. 1823.

JULIEN, CASSIE MASON MYERS, *Biographical Sketches of Bailey-Meyers-Mason Families, 1776–1905*. New York Public Library, Genealogy Room.

KAGAN, SOLOMON R., *Jewish Contributions to Medicine in America from Colonial Times to the Present*. Boston Medical Publishing Co. 1939.

KISCH, GUIDO, *The First Jewish Weekly in N. Y*. Historia Judaica II.

KOHLER, KAUFMANN, *David Einhorn, the Uncompromising Champion of Reform Judaism*. New York. 1909.

KOHLER, MAX J., *Haym Salomon, the Patriotic Broker of the Revolution, His Real Achievements and Their Exaggerations*. A pamphlet. New York. 1931.

KORN, BERTRAM W., *American Jewry and the Civil War*. Jewish Publication Society of America, Philadelphia, 1951.

LEARSI, RUFUS, *The Jews in America*. The World Publishing Co., Cleveland & New York. 1954.

LEBESON, ANITA L., *Jewish Pioneers in America*. New York. Brentano. 1931.

———, *Pilgrim People*, New York. Harper & Brothers. 1950.

LESSER, ALLEN, *Weave a Wreath of Laurel*. New York. The Coven Press. 1938.

———, *The Enchanting Rebel* (Adah Isaacs Menken). New York. Beechhurst. 1947.

LEVINGER, LEE J., *A History of the Jews in the United States*. Cincinnati. Union of American Hebrew Congregations. 1949.

London, Hannah R., *Portraits of Jews by Gilbert Stuart and other Early American Artists*. New York. William Edwin Rudge. 1927.

——, *Shades of My Forefathers*. Springfield. The Pond-Ekberg Company. 1941.

——, *Miniatures of Early American Jews*. Springfield, Mass. Pond-Ekberg Company. 1954.

Lossing, Benson J., *Pictorial Field Book of the War of 1812*.

Makover, A. B., *Mordecai M. Noah, His Life and Works from the Jewish Viewpoint*. New York. Bloch Publishing Co. 1917.

Marcus, Jacob R., *Early American Jewry*. Jewish Publication Society of America, Vol. I. Philadelphia. 1951.

——, *Early American Jewry*. Jewish Publication Society of America, Vol. II. Philadelphia. 1953.

Markens, Isaac, *The Hebrews in America*. New York. 1888.

May, Max B., *Isaac M. Wise, A Biography*. New York. Putnam. 1916.

McCrady, Edward, *The History of South Carolina in the Revolution, 1775–1780*. New York. The Macmillan Co. 1901.

Meade, Robert D., *Judah P. Benjamin, Confederate Statesman*. New York, London. Oxford University Press. 1943.

Mersand, Joseph, *Traditions in American Literature; A Study of Jewish American Authors*. New York. The Modern Chapbooks. 1939.

Moise, Lucius C., *Biography of Isaac Harby*. Central Conference of American Rabbis. Columbia. 1931.

Morais, Henry S., *Eminent Israelites of the 19th Century*. Philadelphia. E. Stern and Co. 1880.

——, *The Jews of Philadelphia*. Philadelphia. 1894.

Mordecai, Alfred, *The Life of Alfred Mordecai as Related by Himself*, Edited by James Padgett. North Carolina Historical Review, Vol. XXII, 1 and 2.

Moultrie, William, *Memoirs of the American Revolution*. New York. D. Longworth. 1802.

Myers, M., *Reminiscences, 1780 to 1814, including Incidents in the War of 1812*. Washington, D.C. The Crane Co. 1900.

Occident and American Jewish Advocate, Edited by Isaac Leeser, 26 Vols. Philadelphia, 1843–1869.

Osterweis, Rollin G., *Rebecca Gratz*. New York. G. P. Putnam's Sons. 1935.

Philipson, David, *Letters of Rebecca Gratz*. Jewish Publication Society of America, Philadelphia, 1929.

——, *The Reform Movement in Judaism*, New York, Macmillan Co. 1907.

——, *Max Lilienthal, American Rabbi*. Bloch Publishing Co. 1915.

Poems of Penina Moise, Charleston Section, Council of Jewish Women, Nicholas G. Duffy, 1911.

POLLAK, GUSTAV, *Michael Heilprin and His Sons.* New York. Dodd, Mead and Company. 1912.

POOL, DAVID DESOLA, *Portraits Etched in Stone.* Columbia University Press. New York. 1952.

RAPHALL, MORRIS J., *The Bible View of Slavery.* New York. Rudd and Carleton. 1861.

REZNIKOFF, CHARLES, *The Jews of Charleston.* Jewish Publication Society of America, Philadelphia, 1950.

RODDIS, LOUIS H., *Phineas J. Horwitz,* United States Navy Bulletin, 1935.

ROSENBACH, HYMAN P., *The Jews of Philadelphia Prior to 1800.* Philadelphia. E. Stern and Co. 1883.

ROSENBAUM, GEANETTE W., *Myer Myers, Goldsmith.* Jewish Publication Society of America, Philadelphia, 1954.

RUSSELL, CHARLES E., *Haym Salomon and the Revolution.* Cosmopolitan Corporation, New York, 1930.

RUSSO, JOSEPH LOUIS, *Lorenzo da Ponte, Poet and Adventurer.* New York. Columbia University Press. 1922.

SCHAPPES, MORRIS U., *Documentary History of the Jews in the United States.* The Citadel Press, New York, 1952.

SHEPPARD, L. A., *Memoirs of Lorenzo da Ponte.* 1929.

SHPALL, LEO, *The Sheftalls of Georgia.* The Geogia Historical Quarterly, XVII, 1943.

STANTON, ELIZABETH CADY, *Eighty Years and More, 1815–1897, Reminiscences,* (Ernestine Rose). London, T. F. Unwin. 1898.

STANTON, ELIZABETH CADY, Susan B. Anthony, and Matilda Joslyn Gage, *History of Woman Suffrage,* (Ernestine Rose), 2nd Edition, Vol. 1, Rochester, 1889.

THE ASMONIAN, 1849–58, New York.

THE GEORGIA HISTORICAL QUARTERLY, *The Minis Family,* Vol. 1, 1917.

THE ISRAELITE (The American Israelite), Cincinnati, 1854–1860.

THE JEW, New York, 1823–25.

UNIVERSAL JEWISH ENCYCLOPEDIA, 10 vols. New York, The Universal Jewish Encyclopedia, Inc., 1939–1943.

VAXER, M., *The First Hebrew Bible Printed in America.* Vol. 2, No. 1. Journal of Jewish Bibliography.

VILLARD, OSWALD GARRISON, *John Brown,* 1800–1859 New York Alfred A. Knopf, 1943.

VOLWILER, ALBERT T., *George Crogham and the Westward Movement* (Gratz Brothers) Cleveland, The Arthur M. Clark Co. 1926.

WALLACE, WILLARD W., *Transitory Hero, The Life and Fortunes of Benedict Arnold.* New York. Harper and Brothers, 1954.

WASSERMAN, JACOB, *Judah Touro.* New York, Bloch Publishing Co. 1925.

WATTERS, LEON L., *The Pioneer Jews of Utah.* American Jewish Historical Society, New York, 1952.

WAX, J. A., *Isidor Bush, American Patriot and Abolitionist.* Historia Judaica V, 1943.

WHITE, GEORGE, *Historical Collection of Georgia,* 1854.

WIERNIK, PETER, *History of the Jews in America from the Period of the Discovery of the New World to the Present Time.* The Jewish History Publishing Company, New York, 1931.

WISE, ISAAC M., *Reminiscences,* Cincinnati, L. Wise & Co., 1901.

WOLF, EDWIN 2nd and MAXWELL WHITEMAN, *A History of the Jews of Philadelphia.* Philadelphia, 1654–1830, The Jewish Exponent, 1954–55.

WOLF, SIMON, *The American Jew as Patriot, Soldier and Citizen.* Brentano, New York, 1895.

———, *Selected Addresses and Papers.* Union of American Hebrew Congregations, Cincinnati, 1926.

YULEE, C. WICKLIFFE, *Senator Yulee.* The Florida Historical Quarterly, Vol. II, nos. 1 and 2, 1900.

INDEX

394

402